Who Counts?

Sheena

with best wishes

Robert

Praise for this book

'This is a timely compilation of ground-breaking work which adds up to a powerful agenda for transformation. This book shows how we can quantify the qualitative, build the active agency of excluded groups, and generate participatory statistics that have greater rigour and legitimacy than most conventional statistics.'

David Archer, Head of Programmes, ActionAid

'An extremely rich compendium – completing and correcting conventional statistical and evaluative practice.'

Professor Helmut Asche, Director, German Institute for Development Evaluation

'This important collection shows how the process of organizing to "count" can help people mobilize for action, as well as producing reliable information at scale. Holland's introduction is a great summary of the range of practice – taking on new development such as ICTs and approaches to standardization of data from participatory exercises at scale, as well as showing the depth of experience that now exists in participatory statistics.

Andrew Norton, Director of Research, Overseas Development Institute

'This is a very welcome and timely addition to current debates about generating rigorous evidence, providing a set of highly practical examples that demonstrate how participatory statistics can improve our understanding of what works for poor people, in ways that are more transformative. It is an important contribution to evaluation practice.'

Lina Payne, Evaluation Adviser, DFID

Who Counts?

The power of participatory statistics

Edited by Jeremy Holland
with an Afterword by Robert Chambers

PRACTICAL ACTION
Publishing

Practical Action Publishing Ltd
The Schumacher Centre
Bourton on Dunsmore, Rugby,
Warwickshire CV23 9QZ, UK
www.practicalactionpublishing.org

ISBN 978 1 85339 772 1 Paperback
ISBN 978 1 85339 771 4 Hardback
ISBN 978 1 78044 771 1 Library Ebook
ISBN 978 1 78044 772 8 Ebook

Jeremy Holland, ed. (2013) *Who Counts? The Power of Participatory Statistics*,
Practical Action Publishing, Rugby, UK.

Since 1974, Practical Action Publishing (formerly Intermediate Technology
Publications and ITDG Publishing) has published and disseminated books and
information in support of international development work throughout the world.
Practical Action Publishing is a trading name of Practical Action Publishing Ltd
(Company Reg. No. 1159018), the wholly owned publishing company of Practical
Action. Practical Action Publishing trades only in support of its parent charity
objectives and any profits are covenanted back to Practical Action (Charity Reg. No.
247257, Group VAT Registration No. 880 9924 76).

Indexed by Liz Fawcett, Harrogate, North Yorkshire
Typeset by Bookcraft Ltd, Stroud, Gloucestershire
Cover photo: Self-help group from El Salvador
Photo credit Jeff Ashe, Oxfam America
Cover design: Mercer Design, London

Printed and bound in India by Replika Press Pvt. Ltd.

Contents

Photos and figures   vii
Tables and boxes   viii
Acronyms and abbreviations   x
Acknowledgements   xii

1   Introduction
Participatory statistics: a 'win–win' for international development   1
Jeremy Holland

PART I
Participatory statistics and policy change   **21**

2   Participatory 3-dimensional modelling for policy and planning:
the practice and the potential   23
Giacomo Rambaldi

3   Measuring urban adaptation to climate change: experiences in
Kenya and Nicaragua   37
Caroline Moser and Alfredo Stein

4   Participatory statistics, local decision-making, and national policy
design: *Ubudehe* community planning in Rwanda   49
Ashish Shah

5   Generating numbers with local governments for decentralized
health sector policy in the Philippines   65
Rose Marie R. Nierras

6   From fragility to resilience: the role of participatory community
mapping, strategic planning and knowledge management in
Sudan   79
Margunn Indreboe Alshaikh

Part II
Who counts reality? Participatory statistics in monitoring
and evaluation   **95**

7   Accountability downwards, count-ability upwards: quantifying
empowerment outcomes in Bangladesh   97
Dee Jupp with Sohel Ibn Ali

8   Community groups monitoring impact with participatory
    statistics in India: reflections from an international NGO
    collective   113
    Bernward Causemann, Eberhard Gohl, Chinnapillai Rajathi,
    Abraham Susairaj, Ganesh Tantry and Srividhya Tantry

9   Scoring perceptions of services in the Maldives: instant feedback
    and the power of increased local engagement   125
    Nils Riemenschneider, Valentina Barca, and Jeremy Holland

10 Are we targeting the poor? Lessons with participatory statistics
    in Malawi   137
    Carlos Barahona

PART III
Statistics for participatory impact assessment   **147**

11 Participatory impact assessment in drought policy contexts:
    lessons from southern Ethiopia   149
    Dawit Abebe and Andy Catley

12 Participatory impact assessment: the 'Starter Pack Scheme' and
    sustainable agriculture in Malawi   163
    Elizabeth Cromwell, Patrick Kambewa, Richard Mwanza, and
    Rowland Chirwa with KWERA Development Centre

13 Participatory impact assessments of farmer productivity
    programmes in Africa   183
    Susanne Neubert

    Afterword   197
    Robert Chambers

    Practical and accessible resources   207
    Index   209

Figures

1.1 Dimensions of methodology and outcome   2
1.2 A social map   4
2.1 Local analysts with P3DM, Telecho, Ethiopia   29
2.2 The global spread of P3DM application   30
4.1 *Ubudehe* data used by the Ministry of Health following persistent
      influence by *Ubudehe* protagonists   60
4.2 Using *Ubudehe* data to offer targeted social protection to
      marginalized and vulnerable households under the VUP   61
4.3 Analysis of participatory trend statistics in Mugunga Village,
      Busengo Sector   61
5.1 PTB mortality map, Cotabato Province   71
6.1 Thematic distribution of crisis and recovery risks in West Darfur
      State   85
6.2 Mapping post-conflict recovery in Eastern Sudan   86
7.1 Empowerment in three acts   101
7.2 An example of quantifying qualitative changes   108
7.3 Literacy levels correlated with GDI achievement   108
8.1 Changes in poverty status, 2006–09   116
8.2 Women's Association goal achievement, 2006–09   117
9.1 Example of a scorecard question   127
9.2 Comparing group-based and survey-based scorecards methods   128
9.3 Comparing group-based scores and survey-based scores   130
9.4 Scorecards used in extractive mode   131
9.5 Scorecards in participatory mode   133
11.1 Mean proportion (%) of household income by income source
      for destocked households during the drought   152
11.2 Proportional (%) use of income derived from commercial
      destocking   153
12.1 Pie chart of Starter Pack contents   176
13.1 Quality of life trend curve produced by COMPACI farmers in
      Zambia   186
13.2 Quality of life trend curve produced by COMPACI farmers in
      Malawi   187

Tables and boxes

Tables

3.1 Composite matrix of perceptions of the most significant weather
hazards in Mombasa and Estelí   41
3.2 Focus group matrices identifying asset actions before, during,
and after severe weather at household, small business, and
community level in Mombasa, Kenya   41
3.3 Composite matrix of important assets in the four study
communities in Mombasa, Kenya   42
3.4 Institutions in the four study communities in Mombasa, by
general importance and in adapting to severe weather   43
4.1 Poverty characteristics of households in Rwanda as defined by
communities and households marked on village social map   54
4.2 Headings of citizen-generated data beyond six household socio-
economic categories (recorded on *Ubudehe* social maps where
relevant)   58
5.1 Levels of administrative authority and persons responsible
within local governments for the health sector by type of local
government unit   66
5.2 Participatory analysis of the top five leading causes of mortality
in municipalities represented   69
5.3 Participatory analysis of the top five leading causes of morbidity
in municipalities represented   69
7.1 Matrix showing distribution of indicators across categories   105
8.1 Cause–effect analysis on access to water, analysed by a women's
self-help group   118
8.2 Impact indicator achievement 2006–09   119
10.1 Correlation between receipt of TIP and food security status   142
11.1 Participatory methods used in the assessment of commercial
destocking in Moyale woreda   151
11.2 Community perceptions of interventions before and after the
drought   156
12.1 Sustainability indicators of Farming Practice Groups   168
12.2 Total households in study villages, by region   171
12.3 Importance of sustainability indicators ranked by study villages   172
12.4a Distribution of study households between Farming Practice
Groups (%) – perceptions of male key informants   173

12.4b Distribution of study households between Farming Practice
       Groups (%) – perceptions of female key informants   173
12.5 Trends in sustainability indicators in study villages, 1970–2000   175
13.1 Overall trends in COMPACI communities in six countries   188
13.2 Trend analysis for three sub-categories conducted by farmers in
       COMPACI communities in six countries   189
13.3 Influence matrix produced by farmers in Zambia   191

Boxes

1.1   Participatory methods that generate numbers   3
6.1   Ten critical issues from Nyala Locality, South Darfur   84
7.1   A short history of the social movement   99
11.1 Key steps in a successful policy process in Ethiopia   160
12.1 Key features of participatory approaches for impact assessment   165
12.2 Dream Pack contents, ranked in order of importance to farmers
       in study villages   177
13.1 Zambian farmers' comments on influence matrix   193

Acronyms and abbreviations

A   awareness level of achievement
ARD Inc   Associates in Rural Development
BMGF   Bill and Melinda Gates Foundation
CAADP   Comprehensive Africa Agriculture Development Programme
CC   confidence and capability level of achievement
CLTS   Community-Led Total Sanitation
COMESA   Common Market for Eastern and Southern Africa
COMPACI   Competitive African Cotton Initiative
CPA   Comprehensive Peace Agreement
CRMA   Crisis and Recovery Mapping and Analysis
CRP   Conflict Reduction Programme
CTA   Technical Centre for Agricultural and Rural Cooperation ACP-EU
DEG   Deutsche Entwicklungsgesellschaft / KfW group
DFID   Department for International Development
DIE   German Development Institute
DRC   Democratic Republic of the Congo
EFI   extremely food insecure
ESS   effectiveness and self-sustaining level of achievement
FI   food insecure
FS   food secure
GDI   Group Development Index
GIS   geographic information systems
GIT   geospatial information technologies
GIZ   German Development Cooperation
GOLD   Governance and Local Democracy project
GoR   Government of Rwanda
GPS   global positioning systems
ICTs   information and communication technologies
IHDP   Integrated Human Development Project
IMWG   Information Management Working Group
INGO   international non-governmental organization
ISK   indigenous spatial knowledge
KRWCDS   Karwar Rural Women and Children Development Society
M&E   monitoring and evaluation
MAPP   Method for Impact Assessment of Programs and Projects
MINALOC   Ministry of Local Government
NGO   non-governmental organization

NGO-IDEAs NGO Impact on Development, Empowerment and Actions
NISR National Institute of Statistics
NITLAPAN Institute for Applied Research and Local Development
NORC National Opinion Research Centre at the University of Chicago
OPM Oxford Policy Management
OSM OpenStreetMap
P3DM participatory 3-dimensional modelling
PAC Public Affairs Centre
PAG performance assessment by groups
PCCAA urban participatory climate change adaptation appraisal
PGIS participatory geographical information systems
PIA participatory impact assessment
PLA participatory learning and action
PPGIS public participation GIS
PRA participatory rural appraisal
RPCM Reconciliation and Peaceful Co-existence Mechanism
SAGE situational analysis and goal establishment
SC US Save the Children US
SDC Swiss Agency for Development and Cooperation
SfAA US-based Society for Applied Anthropology
TIP Targeted Inputs Programme
UNDAF UN Development Assistance Framework
UNHS Uganda National Household Survey
UPPR Urban Partnerships for Poverty Reduction programme
USAID United States Agency for International Development

Acknowledgements

This book is the result of the groundbreaking efforts of many committed professionals and I feel privileged to have been able to bring this collection together. I am grateful first and foremost to the Participation, Power and Social Change team at the Institute of Development Studies (IDS) for inviting me to be a Visiting fellow and for providing the space and institutional connectivity that has brought this book to fruition.

Beyond the authors whose work is represented in this volume, the field of participatory statistics owes a huge debt to the pioneers of participatory research, too many to mention by name here. In the past decade the Parti-Numbers Network of southern and northern practitioners, drawn from a wide range of disciplinary backgrounds, took a step forward in trying to systematise and promote participatory statistics as a methodology and philosophy.

More recently still, fresh momentum for this book was provided by a DFID-hosted Seminar on Participatory Statistics in London in April 2011 organised by Lina Payne (DFID Evaluation Department). I would like to thank Lina and her colleague Kirsten Hinds for their insightful comments on a concept paper that was converted into the General Introduction to this book. Funding for the publishing of this book was kindly provided by the Swiss Agency for Development and Cooperation (SDC) and Swedish International Development Cooperation Agency (Sida) through the Participation and Development Relations (PDR) grant support to IDS. We are grateful to Laurent Ruedin (SDC) and Brigitte Junker (Sida) for approving a budget line to publish this book.

I would like to thank wholeheartedly all at Practical Action Publishing who have provided patient support and oversight through the whole publishing process. I am particularly grateful to an anonymous reviewer, contracted by the publisher, for an excellent critique of an earlier draft of this book.

Last but by no means least my thanks go to Robert Chambers. This collection is the result of his tireless championing of participatory statistics. Without his energy, enthusiasm and good-humoured bullying, this book would *still* be 'in the pipeline'!

Jeremy Holland,
November 2012

Chapter 1

Introduction
Participatory statistics: a 'win–win' for international development

Jeremy Holland

The practice and potential of participatory statistics in development research

Participatory statistics have gained a methodological foothold in the pluralistic world of development research. In recent years participatory research has established its credentials as an approach – with an accompanying set of tools – in which local people themselves generate statistics. Since the early 1990s there has been a 'quiet tide of innovation' (Chambers, 2008) in generating statistics using participatory methods, with diverse examples of cutting-edge and transformative participatory research that can be plotted in the NE quadrant of Figure 1.1. This tide has captured methodological innovation at all levels and in all spheres of development activity. Development practitioners are supporting and facilitating participatory statistics from community-level planning right up to sector- and national-level policy processes. Statistics are being generated in the design, monitoring and evaluation, and impact assessment of policies, programmes, and projects.

Reflecting on this accumulation of experience, this book suggests that a wider and more systematic use of participatory statistics would benefit both development agencies and local communities. The book makes the following claims for a 'win–win' perspective on participatory statistics:

- Participatory research can generate accurate and generalizable statistics in a timely, efficient (value for money), and effective way; and
- Participatory statistics empower local people in a sphere of research that has traditionally been highly extractive and externally controlled.

This book seeks to provide impetus for a step change in the adoption and mainstreaming of participatory statistics within international development practice. There is a wonderful opportunity for donors, partners, and development practitioners to reflect jointly on what an institutionalized approach to participatory statistics might look like and to agree a radical agenda for action. The challenge here is to foster institutional change on the back of the

http://dx.doi.org/10.3362/9781780447711/001

methodological breakthroughs and philosophical commitment described in this book. The prize is a 'win–win' outcome in which statistics are a part of an empowering process for local people and part of a real-time information flow for those aid agencies and government departments willing to generate statistics in new ways.

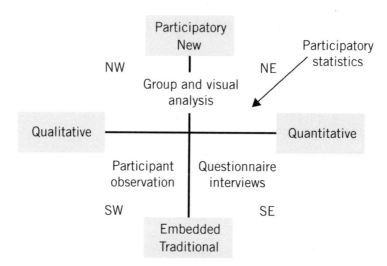

Figure 1.1 Dimensions of methodology and outcome

Source: adapted from Chambers, 2008

Participatory research is different from 'conventional' research

Participatory statistics are generated within a 'paradigm' of participatory research. This paradigm has long challenged a 'top-down' approach to knowledge generation that institutionalizes control of knowledge amongst powerful development professionals. Participatory approaches reposition ownership and control by asking 'whose reality counts?' (Chambers, 1997) and 'who counts reality?' (Estrella and Gaventa, 1998). In this way, participatory research respects local knowledge and facilitates local ownership and control of data generation and analysis.

In contrast to the individualized observation and discussions in much top-down investigation, participatory research also focuses on public and collective reflection and action. At its most political, participatory research is a *process* in which reflection is internalized and promotes raised political consciousness. In this way, population involvement in research shifts from *passive* to *active*. Participatory research supports empowerment by providing opportunities for local agency and shifting power dynamics in aid and development relationships (Eyben, 2006).

Participatory statistics come in many forms

Local people generate statistics in many ways, through mapping, measuring, estimating, valuing, and comparing, and combinations of these (Chambers, 2008, see Box 1.1). They do so through open-ended group-based data generation and analysis, accompanied by in-depth diagnostic or evaluative discussion. This is in contrast with conventional survey-based research, which is typically one-on-one and collects simple pieces of data using questionnaires with closed-ended questions (Barahona and Levy, 2003: 9). Crucially, when participatory numbers are compiled or aggregated, for example from a series of focus group discussions, they can be subjected to statistical analysis.

Box 1.1 Participatory methods that generate numbers

Methods often used to generate numbers include:

- participatory mapping (ActionAid-Nepal, 1992; Chambers, 1997; Barahona and Levy, 2003)
- participatory modelling (Rambaldi and Callosa-Tarr, 2000, 2002)
- proportional piling (Watson, 1994; Jayakaran, 2002, 2003, 2007; Sharp, 2005: 20–4)
- card writing, marking, sorting, ordering, and positioning (Kagugube et al., 2007)
- matrix ranking and scoring (Abeyasekera, 2001; Abebe et al., 2008)
- pair-wise ranking (Mukherjee, 2001)
- linkage diagramming (Burn, 2000; Galpin et al., 2000)
- pocket voting (van Wijk, 2001).

Source: Chambers, 2008: 111

Powerful examples of **counting** are social and census maps (see, for example, Figure 1.2). Conducted in group mode, social mapping generates very accurate data in contexts where there is 'community owned' (public) knowledge, for example when listing and categorizing households in small rural communities. Through a process of 'group-visual synergy' (Chambers, 2008: 99), participants can 'see what is being said' and correct and add detail. For community census purposes, the outcomes have proven very accurate, and where there have been discrepancies, community analysts have wanted to check until they reach agreement.

An example of **calculating** comes from Community-Led Total Sanitation (CLTS), where as part of an appraisal process, local people worked out the quantities (e.g. cartloads for the whole community) of shit (the crude word is used) produced by their households in a day, multiplied out for longer periods, and added up for the whole community, concluding sometimes with community cartloads per annum (Kar, 2008).

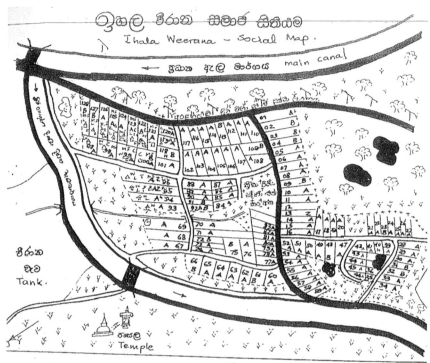

ඉහල වීරාන සමාජ සිතියම
Ihala Weerana - Social Map.

← පුබඛ ඇල මාර්ගය main canal

මුල්ලේ ඇල මාර්ගය

වීරාන
වැව
Tank.

රජමහ විහාරය Temple

SYMBLE සංකේත	DESCRIPTION.	Nos. ගණන
⌂	PERMANANT HOUSES.	51
▢	SEMI PERMANANT HOUSES	22
△	TEMPORARY HOUSES	12
Ⓦ	WELLS WITH WATER	01
Ⓦ	WELLS WITHOUT WATER	17
Ⓛ	PERMANANT LATRINES	44
L	TEMPORARY LATRINES	69
✳	EMPLOYMENT	18
Y	UNEMPLOYMENT (GCE-O/L)	03
S	BOUTIQUES	04
R.M	RICEMILLS.	02
Ⓣ	FOUR WHEEL TRACTORS	01
T	TWO WHEEL TRACTORS	21
TV	TELE··SIONS	45
RR	RADIO	98
⌒	DRAUGHT CATTLE	54
🐂	MILK CATTLE	28
✖	BRIDGES	02
♉ ♉	FOREST RESEVATION	
⋎ ⋎ ⋎	CANAL RESEVATION	
⫰	HITENTION ELECTRICITY LINE	
▱	ROCK	
∽	MAIN CANAL	
≈	TAR ROADS.	
⩫	GRAVEL ROADS	
M	ADULT MALES	
F	ADULT FEMALES	
C	SCHOOLING CHILDREN	
A	FARMER FAMILIES	105
B	SECOND GENARATION FAMILIES	
Z	MARRIED-WITHOUT LANDS	09
N	UNOCCUPIED LANDS.	13
K	CARPENTRY SHOPS.	05

STATISTICS FROM A SOCIAL MAP

1999 · 06 · 11 දින

සහභාගී වූවන් —PARTICIPANTS.

N. G අනෝසි උදය කාන්දා 87
K. H ලාල් කුමාර 195
J. M නිමාල් බණ්ඩාර 112
W. L. G නිලන්ත කුමාර 85
M. P. G රත්නසිරිස 62
K. G සුනිල් කුමාර 03
S. M සරත් බණ්ඩාර 58
K. G ලාල් ශ්‍රීමති 106
K. P. G සරත් කුමාර 17

⌂ permanent houses
Ⓦ wells with water.
Ⓛ permanent latrines
T tractors (2-4 wheel)
⊂ reservation
∽ main canal

WEERANA-SRI LANKA - 1999

Figure 1.2 A social map

Examples of participatory **measuring** can be found in natural resource management and planning, including the use of participatory GIS modelling (e.g. Rambaldi et al., 2007). Through group-based analysis, local people measure natural resources and map and model land use. Examples of participatory measuring can be found with timber stocks, water flows, crop yields, arm circumferences, and land-use areas from participatory GIS mapping and modelling.

Participatory **estimating** uses comparative and relative proportions to indicate trends and changes, for example in production or consumption resources. Historical matrices (e.g. Freudenberger, 1995; PRAXIS, 2001) indicate trends and changes, while seasonal food calendars show seasonal variations in things like amount and type of food consumed (e.g. Mukherjee and Jena, 2001) and health problems (Shah, 1999). Proportional piling has been widely used to estimate income and food sources (e.g. Watson, 1994; Eldridge, 2001). There are many applications with variants of methods such as the Ten Seed Technique (Jayakaran, 2002) or the allocation of 100 seeds, stones, or other counters to give percentages. At the time of writing, this technique was being used in a DFID-funded, six-country impact assessment of cash benefit transfers on beneficiary household income and expenditure patterns. The research was using 'cluster sampling' to generate participatory statistics for over 10 per cent of the beneficiaries in each sampled community. During the fieldwork, beneficiaries conducted individual income and expenditure analysis and then participated in group analytical discussion to validate, explain, and interpret the data generated.

Valuing and scoring methods allow local analysts to categorize and place a value on qualitative dimensions of their social, economic, and political lives. Examples of valuing and scoring methods are preference ranking, matrix ranking, and matrix scoring (Jones, 1996). Things valued include problems with water supply management in China (Vernooy et al., 2003), police–youth relations in Jamaica (Holland et al., 2007), household spending priorities in Maharashtra, India (Kapadia-Kundu and Dyalchand, 2007), crop varieties in Zambia (Drinkwater, 1993) and India (Manoharan et al., 1993) to contraceptive methods in Bangladesh (Kar and Datta, 1998). They range from girls' preferences for sex-partners in Zambia (Shah, 1999) to local preferences for wild plants collected for winter feeding of goats in Afghanistan (Leyland, 1994).

Comparing is widely used in participatory research and is often a significant part of the activities summarized above. Comparisons are made in many ways, often directly through the statistics. Numbers or scores can also be generated as a second stage of a physical activity of grouping or positioning, in many instances with cards representing households. Perhaps the best-known and most widespread example is wealth or well-being ranking, where analysts group households according to their judgements of personal or household conditions. This method has been in use for over 20 years by NGOs and INGOs (see, for example, *RRA Notes* 15, 1992, for an introduction). Plan International and ActionAid, for example, have for many years used wealth ranking as standard practice when first engaging with a community. Placing on a scale is another. In Uganda small groups have placed household cards on a rope symbolizing climbing out of poverty, with the best condition at one end, and the worst at the other, leading to scores between 0 and 10. This method was included as a participatory module in a sub-sample of the Uganda National Household Survey, with major differences emerging between income findings from the UNHS questionnaire and 'having enough money' in the qualitative module (Kagugube et al., 2007). Wealth ranking was conducted as part of the participatory *Consultations with the Poor on Safety Nets* study in Malawi, which fed into the classification of poor households for a poverty-targeting impact assessment in Malawi (see Barahona, Chapter 10). Through participatory studies of urban violence during the past two decades, urban residents in Jamaica and Latin America have estimated the frequency of different types of violence and ranked them according to their seriousness alongside the importance, positive and negative, of different institutions. These have been aggregated to show patterns and compare priorities across communities (see, for example, Moser and McIlwaine, 2004).

Participatory research can measure qualitative changes in processes and relationships

Building on the principle of valuing introduced above, participatory methods are increasingly being used to generate data that quantifies the qualitative (as above) and then measures qualitative changes. Development agencies recognize the importance of measuring changes in processes and relationships, such as empowerment, governance, and accountability. However, donor and government agencies are more used to measuring observable outcomes – metrics such as household income or school attendance. Measuring changing relationships – some of which are linked to these observable outcomes – enables donors and governments to understand their contribution to complex change processes and (predicted and unpredicted) outcomes. Recent and ongoing donor efforts to measure and track qualitative changes have focused on empowerment (see, for example, Alsop et al., 2006) and on voice and accountability (see, for example, Holland and Thirkell, 2009).

Scoring of qualitative changes in relationships, generated through participatory processes, creates space and legitimacy in project monitoring frameworks for these difficult-to-measure changes, while opening the door to in-depth participatory diagnostic analysis. More generally, the use of quantification can be very effective in opening up policy space for discussing non-monetary impacts and linking this discussion to a broader policy debate that incorporates process issues of governance, empowerment, social inclusion, and so on. Recent examples within DFID's portfolio of programmes include methodological innovations with participatory research in a huge global initiative to empower adolescent girls and flagship civil society strengthening programmes in Burma, Afghanistan and Vietnam.

A lot of the innovation and credibility with 'qualitative indicators' has come through the emergence of standardized and aggregated governance indicators for regional or global benchmarking – such as the Afrobarometer indicators, the Ibrahim Index of African Governance, and the World Bank's Worldwide Governance Indicators. The Afrobarometer, for example, includes indicators based on recall data (e.g. 'in the past year, how many times have you paid a bribe to an official for service X?') and on perception scoring of qualitative relationships (e.g. on a scale of 1–4, how much do you trust your local service provider?).[1]

At community level in different contexts, scorecards have emerged as powerful tools for quantifying and monitoring service provider performance. At the interface of 'rights holders' and 'duty bearers', participatory statistics serve as powerful tools for oversight, advocacy, and accountability. Emerging from the innovative work of the Public Affairs Centre (PAC) in Bangalore (Gopakumar and Balakrishnan, n.d.), citizen report cards are now widely used for participatory monitoring and evaluation. Innovative design of scorecards can mix group discussion with secret balloting and can triangulate group scoring with report card survey modules. The data and analysis generated from these types of scoring processes can be used for local reflection and action and for national oversight of policy implementation.

Participatory statistics can be standardized and taken to scale

Methodological and ethical debates over the application of participatory research have surfaced and re-surfaced during the past three decades. Many of these debates have been brought into sharper focus within participatory statistics by the tensions and apparent trade-offs in meeting statistical principles, while ensuring locally embedded and owned data collection and analysis. These trade-offs, once so vexing and seemingly insurmountable, have been tackled with a refreshing vigour by social statisticians who have entered the field of participatory research with a new mindset. They have successfully applied statistical principles to participatory numbers, helping to demythologize statistics and expand the methodological horizons. Largely as a result of their efforts, over the past decade participatory statistics have been used with greater confidence, rigour, and on a larger scale, with methodological and ethical tensions recognized.

From its roots in local community reflection and action, the use of participatory statistics has grown in its scope, purpose, and ambition. Numbers generated locally have long served the purpose of facilitating local analysis and action. Farmers in Kenya map their land-use patterns and produce matrices of seasonal crop productivity levels, while young people in inner-city Jamaica analyse the frequency and cyclical nature of political violence in their ghetto communities. In this way, numbers add to local knowledge and fuel local reflection and action. Numbers in these contexts are fit-for-purpose, powerful stimulants of change.

For outside agencies seeking to understand patterns and trends for poli-cymaking and programming, however, questions emerge relating to the standardization, representativeness, reliability, and objectivity of participa-tory statistics. Survey-based research as a default methodology can generate statistics that are representative of a population, while participatory research is more likely to be viewed as locally valid but not easily generalizable for a larger population. The challenge laid down by these default positions is for participatory researchers to incorporate statistical principles and demonstrate that participatory statistics can meet the demands of standardization and comparability of data across sites:

> There are major differences between survey-based and research using participatory methods, but these should not be because one approach is representative while the other is a collection of 'case studies'. By adopting certain statistical principles and making some adaptations to the PRA tools, this difference disappears. (Barahona and Levy, 2003: 9)

Participatory research can accommodate both the contextual and the standardized

In this way, participatory research that produces statistics can be generalized and used to influence decision making. With externally motivated research, the research agenda and research questions are set by outsiders such as programme managers, policymakers, or donor evaluation units. What does participatory research mean in this context? In many cases the identification and categorization of what should be measured is best left to local people in a process of 'learning reversal'. Who decides what empowerment means? Who decides the characteristics of the poorest? Who decides what it means to be food insecure? With participatory research this kind of contextualized under-standing can emerge through local knowledge before being standardized and subjected to wider investigation – using participatory research approaches and methods – but using a robust sampling protocol.

Given the demands of sampling protocols that meet statistical principles, certainly there remains a tension between depth (allowing analysis, diagnosis, and a participatory process) and coverage (increasing the precision of infer-ence while allowing generalization). Smaller-scale research processes invest time and resources in higher-quality analysis linked to deeper local ownership and impact, but with loss of 'precision of inference'; and vice versa.

But participatory statistics *can* be taken to scale while also stimulating local reflection and action. Breakthroughs in the past decade have demonstrated powerfully that through careful sampling protocols, participatory research can generate statistics that are generalizable. In Malawi in 1999–2002, a research team from the Statistical Services Centre at the University of Reading conducted studies using participatory methods to generate population esti-mates, specifically estimates of the proportion of people in a population with certain characteristics (e.g. the very food insecure) and estimates of the proportion of people in a population that should be targeted by an intervention (Barahona, Chapter 10; Barahona and Levy, 2003). A key requirement was to produce results from a representative sample from which conclusions for the population of interest could be inferred. This meant removing researcher bias in the selection of sites, sampling from classified sites to represent the study population and working in a larger number of sites than was common for most participatory studies. Beneath the level of the village, hierarchical statistical sampling (whose lowest unit is usually the household in conventional research) gave way to participatory methods for collecting information within the selected villages.

Here the study design adapted participatory tools to meet the demands of standardization and comparability of data produced across sites. The research team argued that this could be done without undermining participatory approaches, behaviours, and methods, concluding that if research studies using participatory methods followed this approach, the data generated would be suitable for standard statistical analysis. The statistics produced by such studies should be capable of informing policy at national level.

In facilitating group-based participatory research, the study was strong on the principle that quality of facilitation is critical to the reliability of the data. To achieve good facilitation requires time and resources devoted to careful selection of facilitators, their training, and then their supervision in the field. Even though this may add to costs and slow implementation initially, the outcomes are still highly cost-effective compared with alternatives.

In addition to group-based analysis, which generated 'community owned' census mapping data far more efficiently than a standard survey approach, the study implemented a small household questionnaire survey to collect data that was more reliably collected through a survey rather than a group-based methodology. Sequencing was used to good effect, with the participatory census mapping being used to construct an accurate sampling frame for the household survey component. No other tool would have been able to do this, as the participatory mapping was necessary to establish the boundaries of the village, which households belonged to it, and which of them were real households.[2]

New technologies are opening up exciting possibilities for participatory statistics

The tide of innovation in participatory statistics has been swept along in the broader revolution in information and communication technologies (ICTs), with exciting and transformative methods emerging. These technological innovations serve the demand amongst policymakers and service providers for 'just in time' evidence to improve the delivery of policy and enable management for results. Donors also increasingly need ICTs that can facilitate data collection and communication in fragile and conflict-affected contexts where mobility is restricted and information collection can put people at risk.

Spatial information technologies and participatory GIS support accurate and locally owned maps (see, for example, Rambaldi, Chapter 2), while recent advances in mobile telephone software have blown wide open the opportunities for participatory statistics, bringing the promise of efficiency, speed, democratization, and empowerment to data collection. In Kenya, for example, participatory monitoring is being explored with community-led total sanitation to see whether through mobile phones there can be continuous updates from communities to map their progress towards total sanitation.[3]

Innovators in the South have been developing platforms for quickly aggregating and sharing spatially organized data. The *Ushahidi* (Kiswahili for 'testament' or 'witness') platform is an open source project that allows anyone to gather distributed data via mobile phone SMS, email, or the Web, and visualize it on a map or timeline. It has been used with 'crowdsourced' information for election monitoring in Kenya and India, monitoring unrest in DRC, and tracking violence in Gaza. It was the basis of the system used in the Haiti earthquake for locating where people were trapped under the rubble (Okolloh, 2009).

Map Kibera is a project in Nairobi's largest slum, a community that until two years ago remained a 'blank spot' on the map. One Map Kibera team, consisting of 13 young people from the community trained in open source mapping techniques, created topic and sector maps, for instance for health facilities, for schools, for sanitation and water, and for security and vulnerability. This last map contains unsafe spaces (i.e. places where drugs and alcohol are consumed), safe spaces (i.e. girl groups, community centres, lighted areas), resources (gender-based violence clinics), and more. These data are loaded to an online free and open source map, then shared with the community in order to prompt community reflection and action, and empower community members to engage with local authorities.[4]

Sensemaker is a new and exciting software program that allows for immediate update and 'meta analysis' of qualitative M&E or impact assessment data. In Kenya, for instance, thousands of stories have been told and 'signified' by local people affected by project interventions, bridging the gap between case study and survey data. In this way, qualitative data, in the form of stories, pictures, or video clips, can be uploaded and subjected to Sensemaker 'meta analysis' to identify patterns and trends, with rapid feedback possible into participatory processes at all levels (Irene Guijt, personal communication).

The structure of this book

This book has a three-part structure. It follows the policy and programme cycle in discussing and illustrating the generation of participatory statistics for policy and programme analysis, monitoring and evaluation, and impact assessment.

Participatory statistics are timely and powerful for policy and programme analysis

Part 1 of this book presents case studies that demonstrate the power and utility of participatory statistics for diagnostic discussion in policymaking and programming. Statistical analysis from participatory research can contribute to evidence-based decision making, from community-level diagnostics and planning through meso-level policy implementation up to national and even international strategizing and policymaking.

Beyond evidence and insights, the group-based analysis that underpins participatory statistics can include the voiceless in a policy process that challenges bureaucratized behaviour and which unsettles comfortable patterns of decision making. This challenge will often occur in contexts of scarce resources and limited curiosity about alternative visions of development.

In Chapter 2, Giacomo Rambaldi describes the use of participatory 3-dimensional modelling (P3DM), with local people making their own spatially referenced models of their environment. P3DM can support collaborative natural resource management initiatives and facilitate the establishment of a peer-to-peer dialogue among local stakeholders and external institutions and agencies. Drawing on the global spread of P3DM application, including a case of community environmental rehabilitation planning in Oromiya, Ethiopia, Rambaldi reflects on the value of a spatial data tool that stimulates community-level diagnostic discussion and planning, while providing a database for policy beyond the local.

In Chapter 3, Caroline Moser and Alfredo Stein reflect on the use of participatory research for policy insight in the context of the vulnerability of the urban poor. They describe recent research on the implementation of a participatory methodology to quantify adaptation strategies amongst the urban poor to climate change. Conducted by poor people in cities in Kenya and Nicaragua, participatory appraisal enabled local people to list, rank, and analyse their asset vulnerability and actions in the face of climate change risks. The data generated facilitated local analysis and policy discussions between local people and urban and national authorities. It was also aggregated for longitudinal and cross-population comparison.

In Chapter 4, Ashish Shah documents the evolution and application of the *Ubudehe* community mapping process in Rwanda. Drawing on existing research conducted in villages across Rwanda over five years, Shah argues persuasively that local collective analysis and action moves debates about democracy beyond notions of electoral democracy. *Ubudehe* begins with participatory poverty analysis and social census mapping, prompting diagnostic discussion and action planning. These local plans are then linked to a transparent process of community fund disbursement from the Ministry of Local Government in Kigali. Beyond community planning, the nationwide coverage of *Ubudehe* has generated a national resource of citizen-generated statistics. Policy users include the Ministry of Health, which had been lacking data on how to identify poor and marginalized households to benefit from free health insurance.

In Chapter 5, Rose Nierras recalls innovations in participatory planning in the context of health sector decentralization in the Philippines during the 1990s. In an environment of unmotivated and uninformed planning, provincial and local health officials were faced with new levels of authority over health planning and budgeting. A participatory diagnostic mapping workshop with local governmental and non-governmental stakeholders generated accurate and insightful data on the distribution and levels of causes of morbidity and mortality across the province that countered conventional data sources. These mapped data were overlaid on a health 'supply' map to show where policy delivery was failing to match local health priorities. The resulting cross-sector policy changes included a Provincial Traffic Code which cut road mortalities within six months, increasing provision of ambulances, and a shift of health intervention emphasis from communicable to degenerative diseases.

In Chapter 6, Margunn Alshaikh reflects on the process of Crisis and Recovery Mapping and Analysis (CRMA) in post-secession Southern Sudan. In a context of conflict and insecurity where conventional data collection methods are extremely difficult to implement and where the context changes rapidly, participatory methodologies generate accurate and timely statistics for state-level planning frameworks. The mapping technique produces both quantitative and qualitative data, backed by in-depth qualitative analysis, on local priorities – the basis for evidence-based planning. Alshaikh warns of the importance of embedding data production in an institutional process of promoting a knowledge culture and new forms of collaboration and communication.

Participatory statistics are being generated effectively for monitoring and evaluation

Part 2 illustrates the power of participatory statistics for monitoring and evaluation. Development agencies widely recognize the importance of monitoring and evaluating policies and programmes. Monitoring and evaluation tracks progress and generates the evidence that enables development agencies to make 'course corrections' in their programme and project implementation. They continually face the pressure to demonstrate success on the one hand, while at the same time recognizing the need to learn about what can be done better. This twin perspective tends to promote a top-down approach to monitoring and evaluation. Data needs and instruments are identified in development agency and government offices, while information is extracted from passive beneficiaries on the ground by external 'experts' through highly controlled monitoring procedures.

At its best, monitoring and evaluation enables development agencies and partners to understand their influence and to learn from experience to contribute more effectively to change on the ground. This type of continuous reflection, or 'evaluative practice', relies on the generation and communication of 'real-time' M&E data and analysis. The concept of the 'learning organisation' has its roots in mainstream organizational thinking (Senge et al., 1999), but has also been adapted and used widely in development contexts. It builds on the notion of 'double-loop', adaptive learning for organizational change, with stories of failure and success shared and interrogated. Double-loop learning involves questioning the underlying purpose and values behind one's actions, while 'single-loop' learning is restricted to corrective management within a pre-given framework (Argyris and Schön, 1974).

Participatory monitoring and evaluation – increasingly now referred to as 'monitoring, evaluation and learning' – is widespread (Estrella and Gaventa, 1998) and already delivering the promise of a 'win–win' in generating statistics for donors and local people alike. Large bilateral and multilateral donors, including notably the World Bank, have taken giant steps forward in systematizing and implementing participatory evaluation techniques. With participatory M&E, local people identify, monitor, and evaluate their own indicators of change. Participatory M&E produces numerical data in ways that empower local people to take action and to transform their relationships with service providers and officials. Rapid feedback, participatory statistics provide the evidence and accompanying insights for evaluative discussions. Crucially, they can release 'higher status professionals' from a one-stop, linear, 'neo-Newtonian' straitjacket and allow them to connect with 'adaptive pluralism' to what is local, complex, diverse, dynamic, uncontrollable, and unpredictable (Chambers, 2010). This involves a management shift from rigid, linear, path-dependent, and purposeful planning to adaptive management of complexity (Eyben et al., 2008).

In Chapter 7, Dee Jupp and Sohel Ibn Ali describe participatory M&E conducted with a land rights social movement in Bangladesh in 2007. This research generated a set of quantitative indicators for monitoring and evaluating empowerment, mapped onto a matrix, as a baseline for annual participatory M&E. Participants assigned a happy face to those indicators that had been achieved and an unhappy face to those that had not been achieved, prompting an action plan for making better progress on those indicators. Data were aggregated and used by outside project managers for results-based management. This measuring empowerment methodology has subsequently been taken up by large development agencies such as Trocaire and the UNDP. Trocaire piloted the approach in India in a monitoring framework for a human rights programme with women, tribal, and Dalit communities. Trocaire is currently reviewing the approach in order to produce a manual for a more comprehensive roll-out (Carol Ballantine, pers. comm.). The UNDP's Urban Partnerships for Poverty Reduction (UPPR) Programme in Bangladesh has adopted a community-led process of empowerment in the largest cities and towns in which it works. In this programme, Community Development Committees are supported to identify their problems, develop action plans to solve them, and prepare and manage small contracts to deliver basic infrastructure and services. The UNDP's

Programme Manager is very enthusiastic about Jupp's methodology for quantifying qualitative outcomes from people's own analysis, seeing it as 'a great
substitute for more formal and top down approaches and [which] in itself can
be seen as an empowering process' (Richard Geier, pers. comm.).

In Chapter 8, Bernward Causemann and colleagues describe the collaborative activities of a network of Southern and Northern NGOs on a programme
to develop instruments for regular participatory monitoring and learning
against outcomes and impacts. Local NGOs in different contexts and sectors
in South Asia, the Philippines, and East Africa set goals for their members and
used a system of rating to assess their own performance on these goals over
time. Goals were frequently linked to processes of social change and behaviour. Over time, this generated data on change, which prompted reflection
amongst local people and enabled the NGOs themselves to aggregate, analyse,
and reflect on their interventions.

In Chapter 9, Nils Riemenschneider and colleagues describe the integration
of a scorecard into longitudinal survey conducted at three points between
2006 and 2011 in the Maldives to monitor and evaluate the World Bank's
Integrated Human Development Project. The scorecard was included as a
module of a survey and also used in a group setting. The group-based scoring
of satisfaction with education and health services generated perception data
that could be triangulated with the survey data, while prompting a deeper
evaluative discussion on the quality and accessibility of those services to
justify and explain the satisfaction scores that the groups had given. In this
way, scoring was intrinsically useful to the qualitative exercise, because the act
of being required to score something that was subjective sharpened the qualitative analysis that followed, as participants justifed their scores.

Sarah Levy and Carlos Barahona have brought social statistics rigour and a
fresh perspective to thinking on participatory research. In Chapter 10, Carlos
Barahona describes Sarah Levy's experience of conducting a participatory
evaluation of the DFID-funded Malawi Targeted Inputs Programme, between
1999 and 2002. This research aggregated household food security categorized
data generated by group-based social mapping with cards. The research was
conducted in a representative sample of rural communities as a standardized
sub-component of a flexible participatory process. Analysis of these data, too
complex to be collected with a conventional survey, showed that the community targeting process for the TIP had been generally unsuccessful in targeting
the most food-insecure households. Ten years on, Barahona reflects on what
challenges need to be tackled in the push to mainstream participatory statistics within development decision making.

Participatory impact assessment can generate statistics to identify how much has changed and to understand attribution

Part 3 presents innovative cases of participatory statistics in impact assessment. While monitoring measures ongoing activities and evaluation measures

performance against objectives, impact assessment assesses 'lasting or significant change – positive or negative, intended or not – in people's lives' (Roche, 1999). In this way, impact assessments attempt to attribute final impacts to external interventions and explain what worked and why.

Participatory impact assessment (PIA) has demonstrated how participatory statistics can empower local communities while generating externally meaningful empirical data and analysis. PIA is fast maturing, with proponents systematizing PIA approaches and developing guides for practitioners (see, for example, Catley et al., n.d.; see also the work of the University of Amsterdam and partners on Participatory Assessment of Development[5]). Data collection around locally identified indicators describes the nature and magnitude of longer-term and broader change processes to which external interventions contribute. Group-based diagnosis of these data untangles and explains pathways of change, and generates policy recommendations.

Notably, the work of Tufts University's Feinstein International Center in the horn of Africa has demonstrated the efficiency and effectiveness of PIA in understanding impact linked to learning and policy change. Research teams successfully standardized PIA methods in two livestock-related studies of the impact of Community-Based Animal Health Workers on animal diseases in Ethiopia (Abebe et al., 2008; Catley, 2007). The PIA findings influenced policy, including the official recognition of Community-Based Animal Health Workers in national legislation and guidelines. A similar piece of PIA assessed the impact of an innovative habitat management approach to cropping systems (reaching 25,000 farmers between 1997 and 2009) in Kenya, introduced by the International Centre of Insect Physiology and Ecology (icipe, Kenya). A recent farmer-to-farmer participatory peer assessment generated quantitative data on increased crop yields under new technology and qualitative analysis of knock-on benefits, as well as concerns about the limitations of this technology, its uptake, and its impact. It also generated valuable learning and recommendations for further research, up-scaling and policymaking. All participating actors perceived the participatory assessment method as an eye-opener, fostering mutual learning and capacity building (Martin Fischler, pers. comm.).

In Chapter 11, Dawit Abebe and Andy Catley describe a PIA of a commercial destocking intervention in drought conditions in southern Ethiopia, feeding policy discussions on national guidelines on destocking in pastoral areas of Ethiopia, as well as informing the development of global Livestock Emergency Guidelines and Standards. During this PIA, pastoralists identified 8 qualitative impact indicators against which to compare different food and non-food interventions, using matrix scoring (using 30 stones allocated across 8 sources of support for 8 impact indicators). Destocking was considered to be the most useful intervention (mean score 9.1) against the indicator 'Helps us to cope with the effect of the drought', and also the most valuable intervention (score 11.1) against the post-drought recovery indicator 'Helps fast recovery and herd rebuilding'. Follow-up interviews confirmed the value of destocking over food aid.

In Chapter 12, Elizabeth Cromwell describes an early innovation with PIA applied to an agricultural starter pack programme in Malawi between 1999 and 2000. Farmers identified 15 indicators of sustainability during piloting and for each indicator developed qualitative statements that described what characterized 'high sustainability', 'medium sustainability', and 'low sustainability'. The farmers then analysed each sustainability indicator and generated scores for their importance. These scores placed 'crop diversification' and 'access to seeds' at the top, with agroforestry and fallow at the bottom, revealing a conflict with professional views and indicating an overriding short-term priority given to adequate food.

In Chapter 13, Susanne Neubert describes a PIA conducted in the context of a regional initiative to support cotton farmers across Africa. Cotton farmers in 'intervention' communities analysed changes in their lives and gave value scores to the contribution of COMPACI interventions to different aspects of economic and social well-being. The quantitative data were used for local reflection amongst farmers and by programme managers and implementing partners to reflect on programme design and prioritize future interventions. The standardization of aspects of the methodology allowed for an aggregation of data across programme sites and even across countries.

Conclusion

The increasing visibility and strengthening legitimacy of participatory statistics in development research and practice are certainly encouraging, but will remain fragile without a step change in methodological adoption and adaptation. The chapters pulled together for this volume represent over a decade of innovation, implementation, and reflection by a wide range of development researchers from many different backgrounds working in very different contexts. It is hoped that the cumulative power of this assembled collection will provide learning and inspiration in equal measure for those in the development community who are ready and willing to 'push on' in the pursuit of the institutionalized prize on offer: a 'win–win' in international development.

Notes

1   www.afrobarometer.org; also see UNDP, 2008.
2   This method would not be possible in large rural or urban environments, with difficult-to-access populations (such as stigmatized or illegal groups) or when eliciting private information.
3   Sammy Musyoki, personal communication in R. Chambers (2010).
4   http://mapkibera.org/
5   www.padev.nl/

References

Abebe, D., Cullis, A., Catley, A., Aklilu, Y., Mekonnen, G. and Ghebrechirstos, Y. (2008) 'Livelihoods impact and benefit-cost estimation of a commercial de-stocking relief intervention in Moyale district, southern Ethiopia', *Disasters* 32(2): 167–89.

Abeyasekera, Savitri (2001) *Analysis Approaches in Participatory Work Involving Ranks or Scores*, Statistical Services Centre, University of Reading, UK.

Alsop, R., Bertelsen, M. and Holland, J. (2006) *Empowerment in Practice: From Analysis to Implementation*, The World Bank, Washington, DC.

Argyris, C. and Schön, D. (1974) *Theory in Practice. Increasing Professional Effectiveness*, Jossey-Bass, San Francisco, CA.

Barahona, C. (2010) *Randomised Control Trials for the Impact Evaluation of Development Initiatives: A Statistician's Point of View*, ILAC Working Paper 13, Institutional Learning and Change Initiative, Rome.

Barahona, C. and Levy, S. (2003) 'How to generate statistics and influence policy using participatory methods in research; reflections on work in Malawi, 1999–2002', Working Paper No. 212, Institute of Development Studies, Brighton.

Berg, Christian et al. (1998) 'NGO-based participatory impact monitoring of an integrated rural development project in Holalkere Taluk, Karnataka State, India', Schriftenreihe des Seminars für Ländliche Entwicklung No. S180, SLE, Berlin.

Burn, R.W. (2000) *Quantifying and Combining Causal Diagrams*, Statistical Services Centre, University of Reading, UK.

Catley, A. (2007) 'From marginal to normative: Institutionalising participatory epidemiology', paper to Farmer First Revisited Workshop, Institute of Development Studies, Sussex, December.

Catley, A., Burns, J., Abebe, D. and Suji, O. (no date) *Participatory Impact Assessment: A Guide for Practitioners*, Feinstein International Center, Tufts University, Medford, MA.

Chambers, R. (1997) *Whose Reality Counts? Putting the First Last*, ITDG, London.

Chambers, R. (2007) 'Who counts? The quiet revolution of participation and numbers', IDS Working Paper 296, IDS, Brighton.

Chambers, R. (2008) *Revolutions in Development Inquiry*, Earthscan, London, chapter 6.

Chambers, R. (2010) 'Paradigms, poverty and adaptive pluralism', IDS Working Paper 344, Institute of Development Studies, Brighton.

Cromwell, E., Kambewa, P., Mwanza, R. and Chirwa, R. with KWERA Development Centre (2001) 'Impact assessment using participatory approaches: "starter pack" and sustainable agriculture in Malawi', Network Paper No. 112, Agricultural Research and Extension Network, Overseas Development Institute, London.

Drinkwater, Michael (1993) 'Sorting fact from opinion: the use of a direct matrix to evaluate finger millet varieties', *RRA Notes* 17: 24–8.

Eldridge, C. (1998) 'Summary of the main findings of a PRA study on the 1992 drought in Zimbabwe', Save the Children, UK.

Eldridge, C. (2001) *Investigating Change and Relationships in the Livelihoods of the Poor Using an Adaptation of Proportional Piling*, Save the Children, UK.

Estrella, M. and Gaventa, J. (1998) 'Who counts reality? Participatory monitoring and evaluation: a literature review', IDS Working Paper 70, Institute of Development Studies, Brighton.

Eyben, R. (2006) *Relationships for Aid*, Earthscan, London and Sterling, VA.

Eyben, R., Kidder, T., Rowlands, J. and Bronstein, A. (2008) 'Thinking about change for development practice: a case study from Oxfam GB', in *Development in Practice* 18(2): 201–12 <http://dx.doi.org/10.1080/09614520801898996>.

Freudenberger, K. (1995) 'The historical matrix – breaking away from static analysis', *Forests, Trees and People Newsletter*, 26/27 (April): 78–9.

Gaillard, J. and Maceda, E. (2009) 'Participatory three-dimensional mapping for disaster risk reduction', *Participatory Learning and Action* 60: 109–18.

Galpin, M., Dorward, P., and Shepherd, D. (2000) *Participatory Farm Management Methods for Agricultural Research and Extension Needs Assessment: A Manual*, Departments of Agricultural Extensions and Rural Development, University of Reading, UK.

Germann, D. and Gohl, E. (1996) Participatory Impact Monitoring. Booklet 1: Group-Based Impact Monitoring. Booklet 2: NGO-Based Impact Monitoring. Booklet 3: Application Examples. Booklet 4: The Concept of Participatory Impact Monitoring. Hrsg.: GATE/GTZ und FAKT, Wiesbaden: Vieweg, www.fakt-consult.de

Gopakumar, K. and Balakrishnan, S. (no date) 'Citizens' feedback and state accountability: report cards as an aid to improve local governance', Public Affairs Centre, Bangalore. Citizen Report Card available from: www.citizenreportcard.com/index.html.

Guijt, I. (1999) 'Participatory monitoring and evaluation for natural resource management and research', DFID/NRI, London.

Holland, J. and Thirkell, A. with Trepanier, E. and Earle, L. (2009) 'Measuring change and results in voice and accountability work', DFID Working Paper 34, December.

Holland, J., Brook, S., Dudwick, N., Bertelsen, M., and Yaron, G. (2007) 'Monitoring empowerment in policy and programme interventions: combining qualitative and quantitative approaches', *Q-Squared Working Paper* No. 45, November.

Jayakaran, R. (2002) *The Ten Seed Technique*, World Vision, China. Available from: www.fao.org/participation/Ten-Seed%20Technique-Revised.pdf.

Jayakaran, Ravi (2003) *Participatory Poverty Alleviation and Development: A Comprehensive Manual for Development Professionals*, World Vision, China, and Mekong Institute Foundation, Khon Kaen University, Thailand.

Jayakaran, Ravi (2007) *New Participatory Tools for Measuring Attitude, Behaviour, Perception and Change* (an overview of some of the new participatory tools being used for assessment and evaluation). Available from: Ravi_Jayakaran@online.com.kh; Ravi@Jayakaran.com.

Jones, C. (1996) *Matrices, Ranking and Scoring: Participatory Appraisal 'Methods' Paper*, Participation Group, IDS, University of Sussex, Brighton.

Kagugube, Johnson, Ssewakiryanga, Richard, Barahona, Carlos, and Levy, Sarah (submitted 2007) 'Integrating qualitative dimensions of poverty into the Third Uganda National Household Survey (UNHS III)', *Journal of African Statistics* 8: 28–52.

Kapadia-Kundu, Nandita and Dyalchand, Ashok (2007) 'The Pachod Paisa Scale: a numeric response scale for the health and social sciences', *Demography India*, June. Available from: www.ihmp.org/pp_scale_demography_india_dec19_2006.pdf [accessed 19 September 2012].

Kar, K. with Chambers, R. (2008) *Handbook for Community-Led Total Sanitation*, Plan International, London.

Kar, K. and Datta, D. (1998) 'Understanding market mobility: perceptions of smallholder farmers in Bangladesh', *PLA Notes* 33: 54–8.

Levy, S. (2007) 'Using numerical data from participatory research to support the Millennium Development Goals: the case for locally owned information systems', in K. Brock and J. Pettit (eds) *Springs of Participation: Creating and Evolving Methods for Participatory Development*, pp. 137–49, Practical Action Publishing, Rugby.

Leyland, T. (1994) 'Planning a community animal health care programme in Afghanistan', *RRA Notes* 20: 48–50.

Manoharan, M., Velayudham, K., and Shunmugavalli, N. (1993) 'PRA: an approach to find felt needs of crop varieties', *RRA Notes* 18: 66–8.

Moser, C. and McIlwaine, C. (2004) *Encounters with Violence in Latin America: Urban Poor Perceptions from Colombia and Guatemala*, Routledge, New York and London.

Mukherjee, N. (1995) *Participatory Rural Appraisal and Questionnaire Survey: Comparative Field Experience and Methodological Innovations*, Concept Publishing Company, New Delhi.

Mukherjee, N. (2001) *Participatory Learning and Action – With 100 Field Methods*, Concept Publishing Company, New Delhi.

Mukherjee, Neela and Jena, Bratindi (eds) (2001) *Learning to Share: Experiences and Reflections on PRA and Other Participatory Approaches*, Concept Publishing Company, New Delhi.

Okolloh, O. (2009) 'Ushahidi or "testimony": Web 2.0 tools for crowdsourcing crisis information', *PLA* 59: 65–70. Available from: www.ushahidi.com/.

PRAXIS (2001) *The Politics of Poverty: A Tale of the Living Dead in Bolangir*, Books for Change, Bangalore.

Rambaldi, Giacomo and Callosa-Tarr, Jasmin (2000) *Manual on Participatory 3-Dimensional Modeling for Natural Resource Management*, Essentials of Protected Area Management in the Philippines, Vol. 7, NIPAP, PAWB-DENR, Philippines. Available from: www.iapad.org/publications/ppgis/p3dm_nipap.pdf [accessed 19 September 2012].

Rambaldi, Giacomo and Callosa-Tarr, Jasmin (2002) *Participatory 3-Dimensional Modelling: Guiding Principles and Applications*, ASEAN Regional Center for Biodiversity Conservation, Los Banos, Philippines.

Rambaldi, G., Muchemi, J., Crawhall, N., and Monaci, L. (2007) 'Through the eyes of hunter-gatherers: participatory 3D modelling among Ogiek indigenous peoples in Kenya', *Information Development* 23 (2–3): 113–28.

Roche, C. (1999) *Impact Assessment for Development Agencies*, Oxfam, Oxford.

Schürmann, Anke (2002) *Participatory Impact Monitoring of Self-Help Groups and Watersheds. A Users' Handbook*, Welthungerhilfe, Bonn.

Senge, P., Kleiner, A., Ross, R., Roth, G., and Smith, B. (1999) *The Dance of Change*, Currency Doubleday, New York.

Shah, M. Kaul (1999) 'A step-by step guide to popular PLA tools and techniques', in M. Kaul Shah, S.D. Kambou, and B. Monahan (eds), *Embracing Participation in Development: Worldwide Experience from CARE's Reproductive Health Programs*, CARE, USA.

Sharp, Kay (2005) *Squaring the 'Q's? Methodological Reflections on a Study of Destitution in Ethiopia*, Q-Squared Working Paper 7, Centre for International Studies, University of Toronto. Available from: www.q-squared.ca/pdf/Q2_WP7_Sharp.pdf [accessed 7 November 2007].

United Nations Development Programme (2008) Governance Indicators: A Users' Guide, 2nd edn, UNDP, Oslo. Available from: www.undp.org/oslo-centre/docs07/undp_users_guide_online_version.pdf.

UNIFEM (2010) 'Gender and democratic governance in development: delivering basic services for women', Global Programme Document, UNIFEM, New York.

Uphoff, N. (1996) *Learning from Gal Oya: Possibilities for Participatory Development and Post-Newtonian Social Science*, 2nd edn, Intermediate Technology Publications, London.

Van Wijk, C. (2001) *The Best of Two Worlds? Methodology for Participatory Assessment of Community Water Services*, Technical Paper Series 38, IRC International Water and Sanitation Centre, Delft, The Netherlands, and World Bank Water and Sanitation Program, Washington, DC.

Vernooy, Ronnie, Qiu, Sun, and Jianchu, Xu (eds) (2003) *Voices for Change: Participatory Monitoring and Evaluation in China,* Yunnan Science and Technology Press, Kunming, and International Development Research Centre, Ottawa.

Watson, K. (1994) 'Proportional piling in Turkana: a case study', *RRA Notes* 20: 131–2.

About the author

Jeremy Holland is a social development consultant and a Visiting Fellow with the Participation, Power, and Social Change team at the Institute of Development Studies, University of Sussex. He has 20 years' research and advisory experience in developing and transitional countries, working on poverty and policy analysis, gender equality, rights, participatory governance, and political economy. Jeremy has a particular interest in participatory and combined methods for measuring and analysing non-material dimensions of poverty.

PART I

Participatory statistics and policy change

Chapter 2

Participatory 3-dimensional modelling for policy and planning: the practice and the potential

Giacomo Rambaldi

Participatory Geographical Information Systems (PGIS) are empowering for margin-alized communities, and increasingly accessible as hardware and software become cheaper and more user-friendly. One extraordinary application is that of participa-tory 3-dimensional modelling (P3DM), with local people making their own spatially referenced models of their environment. P3DM has been gaining increased recognition as an efficient method to facilitate geo-referenced data generation, spatial learning, analysis, and community involvement in dealing with spatial issues related to a territory. P3DM can support collaborative natural resource management initiatives and facilitate the establishment of a peer-to-peer dialogue among local stakeholders and external institutions and agencies. Drawing on the global spread of P3DM application, including a case of community environmental rehabilitation planning in Oromiya, Ethiopia, this chapter reflects on the value of a spatial data tool that stimulates community-level diagnostic discussion and planning, while providing a database for policy beyond the local.

The participatory creation of maps began in the late 1980s. At that time, development practitioners were inclined to use participatory rural appraisal (PRA) methods, such as sketch mapping (Mascarenhas, 1991), rather than scale mapping which is more complex and time-consuming. They preferred to elicit local knowledge and build on local dynamics to facilitate communication between insiders (e.g. villagers) and outsiders (e.g. researchers and government officials). This approach placed little emphasis on charting courses of action that would enable ordinary people to interact efficiently with policymakers (Rambaldi, 2005). The situation was further compounded by state control of aerial photography, satellite imagery, and large-scale topographic maps, under the pretext of national security concerns.

The state of affairs in mapping changed in the 1990s, with the diffusion of modern spatial information technologies, including geographic informa-tion systems (GIS), global positioning systems (GPS), remote-sensing image

http://dx.doi.org/10.3362/9781780447711/002

analysis software, and open access to spatial data and imagery via the Internet. With the steadily decreasing cost of computer hardware and the availability of user-friendly software, spatial data that were previously controlled by government institutions became progressively more accessible to, and mastered by, non-governmental and community-based organizations, minority groups, and sectors of society traditionally disenfranchised and excluded from spatial decision-making processes (Fox, 2003).

The new environment facilitated the integration of geospatial information technologies (GIT) into community-centred initiatives. Practitioners and researchers around the world were able to adopt a range of GIT to integrate multiple realities and diverse forms of information. Their objectives were to empower underprivileged groups, promote social learning, support two-way communication, and thereby broaden public participation across socio-economic contexts, locations, and sectors. This merging of community development with geospatial technologies to empower less-privileged communities has come to be known as Participatory GIS (PGIS) practice.

In recent times, geographic information created by amateur citizens has been referred to by Michael Goodchild as volunteered geographic information (2007). It represents a shift from authoritative map data towards information generated by the general public through collaboration. The increasing emergence of such user-generated content has been brought about by the advent of Web 2.0 technologies like Wikipedia, Panoramio, and Flickr, where online content is put together in a collaborative mode and widely shared. Such activity has also contributed towards the emergence of *citizen science*, where the general public not only collects scientific data (such as birds' seasonal migrations pattern (Wiersma, 2010), or noise or pollution information), but also participates in its processing and interpretation, benefiting as a group from the resulting outputs. A lot of this information is geographic in nature and can be shared through maps and geographic visualizations.

Intriguing examples include OpenStreetMap (OSM), which was started by volunteers in 2004. The maps are created using data from portable GPS devices, remote sensed images including aerial photography and enriched with local people's knowledge. OpenStreetMap data are available mainly for urban areas and have proven to be as accurate and most frequently more up to date compared to 'official' maps. Other examples include Wikimapia, an online map and satellite imaging resource launched in 2006 which combines Google Maps with a wiki system. It allows users to add information to any location on earth. At the time of writing it had over 15,000,000 entries. Other forms of collaborative mapping like Ushahidi are based on the integration of different technologies which enable people to submit geocoded information using their mobile phones or a Web-based interface, and display these on online maps, thus creating a temporal and geospatial archive of events (Wikipedia, 2011).

About PGIS practice

PGIS is an emerging practice; it is developing out of participatory approaches to planning, documenting, and managing spatial information and communication. The practice merges participatory learning and action (PLA) methods with GIT. PGIS practice combines a range of geospatial information management tools and methods such as sketch maps, participatory 3D models (P3DM), remote sensed imagery, online mapping interfaces, GPS readings, and GIS to represent people's spatial knowledge as virtual or physical, two- or three-dimensional maps. These are used as interactive vehicles for spatial learning, discussion, information exchange, analysis, decision making, advocacy, and action taking. PGIS implies making GIT available to disadvantaged groups in society in order to enhance their capacity to generate, manage, analyse, and communicate spatial information.

PGIS practice is geared towards community empowerment through measured, demand-driven, user-friendly, and integrated applications of geospatial technologies. GIS-based maps and spatial analyses become major conduits in the process. A good PGIS practice is embedded into long-lasting spatial decision-making processes, is flexible, adapts to different sociocultural and biophysical environments, depends on multidisciplinary facilitation and skills, and builds essentially on visual language. The practice integrates several tools and methods, while often relying on combining 'expert' skills with socially differentiated local knowledge. It promotes interactive participation of stakeholders in generating and managing spatial information, and it uses information about specific landscapes to facilitate broadly based decision-making processes that support effective communication and community advocacy.

If appropriately used, the practice exerts profound impacts on community empowerment, innovation, and social change. More importantly, PGIS practice could protect traditional knowledge and wisdom from external exploitation by placing control for access and use of culturally sensitive spatial information in the hands of those who generated it.

Communication as a key ingredient

Cartographers convey spatial information through a visual language[1] that consists of a combination of symbols (e.g. points, lines, polygons, and volumes[2]), their variables (e.g. hue, orientation, shading value, shape, size, and texture), and interpretation keys printed on maps. Three-dimensional elevation models of the landscape offer additional enhancements to facilitate efficient interpretation and mental processing of spatial data. A map's communication capabilities depend on the selection of features, the manner in which the features are depicted,[3] and the capability of users to objectively understand and relate these to their life-worlds. It is important that a map's graphic vocabulary be fully understood by all parties involved and that each feature be provided with a commonly defined key to be interpreted (Carton, 2002). This is particularly critical when a map is being used to support a dialogue.

Producing, georeferencing, and visualizing indigenous spatial knowledge (ISK) helps communities engage in peer-to-peer dialogue, promote their particular issues and concerns with higher-level authorities, and address economic forces. Maps based on ISK are used also in adversarial contexts, such as in counter mapping where indigenous communities adopt participatory mapping methodologies to regain a measure of control over ancestral lands and resources (De Vera, 2005; Denniston, 1995; Indigenous Peoples of Africa Coordinating Committee, 2009; Rambaldi et al., 2002; Zingapan and De Vera, 1999).

PGIS is a component of an integrated and multifaceted process that provides legitimacy for local knowledge and generates a great sense of confidence and pride among people who are involved in the process, and which prepares them to deal with outsiders. The process fuels self-esteem and raises awareness about pressing issues in the community. Experiences from the various countries have shown that exercises conducted at the community level in response to local needs have fostered community cohesion and identity building (Rambaldi et al., 2007). As Janis Alcorn (2000) puts it, 'old people share history with young people, passing on legends and religious beliefs, sacred rites and places so essential to conserving tradition'.

Contexts

PGIS practice implies making GIT available to less-favoured groups in society to enhance their capacity to generate, manage, and use their own ISK and externally generated spatial information in contexts such as:

- self-determination (e.g. protecting ancestral land and resource rights and entitlements);
- management and amelioration of conflicts among local community groups and between communities and local authorities regarding access, use, control, and allocation of natural resources;
- collaborative research;
- collaborative resource-use planning and management;
- preservation of intangible cultural heritage and identity building among indigenous people and rural communities;
- good governance regarding transparency and consensual spatial decision making;
- raising awareness and assisting with education and social learning for new generations;
- community-based hazard management and risk reduction (Gaillard and Maceda, 2009);
- promotion of equity regarding ethnicity, culture, gender, and environmental justice.

Building on indigenous spatial knowledge

PGIS builds on socially differentiated ISK and the willingness of custodians of such knowledge to share it. Typically, ISK covers the following areas in rural settings:

- resource distribution: land cover and use, water sources, habitats;
- resource use, control, and access:[4] hunting, fishing, farming, grazing, mining, gathering, and harvesting from the wild, etc.;
- places of historic, cultural, and religious significance, ancestral grounds, and sacred areas;
- indigenous names; cosmovisions, creation and origin myths, etc.;
- hazard perception (e.g. landslides, floods, malaria).

ISK may complement 'scientific knowledge' in cases related to resource location, water conservation or livestock management. In such cases, ISK might be considered more relevant to the participatory processes than the technology because it embodies generations of people's practical knowledge. Some ISK is cognitively different from scientific knowledge (i.e. mental maps). Mental maps may incorporate overlapping or layered zones, blurred or multiple boundaries and uncertain or restricted locations (McCall, 2004).

The importance of the 'P'

Effective participation is the key to good PGIS practice. While traditional GIS applications often focus on the outcome, PGIS initiatives tend to emphasize the processes by which outcomes are attained. At times, the participatory process can obfuscate systematic inequalities through unequal and superficial participation. For example, PGIS applications may be used to legitimize decisions which in fact were taken by outsiders. The process also can be hijacked easily by community elites (Kyem, 2004; Rambaldi and Weiner, 2004).

For the PGIS practice to be successful, it has to be part of a well-conceived and demand-driven process based on proactive collaboration between the custodians of local and traditional knowledge, and facilitators skilled in applying PGIS and transferring technical know-how to local actors. Participation takes place throughout the process – from gaining a clear understanding about the existing legal and regulatory frameworks, to jointly setting project objectives, to defining strategies and choosing appropriate geospatial information management tools.

Data, information, and knowledge

When it comes to dealing with geospatial issues, it is important to distinguish between data, information, and knowledge. 'Data are often associated with observation, while information implies that data have been manipulated, filtered, processed and interpreted into a form that addresses some definite use' (Goodchild, 2009). Knowledge can be considered as how we understand, give meaning to, perceive, or interpret the world around us (Leeuwis, 2004). Knowledge is what we store in our mind and what leads us to take decisions, act, and react to stimuli received from the external world. Knowledge is very subjective and builds up in everybody's mind through a continuous learning process involving, among others, concrete experiences, interaction and communication with others, observations and reflections, and formation of concepts and their testing.

Participatory 3D modelling

Participatory 3D modelling or P3DM[5] is a mapping method based on merging spatial information (e.g. contour lines and people's spatial knowledge, or mental maps); the outputs are solid 3D models and their derived maps. The models are used in development and natural resource management contexts and have proved to be excellent media and user-friendly, relatively accurate data storage and analysis devices. 3D models work best when used jointly with global positioning systems (GPS), multimedia documentation, and GIS.

P3DM has been gaining increased recognition as an efficient method to facilitate geo-referenced data generation, spatial learning, analysis, and community involvement in dealing with spatial issues related to a territory. P3DM can support collaborative natural resource management initiatives and facilitate the establishment of a peer-to-peer dialogue among local stakeholders and external institutions and agencies.

Representatives from local communities manufacture scaled 3D models by merging spatial information (i.e. contour lines) with their location-specific knowledge. Contour lines are used as templates for cutting out sheets of carton board or other materials of a given thickness (i.e. expressing the vertical scale). Cut-out sheets are progressively superimposed to build the model.

Local knowledge holders first develop the map legend (i.e. the visual language of the map) through a consultative process. Based on its elements, they depict land use, land cover, and other features on the model by using pushpins (for points), yarns (for lines), and paint (for polygons).

Once the model is completed, participants apply a scaled grid to transpose geo-referenced data into a GIS. The grid offers the opportunity to add other geo-coded data generated by GPS readings or obtained from secondary sources. The grid also allows participants to take approximate coordinates on the model and verify these on the ground by using a GPS. These functionalities are extremely useful when models are used to support boundary negotiations. Data on 3D models can be extracted by digital photography and imported into a GIS.

To upgrade its potential, P3DM is best integrated with GPS and GIS. Such integration allows participants to add precisely geo-referenced data, conduct additional analysis, and produce impressive cartographic outputs. Resulting synergies make community knowledge portable and sharable at all levels of

Figure 2.1 Local analysts with P3DM, Telecho, Ethiopia

society and, more importantly, add veracity and authority to it, paving the way for peer-to-peer dialogue and more balanced power sharing when territorial issues are at stake.

Because 3D models augment the power of the mind and facilitate scaling, they allow participants to complete information more fully and accurately on a given area. Generally this is not the case with sketch mapping, which has been widely used to represent spatial knowledge in the context of participatory action research. The difference between a blank contour map and the corresponding 3D model is that the vertical dimension provides essential cues for stimulating memory, establishing spatial associations, and depicting mental maps.

P3DM has been widely deployed and has been adopted as a participatory mapping method in many parts of the world.

P3DM applied for community environmental rehabilitation planning in Oromiya, Ethiopia

In December 2010, some 120 villagers constructed a 3D model in Oromiya, Ethiopia covering a total area of 672 km² at 1:10,000 scale. Once completed, the model stored 48 layers of information, including 25 point, 5 line, and 18 area types.

A count of point data revealed that within the area there were among others 38 schools, 23 health posts, 113 sacred trees, 8 markets, and 861 settlements.

The exercise – organized by MELCA-Ethiopia, a national NGO and supported by the Technical Centre for Agricultural and Rural Cooperation ACP-EU (CTA) – was a response to a call by the community for assistance in rehabilitating its environment, which suffered heavy deforestation and soil degradation over

Figure 2.2 The global spread of P3DM application

the past decades. After several months of preparation, the exercise took place in the village of Telecho, Ethiopia on 8–18 December 2010.

The villagers worked in shifts on the model. Elders representing 28 kebeles contributed to the elaboration of the map legend and to depicting of their mental maps onto the model.

Participating villagers reported that working on the model elicited powerful memories of a past landscape characterized by lush forests and permanent river courses, and made them realize how much the almost total conversion of the natural forest into farmland had impacted (negatively) on their life. Participants stated that while making the map, through a self-reflection process they realized that their non-sustainable handling of the resources base had led to impoverishment of soils and a decrease in crop yield, and that the present situation was threatening their livelihoods and mere subsistence. They stated that the process of model building created a learning environment and gave them a sense of purpose. 'The P3DM process enables the community to look at itself using the model as a mirror', wrote a villager on a card featuring on the 'Democracy Walls'.

As a follow-up to model making, the community planned out rehabilitation works. MELCA-Ethiopia was able to mobilize funds from the Finnish embassy to follow up on the new community aspirations.[6]

Discussion

Collective spatial knowledge

Compared to conventional surveying methods, P3DM offers the opportunity of generating vast amounts of data in a relatively short time. It is quite common for participants in P3DM exercises to develop map legends including tenths legend items, and to locate such features on the model, thus generating a corresponding number of data layers.

Scaling the territory

By miniaturizing (i.e. 1:5,000–1:20,000) real-world features as they are known and perceived by knowledge holders, P3DM has proved to be particularly effective in dealing with relatively large and remote areas, and overcoming logistical and practical constraints to public participation in data generation related to land- and resource-use planning and management.

Data generation

In developing countries, baseline data available from official sources are frequently limited, inconsistent, outdated, scarce, and inaccurate. Immaterial features like 'customary tenure', 'resource control', 'values', and 'perceptions' are not visible and, if unmapped, are passed over from generation to generation orally, through tales, songs, myths, and legends. Local georeferenced knowledge is extremely valuable in such contexts. When P3DM is applied in a genuinely participatory manner, it generates relatively accurate qualitative and quantitative georeferenced data that are intellectually owned and understood by those who have compiled them.

Articulating tacit knowledge

Tacit knowledge corresponds to knowledge which is difficult to articulate, about which individuals are not immediately aware, and on which they base their day-to-day actions. This kind of knowledge can be elicited through in-depth discussions and interactive exercises. In many instances, 3D models proved to be catalysts in stimulating memory and making such knowledge explicit. Participants in P3DM exercises become aware of what they know and the importance such knowledge has for them and their community. Usually this gained awareness triggers great excitement among participants and stimulates their desire to 'discover' and learn more by doing.

3D models offer an efficient base for spatial interpretation by displaying the vertical dimension, which provides additional cues to memory and facilitates mental spatial knowledge processing. Thanks to the different means of coding (e.g. paint, yarns, and pins), a 3D model can accommodate overlapping layers of information like, for example, 'land use' and 'land tenure' depicted by colour-coded paints and yarns respectively. 3D models often visualize invisible features like values, tenure, cultural domains, and sacred areas.

By providing a bird's-eye view, and by accommodating different layers of information, 3D models contribute to widening the users' evaluative frame of reference on spatially defined issues, and thus stimulate learning and analysis. In other words, scaled 3D models help participants understand biophysical and socio-economic dynamics that go beyond their individual cognitive boundaries.

Participatory legend making and visual language

Participatory legend making is vital for the process to be genuinely participative and owned by the map makers. It is critically important that legend items are generated by the community members in their own language.

To facilitate a good legend-making process does not necessarily require prior exhaustive knowledge of the particular language. Nonetheless, it helps to have some appreciation of the variety of cultural systems and how natural resources are considered and used. The process of legend making provides a helpful framework on which local people can overlay the distinctiveness of their culture. It does not necessarily capture all of the complexity of the cultural systems, but with additional tools such as a matrix, it allows complex knowledge to surface and be captured and represented in a medium that can be understood by people with different cultural backgrounds.

Legend making is perhaps the most important element of the P3DM process. If done correctly, it puts the knowledge holders in the driver's seat. It allows them to express a complex network of ideas, concepts, and interlocking criteria that will be visualized and coded on the model. A well-prepared legend allows clearer meanings, and maps out the relationships between natural and cultural features.

More than data

In addition to data generation, the P3DM process has other value-added outcomes, which include building up of self-esteem and social cohesion, communication, intra- and intergenerational knowledge exchange, and conflict management.

Self-esteem and social cohesion

P3DM processes and outputs fuel self-esteem, raise local awareness of linked ecosystems, and strengthen intellectual ownership of the territory. Experience documented in the Philippines, Fiji, Kenya, and Ethiopia has shown that P3DM exercises – conducted at the community level and as a response to local needs versus external threats – have yielded positive effects in terms of community cohesion and identity building, by reviving local knowledge.

Communication

Different opinions are frequently based on different perspectives and the quality of the media used to communicate. When a process is geared towards addressing conflicts bound to the territory, appropriate communication channels are essential to grant all parties equal access to information in order to develop a common understanding of the issues at stake. An example is the so-called 'bird's-eye view' offered by a scaled 3D model through which a viewer acquires a holistic view of the landscape wherein landmarks and salient features are equally visible to everyone. When language barriers represent a constraint, the best exchange of information occurs by visual communication based on colour, shape, and texture, like in a 3D model.

Intra- and intergenerational knowledge exchange

The P3DM process helps reclaim lost memories about the traditional ways of living. In the presence of elders (i.e. custodians of traditional knowledge) and youth, it facilitates intergenerational knowledge exchange and raises awareness across generations about the status of the environment. In many instances, participants concluded that they gained a more holistic under-standing of their social, cultural, and biophysical environments, and that they realized the importance of working together towards a common goal. They further stated that they became aware of the value and potential authority of their spatial knowledge once it was collated, geo-referenced, documented, and visualized.

Conflict management

Resource use, control, and access are increasingly the issues at stake in latent or explicit conflicts. P3DM has been successfully used in several countries to deal with such controversies. By creating shared vantage points and offering a common visual vocabulary, 3D models and derived maps are instrumental in bridging communication barriers, facilitating dialogue, and limiting subjec-tive interpretations, thus setting the basis for fruitful negotiations.

Conclusion

P3DM has proved its worth as a tool that generates spatial data while stimu-lating community-level diagnostic discussion and planning at the local level, while providing a database for policy beyond the local. Based on documented case studies, the range of applications of P3DM, the method, is impressive and includes:

- complementing collaborative research on biodiversity, land use, resource tenure, cultural heritage, demography, health, poverty, etc.;
- supporting the development of resource uses, protected areas, cultural heritages, or ancestral domain management plans;
- supporting self-determination (e.g. tenure mapping, ancestral domain mapping);
- managing and ameliorating territorial conflicts;
- safeguarding ever-evolving intangible cultural heritage and building identity;

- supporting good governance in regards to transparency and consensual spatial decision making;
- raising awareness and assisting with education and social learning; and
- developing Community-Based Disaster Risk Reduction plans.

While there are many opportunities for P3DM application in community resource management, planning, and education, there are also risks associated with the 'mainstreaming' of this methodology. Because of their accuracy, 3D models, like other repositories of geographic information, pose some risks in terms of disclosing sensitive information. Alone or combined with GIS, 'they turn local knowledge into public knowledge and conceivably out of local control. This can be used by outsiders to locate resources and meet development needs, or merely, to extract more resources, or increase outside control' (Abbot et al., 1998). Therefore, exercises dealing with sensitive issues should be carried out with caution and behind closed doors during focus group discussions. Culturally sensitive data or data at risk of abuse should be removed from the model and eventually stored as confidential GIS layers with limited or protected access (Harmsworth, 1998). Researchers, planners, and practitioners should be aware of these possible drawbacks and be careful applying the method.

Notes

1 Topology, the names of things, is used less often than graphic symbols.
2 Pebbles, push pins, yarns, oil-based modelling clay, and 3D cartographic images are considered to be 'volume' symbols.
3 The symbols used to depict real-world features are frequently not at scale; they reflect a selected interpretation of reality made by those who composed the map.
4 Different maps on resource-use control and access can be produced for the same area by different groups in society. Of particular interest are the differentiated spatial perspectives of women, elderly people, youth, and children (re: gender- and age-related areas).
5 On 5 November 2007, Participatory 3D Modelling (P3DM) was granted the World Summit Award 2007 in the category of e-culture. P3DM was considered to be one of the 40 best practice examples of quality e-content in the world.
6 A video documentary of the exercise is available at http://vimeo.com/channels/pgis#22123738

References

Abbot, J., Chambers, R., Dunn, C., Harris, T., de Merode, E., Porter, G., Townsend, J., and Weiner, D. (1998) 'Participatory GIS: opportunity or oxymoron?' *PLA Notes* 33: 27–33.

Alcorn, J. (2000) 'Borders, rules and governance: mapping to catalyse changes in policy and management', *Gatekeeper Series* 91, International Institute for Environment and Development, London.

Carton, L. (2002) 'Strengths and weaknesses of spatial language: mapping activities as debating instrument in a spatial planning process', *FIG XXII International Congress*, Washington, DC.

De Vera, D. (2005) 'Mapping with communities in the Philippines: rolling with the punches', *PGIS'05 Mapping for Change Conference*, Nairobi.

Denniston, D. (1995) 'Defending the land with maps', *PLA Notes* 22, 36–40.

Fox, J.E. (2003) 'Mapping power: ironic effects of spatial information technology', *Ethics, Values and Practice Papers*.

Gaillard, J., and Maceda, E.A. (2009) 'Participatory three-dimensional mapping for disaster risk reduction', *Participatory Learning and Action* 60: 109–18.

Goodchild, M. (2007) 'Citizens as sensors: the world of volunteered geography', *GeoJournal* 69 (4); 211–21.

Goodchild, M.F. (2009) 'Neogeography and the nature of geographic expertise', *Journal of Location-Based Services* 3 (2): 82–96.

Harmsworth, G. (1998) 'Indigenous values and GIS: a method and a framework', *Indigenous Knowledge and Development Monitor* 6 (3).

Heywood, I., Oliver, J., and Thompson, S. (1995) 'Building and exploratory multi-criteria modeling environment for spatial decision support'. In P. Fisher (ed.), *Innovations in GIS 2*, Taylor & Francis, London.

Indigenous Peoples of Africa Coordinating Committee (2009) *African Indigenous Peoples' Workshop on Effective Use of Information Communication Technology (ICTs) in Environmental Advocacy*, IPACC and CTA, Cape Town.

Kyem, P. (2001) 'Embedding GIS applications into resource management and planning activities of local communities: a desirable innovation or a destabilising enterprise?', *Journal of Planning Education and Research* 20 (1): 176–86.

Kyem, P. (2004) 'Power, participation and inflexible social institutions: an examination of the challenges to community empowerment in participatory GIS applications', *Cartographica, the International Journal of Cartography* 38 and 39 (4): 5–17.

Leeuwis, C. (2004) *Communication for Rural Innovation. Rethinking Agricultural Extension*, Blackwell Science, Oxford, and CTA, Wageningen.

Mascarenhas, J.A. (1991) 'Participatory mapping and modelling users' notes', *RRA Notes*, 12: 9–20.

McCall, M. (2004) 'Can participatory GIS strengthen local-level planning? Suggestions for better practice', *7th International Conference on GIS for Developing Countries (GISDECO 2004)*, Johor, Malaysia.

Minang, P. and Rambaldi, G. (2004) *Summary Proceedings of the Pre-conference Workshop on Participatory GIS, 7th International Conference on GIS and Developing Countries (GISDECO 2004)*, Johor, Malaysia.

Rambaldi, G. (2005) 'Who owns the map legend?' *URISA Journal* 17 (1): 5–13.

Rambaldi, G. and Weiner, D. (2004) *Summary Proceedings of the Track on International PPGIS Perspectives, Third International Conference on Public Participation GIS (PPGIS)*, Wisconsin, USA.

Rambaldi, G., Bugna, S., Tiangco, A., and De Vera, D. (2002) 'Bringing the vertical dimension to the negotiating table. Preliminary assessment of a conflict resolution case in the Philippines', *ASEAN Biodiversity* 2 (1): 17–26.

Rambaldi, G., Muchemi, J., Crawhall, N., and Monaci, L. (2007) 'Through the eyes of hunter-gatherers: participatory 3D modelling among Ogiek Indigenous Peoples in Kenya', *Information Development* 23 (2–3): 113–28.

Sieber, R. (2000) 'Conforming (to) the opposition: the social construction of geographical information systems in social movements', *International Journal of Geographic Information Science* 14 (8): 775–93.

Weidermann, I. and Femers, S. (1993) 'Public participation in waste management decision making: and analysis and management of conflicts', *Journal of Hazardous Materials* 33: 355–68.

Wiersma, Y.F. (2010) 'Birding 2.0: citizen science and effective monitoring in the Web 2.0 world', *Avian Conservation and Ecology* 5 (2): 13.

Zingapan, K. and De Vera, D. (1999) 'Mapping the ancestral lands and waters of the Calamian Tagbanwa of Coron, Northern Palawan', Conference on NGO Best Practices, Davao City, Philippines.

About the author

Giacomo Rambaldi is Senior Programme Coordinator at the Technical Centre for Agricultural and Rural Cooperation (CTA) in the Netherlands. He has 30 years' professional experience in Africa, Latin America, South and South-East Asia, the Pacific, and the Caribbean where he worked for a number of international organizations. Giacomo holds Fellow status in the US-based Society for Applied Anthropology (SfAA). His first involvement in participatory mapping dates back to the 1980s. He developed and promoted participatory 3D modelling (P3DM), a community-based mapping method fully integrated with GIS, now widely used around the world. In 2000 he launched Participatory Avenues www.iapad.org, a website dedicated to sharing knowledge on participatory mapping. Giacomo is the author of a number of publications on these subjects, developer of www.ppgis.net, and administrator of the [ppgis] DGroups.

Chapter 3

Measuring urban adaptation to climate change: experiences in Kenya and Nicaragua

Caroline Moser and Alfredo Stein

This chapter describes the implementation of a participatory methodology – urban participatory climate change adaptation appraisal (PCCAA) – which included quantification of outcomes amongst the urban poor in Kenya and Nicaragua experiencing climate change. The methodology tested in these two case studies enabled local authorities to recognize vulnerabilities to ongoing climate challenges so they could better support the adaptive efforts already employed by citizens. Of the various initiatives currently underway to help urban authorities develop plans and policies to cope with the impacts of climate change, the innovative element of this research process was its combination of three elements: 1) a participatory methodology, generating both quantitative and qualitative data, to understand the lived experience of vulnerability associated with increasing climate variability from the perspective of residents of poor urban areas; 2) linked analysis of the institutional and policy framework for response, including the respective response roles of national governments, urban authorities, communities, and households; and 3) an action component that brought these two elements together in facilitated discussions with urban authorities to support them in thinking through the implications of increasing climate variability for planning and policy.

The context: climate change and urban vulnerability

With climate change[1] firmly established as a major global concern, urban centres in low- and middle-income countries concentrate a large proportion of those most at risk from its effects for a number of reasons, including the following: since 1950, there has been an eight-fold increase in the urban population in these nations, which now have close to three-quarters of the world's urban population. Around the world, over 1 billion (or one in three) urban inhabitants currently do not have adequate access to water and sanitation, live in overcrowded conditions, live in poor-quality, temporary shelters, or lack security of tenure. The number of slum dwellers is predicted to double to 2 billion by 2050 (UN Habitat, 2008/9).

http://dx.doi.org/10.3362/9781780447711/003

Rapid urbanization is perceived as increasing the vulnerability of urban centres to climate change impacts in the context of urban poverty and inequality. It has, for instance, increased the concentration of people in low-lying coastal zones at risk from sea-level rise and severe weather events (on steep slopes vulnerable to landslides and in unserved settlements with little protective infrastructure) (McGranahan et al., 2007). This poor urban population is at greatest risk from the increased intensity and/or frequency of storms, flooding, landslides, heat waves, and constraints on fresh water that climate change is already bringing or will bring in the future.

A very high and growing proportion of global deaths from disasters relating to severe weather occur in the urban areas of these countries, with a large and growing proportion of such deaths in urban areas (UN Habitat, 2007). Although the growing number of severe weather-related disasters is not 'proof of climate change' (which is difficult to ascertain), these disasters **are** proof of the vulnerability of cities and smaller settlements to severe weather events whose frequency and intensity are likely to increase as a result of climate change (Moser and Satterthwaite, 2008).

Climate change imposes additional risks to people and their assets[2] (e.g. buildings, infrastructure) due to the potential impacts of climate change. These risks can be direct, as in larger and/or more frequent floods, or more intense and/or frequent storms, or heat waves, or less direct as climate change negatively affects livelihoods or food supplies (and prices) or access to water needed for domestic consumption or livelihoods. Certain groups may face increased risks from measures taken in response to climate change (for instance, measures to protect particular areas of a city from flooding which increase flood-risks 'downstream', or emphasis on new hydropower schemes that displace large numbers of people) (Moser and Satterthwaite, 2010).

Towards a participatory methodology for analysing climate change adaption in Kenya and Nicaragua[3]

Capturing the perceptions of the urban poor of the impacts of weather change and understanding their adaptive strategies is particularly important in a context of both climate change and rapidly rising numbers of poor and informal urban settlers. In addition, current approaches to urban vulnerability assessments are implicitly or explicitly based on the prospect of climate disasters, e.g. flooding in coastal cities, while no current methodology has been developed to assess the vulnerability of city-dwellers to ongoing adverse or severe changes in weather.

This study focused on secondary cities where much of the anticipated growth in urban populations over the next 20 years will be concentrated. Given the scale of this particular study, priority was given first to a southern African city as an under-researched area, and second, to Central America as an area that has long experienced extreme weather vulnerability. The cities of Mombasa in Kenya and Estelí in Nicaragua were selected for this research as medium-sized but fast-growing urban centres in a flood- and drought-prone region respectively. Mombasa is a coastal town, centred on Mombasa Island, but extending to the mainland. In contrast, Estelí is situated inland in the north central highlands surrounded by forested mountains.

In both cases, city selection was also driven strongly by the availability of a local research partner with the capacity to undertake this research. In Mombasa, the research was undertaken with Eco Build Africa Trust and drew in local CBOs that provided community researchers as well as facilities for training, daily report-back sessions, and final analysis. In Estelí, the Institute for Applied Research and Local Development (NITLAPAN) at the Central American University was the primary research partner.

The study followed discussions held during an international workshop on Social Dimensions of Climate Change held by the World Bank's Social Development Department in March 2008, as well as the 5th Urban Research Symposium on Cities and Climate Change held in Marseilles in June 2009. The authors designed an analytical framework and participatory methodology for implementing an urban participatory climate change adaptation appraisal (PCCAA). The analytical framework incorporated a conceptual analysis of vulnerability and an operational approach to climate change adaptation relating to climate variability. It did so using the perspective of *assets*, linking vulnerability, assets, and climate change. The framework comprises the following two key components:

- At the analytical level it identifies **sources of vulnerability** in terms of the mechanisms through which weather variability associated with climate change impacts lead to the erosion of assets. This framework focused particularly on three types of vulnerability: first, *spatial and physical* vulnerability experienced by local populations as a result of the terrain; second, the *politico-legal* vulnerability relating to insecure tenure rights to housing and land and resulting in inadequate provision of important essential physical infrastructure; and third, *social vulnerability* of those groups most at risk to increasing intensity of severe weather.
- At the operational level it classifies the **sources of resilience** that enable households and communities to protect themselves, or to recover, from the negative effects of severe weather associated with climate change. Three closely interrelated phases of adaptation were usefully identified: first, asset-based adaptation to build long-term resilience; second, asset damage limitation and protection during severe weather events; and third, asset rebuilding after severe weather. In this way, the asset adaptation framework was designed to be instrumental when designing policy solutions for climate change adaptation.

The PCCAA methodology was adapted from a rapid participatory methodology, developed by a range of practitioners including Chambers (1994) and previously used by Moser in research on violence and insecurity, and on peace building (see Moser and Holland, 1997; Moser and McIwaine,[4] 1999, 2004; Moser et al., 2006). The participatory methodology also drew on previous participatory quantification approaches to facilitate local people to categorize and value score attributes of sustainability, vulnerability, and coping/adaptive strategies (see, for example, Cromwell et al., 2001; Kagugube et al., 2007).

Participatory research was conducted over a period of five weeks (including training and piloting) in a stratified sample of urban communities and with a range of different social groups in each community. The research was conducted mainly through participatory group analysis and used a mix of methods to generate both qualitative and quantitative data. We focus here on the quantitative data generated.

Quantification of participatory data

While a detailed description of the implementation and analysis of PCCAA data goes beyond the scope of this chapter (see Moser and Stein, 2011), it is useful to point to the fact that it can take two forms. First, it can identify broad patterns from in-depth content analysis of the focus group exercises. These can then be visually illustrated in the text using the most appropriate tools. Second, in order to move beyond individual focus group experiences at the analysis stage it may be useful to quantify some of the information.

In the PCCAA in both Mombasa and Estelí, all focus groups used the same tools when addressing each issue. This meant that those tools lending themselves to quantification, such as ranking and listing, and institutional mapping, could produce results for statistical cross-comparison – as well as for cross-city comparisons. It is important to stress that quantification depends on focus groups using exactly the same tools, or the data will not be compatible – hence the importance of training.

Using the total number of listings (the number of times a listing was conducted) as the universe, it was possible to conduct some basic statistical analysis. Equally information gained from rankings could be quantified – using the prescribed participatory methodology on ranking information (3 for first priority, 2 for second, and 1 for third) (see Moser, 2002). While this data was only representative for the focus groups, nevertheless it assisted in showing the broader picture.[5] The following examples show how comparative Mombasa/Estelí data was quantified, as well as city-specific data.

Quantification of listings and rankings of weather

As Table 3.1 shows, listings and rankings from participatory focus groups in both cities showed similar perceptions of severe weather. Rain and associated flooding was identified as the most severe problem in both Mombasa (49.8 per cent) and in Estelí (69.8 per cent), with heat/drought/sun of second importance, followed by winds – more evident in Mombasa than Estelí.[6]

Table 3.1 Composite matrix of perceptions of the most significant weather hazards in Mombasa and Estelí

Type of weather	Mombasa[1]		Estelí[2]	
	Ranking totals	%	Ranking totals	%
Flood/rain	166	49.8	312	69.8
Heat/sunny	105	31.4	116	25.8
Strong wind	55	16.4	20	4.4
Cold/chilly	8	2.4	–	–
Total	**334**	**100**	**448**	**100**

1 Mombasa data from listing and rankings in 72 focus groups in four communities
2 Estelí data from listings and ranking in 62 focus groups in four communities

Quantification of listings of asset actions before, during, and after severe weather

The same methodology was used in this case to list actions, quantified in terms of the total number of asset adaptation matrices. As Table 3.2 shows, in Mombasa the majority (88.6 per cent) of households, small business, and community groups were resourceful at developing a range of resilience measures. Yet within the community there were also slight differences among different groups. Households responded more often than other groups (94 per cent), with the greatest number of activities (90.6 per cent) occurring during severe weather itself.

Table 3.2 Focus group matrices identifying asset actions before, during, and after severe weather at household, small business, and community level in Mombasa, Kenya

Focus groups from four communities	Number of assets adaptation matrices	Actions relating to severe weather (in numbers and %)							
		Before		During		After		Average	
Household adaptation	23	21	91%	23	100%	21	91%	22	94%
Small business adaptation	16	15	94%	15	94%	14	88%	15	92%
Community adaptation	32	25	78%	25	78%	27	84%	26	80%
Total	**71**	**62**	**87.6%**	**64**	**90.6%**	**62**	**87.6%**	**63**	**88.6%**

Note: participants from 68 household, 72 small business, and 72 community focus groups undertaken in four communities

Quantification of listing and ranking of assets

Quantification of the listing and ranking of assets again helps identify those assets considered as priorities by households, small-scale business, and communities. In Mombasa, the totals taken from asset listings and rankings show that housing, followed by health, was the most highly prioritized asset, whether owned by individual households or by business owners (see Table 3.3).

Table 3.3 Composite matrix of important assets in the four study communities in Mombasa, Kenya

Category of asset-based adaptation	Asset ranking								
	First	%	Second	%	Third	%	Fourth	%	Total%
Household	House	38	Health	14	Children	9	Others	39	100
Business	Stock[1]	23	Machinery[2]	17	Health	14	Others	46	100
Collective	Wells/ latrines	27	Health/ hospital	18	School/ education	17	Others	38	100

Note: Participants from the focus groups in four communities
1 includes stock itself, source of stock, various materials such as wood, etc.
2 includes sewing machines, fishing gear, and handcarts.

Quantification of institutional maps

Institutions important in the four communities in Mombasa were numerically quantified in terms of the number of times they appeared in the institutional maps. Focus groups first identified institutions that were perceived to be important generally in local communities, and identified whether they were inside or outside the community, and were perceived as positive or negative. The same focus groups then identified those institutions that particularly assisted local communities in adapting or responding to severe weather. This allowed for the quantitative, comparative identification of those institutions important in the community, and the extent to which the same institutions were, or were not, important in adapting to weather.

In Table 3.4 the first number in each column indicates the order of importance from first to third, with the numbers in brackets the absolute numbers. This result shows that institutions considered important by community members were not necessarily the same as those they perceived as assisting them in relation to severe weather. While local government representatives such as chiefs and elders were identified as important local institutions, they did not take an active role in dealing with severe weather problems, except in the community of Tudor.

Table 3.4 Institutions in the four study communities in Mombasa, by general importance and in adapting to severe weather

Name of community	Institution	Important in community	Important in adapting to weather
Bofu	LICODEP	1 (10)	1 (15)
	Women's group	2 (7)	
	CDF	3 (6)	2 (6)
	Schools	3 (6)	
	Church/mosque		3 (4)
Ziwa la Ngombe	Schools	1 (8)	1 (18)
	Chief	1 (8)	
	ActionAid	2 (7)	2 (16)
	Women's groups	3 (6)	3 (14)
	Youth group	3 (6)	
Timbwani	Hospital/health centre	1 (10)	1 (21)
	Schools	2 (9)	
	CDF	3 (8)	
	Chief	3 (8)	
	LICODEP		2 (20)
	Church/mosque		3 (16)
Tudor	Chief	1 (6)	1 (16)
	Elders	2 (5)	1 (16)
	Women's group	2 (5)	3 (8)
	Youth club	3 (4)	3 (8)
	Red Cross	3 (4)	
	Municipality	3 (4)	
	Community group		2 (9)

Note: Participants were the focus groups in the four study communities.
LICODEP is a local CBO; CDF = Community Development Fund.

From participatory research to policy process

Participatory research enables local groups to reflect and act to solve local problems. Through the urban participatory climate change adaptation appraisal,
local groups in urban communities in Kenya and Nicaragua were able to come
together to generate and analyse data on the impact of climate change on
their lives. For an external policy audience, participatory research assists in
identifying interventions from the perspective of the poor, rather than from
that of policymakers or academics. While the quantification of participatory
data presents particular challenges as to its representativeness, as discussed
elsewhere in this volume (see also Moser, 2002), nevertheless it can assist in
providing strong messages, particularly to policymakers who have a tendency
to dismiss such work as anecdotal.

The first-stage generation of quantitative and qualitative data by the PCCAA provided a strong set of policy analysis/statements. This was further strengthened by a second stage of institutional and policy framework analysis that identified the constraints and opportunities for a policy response. A third stage fed this combined analysis into dialogue with national and local urban policymakers.

The first-stage research in Mombasa and Estelí, presented in this study, shows that despite the lack of concrete climate projections, the lives and livelihoods of urban residents are already significantly impacted by incremental shifts in weather, e.g. higher intensity of rainfall causing seasonal flooding, increasing speed of winds, or gradually rising temperatures. These incremental impacts of long-term trends in increasing severity of weather are added to the existing physical, social, and legal vulnerabilities related to their poverty, physical location, and exclusion from most basic services. The lack of formal land tenure rights makes the poor particularly vulnerable to severe weather and they squat on the most vulnerable land; without tenure rights, municipal authorities are less likely to provide municipal services and infrastructure; because they lack tenure households, they are reluctant to invest resources in adaptation measures to build resilience in their plots; the lack of formal tenure impairs their capacity to make claims for services and exercise their voice as citizens. Important public institutions (both state and non-state) identified in local communities did not necessarily assist households, small businesses, and local community groups to adapt either to severe weather or to invidious changes. Indeed, most adaptation measures were local bottom-up initiatives. Nonetheless, the majority of households, small businesses, and community groups were resourceful in developing a range of asset-related strategies including asset adaption to build long-term resilience, asset damage limitation and protection during severe weather events, and rebuilding asset portfolios after severe weather.

The second-stage analysis of the institutional and policy framework for response noted an institutional disconnection between Ministries of Environment mandated to respond to climate change and other relevant legal and policy instruments spread across sector ministries. The research also confirmed that from a policy perspective, clarifying tenure rights and developing coherent urban land policy frameworks is of the utmost importance for building resilience of the urban poor to negative climate change impacts. The lack of comprehensive land policies for the poor, as well as inefficient land management and administration systems, limits the poor's capability to access affordable land or upgrade from squatter status. Furthermore, national governments, local governments, NGOs, donors, the private sector, and even academics very rarely are aware, or see, the asset-based adaptation strategies that community groups, households, and small business are already implementing. Until this range of institutions recognize the initiatives and enterprises of local communities, they will fail to provide effective support for the urgent long-term resilience to cope with climate change.

A third and final stage to validate results was the consultation process, involving local people in dialogue with national and urban policy actors. In Estelí, an action planning exercise was undertaken to triangulate the results. This participatory exercise allowed urban poor communities and public authorities together to start articulating and identifying common problems, and defining and structuring possible strategies and solutions by which to reach consensus, and negotiate collaboration.[7] In Mombasa, where the research process generated less commitment from the local authorities, the post-research consultation process was limited to an information-sharing and capacity-building event attended by some 80 people, including a wide range of local representatives from the communities in which the research took place (such as chiefs, elders, and other prominent community members), members of the Mombasa municipality, as well as other local governments, NGOs, national authorities, and members of the international donor community.

Conclusions

Assessing climate change vulnerability of urban centres has only recently become a focus of concern for development agencies given that national climate change assessments and strategies have primarily concentrated on environmental and agricultural systems. In the past few years, various development institutions have taken up the challenge to provide city governments with the necessary tools to integrate climate change adaptation into their policies. As a result, a number of methodologies for urban vulnerability assessments and disaster and adaptation planning are currently emerging and being piloted in large and mid-size cities in the developing world.[8]

Significantly, however, the perspectives of marginalized urban people themselves on the effects of climate variability on their households and communities are largely absent from these methodologies. The participatory methodology described in this chapter was an attempt to shift the focus of analysis down from the local government level in order to take into account other local points of vulnerability, as well as other local sources of resilience within households and communities. The approach enabled local people to categorize, value, and score their own changing realities, while enabling a degree of standardization and aggregation for cross-comparison for outside policy analysis. Having a powerful analytical asset-based framework helped to interpret the findings for policy audiences. The emphasis on feeding analysis into policy debates through participatory consultations provided at least an initial step towards embedding local statistics into ongoing policy deliberation.

Notes

1 'Climate change' refers to a change in the state of the climate that can be identified (e.g. using statistical tests) by changes in the mean and/or the variability of its properties, and that persists for an extended period of time (typically decades or longer), whether due to natural variability or as a result of human activity (IPCC, 2007).

2 An asset is identified as 'a stock of financial, human, natural, or social resources that can be acquired, developed, improved, and transferred across generations. It generates flows or consumption, as well as additional stock' (Ford Foundation, 2004; Moser, 2009).

3 This section, including the tables, draws heavily on the empirical data from a recently completed study (Moser et al., 2010).

4 See Moser and McIlwaine (1999) for an earlier guideline which describes the participatory methodology for appraisals of urban violence and insecurity. This provided a preliminary structure for the development of this working paper.

5 For other examples of quantification of focus groups, see Moser and McIlwaine (2004).

6 Some bias in the weather data reflected the fact that some of the tenants who, because they did not own their houses, did not care as much as did home owners. As a middle-aged woman from Bofu commented: 'Floods are not such a problem for me, as I am a tenant'.

7 Such a process has already been recognized in Estelí, where for the last fifteen years, municipal investments in infrastructure and basic services (co-financed by a national programme PRODEL) have been identified and approved by the municipality and urban poor communities through an action planning methodology known as 'participatory micro-planning'.

8 These methodologies are summarized in Moser et al. (2010), table 1, page 4.

References

Chambers, R. (1994) 'The origins and practice of participatory rural appraisal', *World Development* 22: 953–69.

Cromwell, E., Kambewa, P., Mwanza, R., and Chirwa, R., with KWERA Development Centre (2001) 'Impact assessment using participatory approaches: "starter pack" and sustainable agriculture in Malawi', *Network Paper No. 112*, Agricultural Research and Extension Network, Overseas Development Institute, London.

Ford Foundation (2004) *Building Assets to Reduce Poverty and Inequality*, New York.

Kagugube, J., Ssewakiryanga, R., Barahona, C., and Levy, S. (2007) 'Integrating qualitative dimensions of poverty into the third Uganda National Household Survey (UNHS III)', *Journal of African Statistics,* 8: 28–52.

McGranahan, G., Balk, D., and Anderson, B. (2007) 'The rising tide: assessing the risks of climate change and human settlements in low-elevation coastal zones', *Environment and Urbanization* 19(1): 17–37.

Moser, C. (1998) 'The Asset Vulnerability Framework: Reassessing urban poverty reduction strategies', *World Development* 26(1): 1–19.

Moser, C. (2002) '"Apt illustration" or "anecdotal information"? Can qualitative data be representative or robust?' in R. Kanbur (ed.), *Qual-Quant: Qualitative and Quantitative Methods of Poverty Appraisal*, Permanent Black, Delhi.

Moser, C. (2009) *Ordinary Families: Extraordinary Lives: Assets and Poverty Reduction in Guayaquil, 1978–2004*, Brookings Press, Washington, DC.

Moser, C. and Holland, J. (1997) *Urban Poverty and Violence in Jamaica*, World Bank, Washington, DC.

Moser, C. and McIlwaine, C. (1999) 'Participatory urban appraisal and its application for research on violence', *Environment and Urbanization* 11(2): 203–26.

Moser, C. and McIlwaine, C. (2004) *Encounters with Violence in Latin America: Urban Poor Perceptions from Colombia and Guatemala*, Routledge, London and New York.

Moser, C. and Satterthwaite, D. (2008) *Towards Pro-Poor Adaptation to Climate Change in the Urban Centres of Low- and Middle-Income Countries*, International Institute for Environment and Development: Human Settlements Discussion Paper Series, Theme: Climate Change and Cities – 3, IIED, London.

Moser, C. and Satterthwaite, D. (2010) 'Towards pro-poor adaptation to climate change in the urban centers of low- and middle-income countries', in R. Mearns and A. Norton (eds), *Social Dimensions of Climate Change*, World Bank, Washington, DC.

Moser, C. and Stein, A. (2011) 'A methodological guideline for implementing urban participatory climate change adaptation appraisals', *Environment and Urbanization* 22(2): 463–86.

Moser, C., Acosta, A., and Vásquez, M.E. (2006) *Mujeres y Paz: Construcción de Consensos, Guía para procesos participativos e incluyentes*, Social Policy International, Bogotá.

Moser, C., Norton, A., Stein, A., and Georgieva, S. (2010) *Pro-Poor Adaptation to Climate Change in Urban Centers: Case Studies of Vulnerability and Resilience in Kenya and Nicaragua*, World Bank Report No. 54947, World Bank, Washington, DC.

UN Habitat (2007) *Global Report on Human Settlement 2007: Enhancing Urban Safety and Security*, Earthscan, London.

About the authors

Caroline Moser is a professor of urban development and director of the Global Urban Research Centre at the University of Manchester. Previously she was at the London School of Economics, World Bank, and Brookings Institution. Her recent research focuses on intergenerational asset accumulation and poverty reduction strategies and its implications for international migration and climate change, as well as on tipping points of urban conflict and violence chains.

Alfredo Stein is an urban development planning specialist with 30 years of experience in the design, management, and evaluation of low-income housing and local development, post-emergency reconstruction, and urban poverty reduction policies and programmes in Latin America, Africa, and Asia. He is a lecturer in urban development planning at the Global Urban Research Centre, University of Manchester.

Chapter 4

Participatory statistics, local decision-making, and national policy design: *Ubudehe* community planning in Rwanda

Ashish Shah

This chapter looks at the practice and potential of participatory statistics generated through a community planning process in Rwanda. The Rwandan word Ubudehe refers to the tradition of collective action, mutual help, and reciprocity to solve community problems. During the past 10 years Ubudehe has been promoted and implemented as a formalized community decision-making process that has created space for more local and democratic deliberation in a centralized and hierarchical governance system. Ubudehe involves social mapping and well-being analysis across all villages in Rwanda, creating a national census and social data set (easily updated) which is both locally relevant and nationally commensurable. Through the persistence of its supporters within the Ministry of Local Government and amongst external allies, the power and potential of this participatory data set is being recognized by policymakers at all levels. To date this has included district-level use of Ubudehe data for targeting and prioritizing district investments and for holding district officials accountable for outcomes under their performance contracts. It has also extended to higher-level sector policy and programming by, amongst others, the Ministry of Health to target its Health Insurance Scheme and by the national Vision Umurenge Programme. There is a huge potential for further uptake of this unique data set and much can be learnt from the experience so far.

Background: negotiating democratic space for participation through *Ubudehe*

The role of Ubudehe *in a reformist agenda*

The Rwandan word *Ubudehe* refers to the traditional practice and culture of collective action, mutual help, and reciprocity to solve community problems. *Ubudehe* emerged in its contemporary form in 2001, in an attempt by reformists within government to secure alternative democratic spaces – within a decentralization policy framework – that would not directly threaten the vested interests of political hardliners.

http://dx.doi.org/10.3362/9781780447711/004

The reformists noted that since the 'colonial encounter', Rwanda had inherited a political administrative structure that was extremely hierarchical, centralized, and authoritarian. This centralized system excluded the participation of Rwandans from determining their socio-economic development and political future. Rwandans, they argued, were both suspicious of the motives of state intervention and suffered from a culture of obedience. It was this that had facilitated the rapid mobilization of the population during the 1994 genocide. They argued that participatory democracy and representative democracy were not mutually exclusive, and that strengthening participatory democracy would in the long run yield a political culture mature enough to engage with electoral politics (RoR, 1999: 42).

By focusing on participatory democracy, reformists managed to secure democratic space and achieve consensus with hardliners to pursue a conceptualization of democracy that was not immediately threatening. The final consensus noted that the aim was to:

> give the floor and freedom to the people so that they can talk about their problems and how they can be solved. A Rwandan citizen has never been given the floor, he has always been waiting for instructions from his superiors and he has always been guided by them. It is necessary, therefore, to look for 'mechanisms' of giving the floor to people. (RoR, 1999: 40)

It was within this context of consensus looking for 'mechanisms of giving the floor to people' that *Ubudehe* was to emerge.

Conceptualizing Ubudehe

In conceptualizing the role of *Ubudehe* in Rwandan governance reform, protagonists envisioned a popular platform for participatory democracy. They believed that only when people experience and engage in self-governing collective action at local level will they be able to build the experience and capabilities of sustaining democratic values and subsequently apply this experience to issues of national concern. Based on these ideas, the purpose of *Ubudehe* would be to 'create foundations of democratic functioning by helping diverse forms of associational experience to express local liberties at the family, neighbourhood and village levels' (MINALOC, 2006: 15).

One of the defining features of *Ubudehe* is its explicitly eclectic design. The traditional term *Ubudehe* was appropriated to capture the imagination of the masses and infused with a sophisticated set of normative principles and design properties seeking to foster citizen participation, self-governance, and collective action amongst Rwandans. Theoretically and methodologically *Ubudehe* draws eclectically from the works of Korten (1980), Uphoff (1996), V. Ostrom (1997), Tocqueville (2002), Gandhi (1997), Chambers (1997), E. Ostrom (1990), and Checkland (1989).

Methodologically, one set of ideas *Ubudehe* draws on is Chambers' (1997) notions of normal professionalism, local knowledge, and power. Professionalism is concerned with how knowledge is generated and which knowledge is seen as important. This set of ideas recognizes the liberating potential of a wide array of participatory methods to counter such challenges. PRA methods are seen as a useful means to support the articulation of local knowledge, with an emphasis on visual tools such as social maps to generate information, analysis, and debate. Sam Joseph (2006: 30), who was actively involved in supporting the emergence of *Ubudehe*, argues that in addition to PRA tools, local groups need to be supported with opportunities, space, and resources to engage in designing their own institutions to deal with local problems. In the context of *Ubudehe*, if participatory methodologies (Chambers, 1997) could help draw out the knowledge and multiple perspectives of local populations, and if there existed an institutional framework (Ostrom, 1990) with which to design local self-governing organizations, soft systems methodologies drawing on the works of Checkland (1989) could help multiple actors to deliberate and act on solving specific problems identified by local populations.

The evolution of Ubudehe

The evolution of *Ubudehe* since it was conceived in 2001 can be categorized into three distinct time periods:

- In an experimental phase between 2001 and 2003, *Ubudehe* was piloted in Butare, one of the then 12 provinces in Rwanda, with European Union funding and a positive assessment. Notably, technocrats in the government bureaucracy were impressed by the data-producing potential of *Ubudehe* based on the social categorization and social mapping carried out by citizens.
- In a second, national roll-out phase under the Ministry of Local Government between 2004 and 2006, *Ubudehe* was adopted officially as a national policy, rolling out nationwide across all 9,175 cellules. Following an aid freeze, the GoR stepped in to fund secretariat and training costs for almost 20,000 facilitators working in some 9,000 cellules (village clusters representing the lowest administrative level) across the country.
- In a third consolidation phase from 2006 to the present, EU funding resumed and training expanded to over 30,000 facilitators as a new, lower level of administration, the *Umudugudu* (Village), was created, prompting the *Ubudehe* focus to shift from cellule level down to these 15,000 villages. By the end of 2008 the first cycle of *Ubudehe* had taken place in all 14,837 villages under the new administrative boundaries, funding livelihoods and public goods and services initiatives across the country.

In 2008 *Ubudehe* was awarded the United Nations Public Service Award for its work in fostering citizen participation and accountability. This accolade gained *Ubudehe* more political goodwill, including recognition by President Kagame. It also convinced the EU to fund an extra 20 million euros for subsequent rounds. By 2010 over 55,000 collective actions had taken place in Rwanda's villages facilitated by a pool of over 30,000 facilitators across the country.

The *Ubudehe* methodology

The critical role of facilitation

An ideal-type *Ubudehe* process hinges on facilitation. Much rests on the identification and equipping of facilitators (at all levels) with the necessary skills and understanding to put the ideas behind *Ubudehe* into practice. Two levels of facilitators would undergo rigorous experiential training in the *Ubudehe* principles and methods. The first would be government facilitators at various administrative levels of government. They would not be expected to directly facilitate community-level processes. The second level of facilitators would be 'community facilitators'. They would be local residents, trained by their nearest government facilitators to facilitate *Ubudehe* amongst their own communities. There would be a minimum of two community facilitators per community representing both sexes. The stipulation that community facilitators be residents of the communities they live in was based on an assumption that they would be more readily accepted and trusted by communities, and that they would be able to sustain *Ubudehe* over a longer period of time compared to the use of external facilitators, who would only have short-term affiliations to communities.

Furthermore, it was expected that community facilitators would be volunteers and view their facilitative role as a vocation. It was assumed that this requirement would be a form of self-screening that would identify committed facilitators as opposed to those motivated by financial self-interest. The requirement of voluntarism would also ensure sustainability and prevent facilitation from being dependent on external financing.

Community facilitators would be elected through a community meeting by residents and could not be local leaders, chiefs, or administrators in positions of power. This requirement was based on the fear of local power dynamics and the ability of powerholders to manipulate participatory deliberations. It was expected that the active role of facilitators would diminish over time as more and more community members became familiar with the principles and methods of *Ubudehe* and felt confident enough to start their own autonomous processes. Community facilitators would then mobilize local residents to come together to engage in facilitated deliberation. The initial start-up phase of *Ubudehe* would entail community discussions organized over a minimum period of eight days (to adequately cover all stages of *Ubudehe* methodology), always at times convenient and suitable to the residents (after farming, etc.).

A step-by-step methodology: from social mapping to community planning

The *Ubudehe* methodology proceeds in a series of steps. This begins with poverty analysis and social categorizing of the population by community participants. In these first stages, facilitators assist the community to deliberate on their understanding of poverty, its causes, and consequences based on *their* experience and realities. They also assist them to determine the categories of poverty and wealth, and categorize people within the community, ranked in hierarchical categories according to their living conditions from poorest to richest. It is assumed that the social categorization is possible because residents of the same locality know one another. Six categories of households in villages were identified: Umutindi nyakujya (those in abject poverty); Umutindi (the very poor); Umukene (the poor); Umukene wifashije (the resourceful poor); Umukungu (the food rich), and Umukire (the money rich). Their detailed characteristics are listed in Table 4.1.

In the next stages, participants conduct a community social census involving social mapping. Participants map out their community in detail on a village social map. All the names of the household heads and their family members residing in the village; their socio-economic categories; type of housing; and all physical and development infrastructure available in the village are marked.

The village social map is first laid out on the ground using local materials, and then transferred onto a piece of cloth measuring a minimum of 2 metres by 1.5 metres. While this may appear to be a trivial exercise, there is an important rationale. Too often in PRA exercises, village maps are facilitated by external actors (such as NGOs) and transferred into the actors' notebooks, and hence the information generated by such exercises is expropriated from the communities involved. In the case of *Ubudehe*, social maps are transferred onto large cloths so that they can be a retained resource belonging to the community. It is expected that by making the social maps more visual and large in scale, more community members would be able to triangulate discussions, verify facts, and prevent knowledge and power from being controlled by those who hold the pen and try to control the discussion (like village elites or facilitators). As a result, large social maps serve both a transparency and accountability function.

Through debate and deliberation, participants then identify and analyse their problems, and then prioritize these problems through preference scoring, allowing the collective energies of the community to be directed at trying to solve one practical problem at a time. Through intense but guided deliberation by the community facilitator, the community then crafts a strategy and action plan to address the prioritized problem. Community members then elect a management committee to implement the process, and a monitoring committee to monitor the process and provide corrective action based on rules agreed upon in earlier stages. The community strategy is then signed off by community members and submitted to the relevant and nearest government

Table 4.1 Poverty characteristics of households in Rwanda as defined by communities and households marked on village social map

Group	Characteristics	
Umutindi Nyakujya (those in abject poverty)	Destitute. Need to beg to survive. Have no land or livestock. Lack adequate shelter, clothing, and food. Fall sick often and have no access to medical care. Children are malnourished and they cannot afford to send them to school. Not respected. Discriminated against.	Below subsistence group
Umutindi (the very poor)	The main difference between the Umutindi and the Umutindi Nyakujya is that this group is physically capable of working on land owned by others, although they themselves have either no land, or very small land holdings, and no livestock. They suffer from low harvests and also have no access to health care or schooling.	
Umukene (the poor)	These households have some land and housing. They live on their own labour and produce, though they have no savings, and they can eat, even if the food is not very nutritious. However, they do not have a surplus to sell in the market, their children do not always go to school, and they often have no access to health care.	Middle peasantry group
Umukene Wifashije (the resourceful poor)	This group shares many of the characteristics of the Umukene and, in addition, they have small ruminants and their children go to primary school. They have a few animals and petty income to satisfy a few other needs.	
Umukungu (the food rich)	This group has larger land holdings with fertile soil and enough to eat. They have livestock, often have paid jobs, and can access health care. They employ others on their own farms and at times have access to paid employment. They have some savings.	Rich and elite group
Umukire (the money rich)	This group has land and livestock, and often has salaried jobs. They have good housing, often own a vehicle, and have enough money to lend and to get credit from the bank. Many migrate to urban centres.	

Source: MINECOFIN, 2002; MINALOC, 2006

office to request funding from the *Ubudehe* Community Development Fund. A village *Ubudehe* bank account is opened based on the contribution fees of the population and the problem being addressed.

As soon as sign-off occurs, funds are disbursed immediately from the *Ubudehe* Community Development Fund account at the Ministry of Local Government in Kigali to the district account and passed on to the village account. The amount of funds received is announced publicly at a community meeting, and the elected implementing committees are mandated to manage and monitor the funds. Once a collective action is completed and a problem successfully addressed, the whole process of community dialogue and preference scoring starts again, as does the process of updating the village social map (to include changes in social category, new residents to the village, etc.). With each new problem prioritized, new plans are developed, new collective action committees are established, and new bank accounts are opened. It is assumed that the more repeated cycles of *Ubudehe* there are, the more confidence communities will gain in managing collective action effectively and strengthening a culture of citizenship.

Community decision-making for participatory democracy?

At its best, *Ubudehe* works as a local-level deliberative and democratic decision-making mechanism, with priorities identified and funded. In an *Ubudehe* community planning process in the village of Kanunga in 2007, for example, the two top priority problems that residents had listed for collective action were the lack of a nursery school in the village, which meant that young children had to walk long distances to reach a nursery, and the lack of clean drinking water. In the second cycle of *Ubudehe*, a village nursery school was built, with the Community Development Fund contributing 700,000 RWf (Rwandan francs) and the community contributing 116,900 RWf. Village residents liaised with the District Education Officer to ensure that at least one member of staff was provided to the nursery. Following the successful completion of the nursery school project, residents decided to implement a water project. The actual costs of implementing the water project were much higher than the standard 700,000 RWf provided by the *Ubudehe* secretariat for each collective action. The residents secured the remaining funding from the District Public Works Office and an international NGO operating in the area. The water project was completed in July 2010 (Shah, 2011: 94).

Of course, for every democratic success story there is likely to be a risk elsewhere of elite capture of the decision-making process and subsequent investments. However, the visual and public nature of social maps tends to make it difficult for local elites to manipulate categories of poor. Similarly, the social maps, by being visual and a resource retained in the cellule, serve a transparent, self-triangulating purpose, as village residents check and verify their own data on the map. The open use of preference voting for community investments, particularly if well facilitated, can also bring greater transparency to the community planning process. Two 'middle poor' residents, reflecting on their *Ubudehe* experience, illustrated this point with the following anecdotes (Shah, 2011: 98):

> When we were designing the water project, one of the church leaders was trying to divert the path of the water pipeline towards his house. If we did that, the pipeline would only serve one part of the village and leave

a large group of people without water. We only realised this because he
had to mark what he was suggesting on the social map. There were many
arguments but in the end he could not get his way.

When we were distributing goats, the head teacher, who is quite senior
in the village, wanted to allocate all goats to his friends. But we had
agreed on a rule that the poorest households would benefit first. The map
prevented him from writing a list on paper and giving it to the officials.

District-level government bureaucrats have also been supportive of *Ubudehe*.
They value the information available from citizens and feel that the popu-
larity of the overall process has earned them respect and trust. As they are
involved in the sign-off process before any collective action can be funded,
they tend to be aware of the general efforts of village residents. However,
they note that they are not engaging with the process as systematically as
they could be and say that more needs to be done. They allude to political
and motivational challenges. As one senior district official noted (Shah,
2011: 103):

Ubudehe is good, but it is also threatening because it challenges our power.

Districts get their power from control of resources and control of ideas.
Ubudehe places the control of both ideas and resources into the hands of
the common people. It is very difficult for the District to give up power in
such a way. This will have to be a gradual process.

A national data source for policymaking

A real-time rural census

By 2010, each of the 14,837 villages in Rwanda had a large social map that
not only listed the number of households in each village, but provided and
offered a basis for capturing a wealth of information ranging from the socio-
economic profiles of households, to listing priority problems that each village
was facing.

The first important fact is that the social maps in *Ubudehe* offer a real-time
census of populations in Rwanda's villages that can be updated regularly – as
such, a ready-made baseline is available for anyone to use. Since the first maps
were drawn in the newly re-ordered villages in 2006, many maps have been
updated biannually if not annually.

Whilst an empirical costing has not been conducted, just from observation, it seems that the financial and time cost of carrying out nationwide
survey-based censuses every 10 years outweighs the cost of village residents
drawing, owning, and updating their own social maps regularly. One of the
reasons updating of maps is possible is the fact that social maps are drawn

on large bed-sheet-size cloth, and the size of each household is drawn with enough space to cross out and update every year as well as add new households. Where maps get messy by too much updating, the cost of buying a new cloth/material is not significantly high, and several villages have invested in new cloths/manila paper to update their maps. In several cases, the fact that residents have chosen to update their social maps on their own without relying on the government to provide materials, highlights the use value that village residents find from the maps themselves.

Well-being categories aggregated for every village in Rwanda

Beyond the fact that social maps can provide a general census of populations in villages, the *Ubudehe* social maps capture detailed household characteristics that can influence resource allocation and public policy. For a start, all 14,837 villages in Rwanda determined their categories of poverty and wealth, and categorized people within their communities ranking them in hierarchical categories using the six generic and traditional categories described above. This meant that it would be possible to aggregate data beyond the village level to achieve higher levels of poverty statistics for policy and programme design, implementation, monitoring and evaluation, and impact assessment.

In addition to these basic social-economic categories, social maps also captured more specific data by going further in categorizing populations according to specific criteria such as land holding size, employment, and physical status. Table 4.2 highlights some of the key basic headings for which village household-level data are now available from each village, mapped onto the cloth using different symbols and keys.

Policymakers engaging with participatory statistics

Above the level of *Ubudehe* community planning and collective action as described above, the participatory data generation from the *Ubudehe* is starting to be used as a statistical evidence base to influence government policy and programme design. One of the key challenges that the *Ubudehe* process has faced is the fact that the rate of data generated from the social maps has been faster than the capacity of the government and key actors to absorb and engage with this data. Given its organic and experimental nature, engagement and strategic use of this wealth of data is still untapped. Nonetheless, there are promising examples of how citizen-generated data from social maps is influencing public policy and resource allocation.

District-level performance contracts

In most districts, the data from maps has been translated into handwritten lists of households noting their different characteristics. These *Ubudehe* data sets have been used for district-level programme implementation and have

Table 4.2 Headings of citizen-generated data beyond six household socio-economic categories (recorded on *Ubudehe* social maps where relevant)

Economic categories	Social categories
Ba Nyakujya bafite ubutaka (<ha) (poorest having land)	Abamugaye (handicapped)
Ba Nyakujya bashoboye gukore (poorest who can work)	Incike (Utagira Abana) (elderly without children)
Ba Nyakujya badashoboye gukora n'impamvu (poorest who cannot work)	Abana Bibana (child-headed households)
Ba Nyakujya bakora indi mirimo itari iy'ubuhinzi (poor who are doing other non-agricultural work)	Abasizwe inyuma n'amateka (Batwa)
Abakene (125–250 Frw/umunsi) bafite ubutaka < ha (poor earning less than 125 Frw/day)	Abasheshe Akanguhe (elderly over 70 years of age)
Abakene (125–250 Frw/umunsi) bashoboye gukora (those poor who can work)	Abacitse kw'icumu (genocide survivors)
Abakene (125–250 Frw/umunsi) badashoboye gukora (impavu) (poor who cannot work and why)	Ababana n'agakoko ka Sida (people living with HIV/AIDS)
Abakene bakora indi mirimo itari ubuhunzi (poor who are doing other work)	Abana Binzererezi (street children)
Abari hejuru y'umurongo w'ubukene (+250 Frw/umunsi) bafite ubutaka (those who are earning more than 250 Frw/day)	Abapfakazi (widows)
Abari hejuru y'umurongo w'ubukene (+250 Frw/umunsi) badashoboye gukora impavu (those earning more than 250 Frw/dau but unable to work)	Impunzi (refugees)
Abari hejuru y'umurongo w'ubukene (+250 Frw/umunsi) bakora indi mirimo itari ubuhinzi (those who are earning more than 250 Frw, but not engaged in agriculture)	Abatahutse 2006 (returnees)
	Abatuye mu bice byinzara (high hunger period sufferers)
	Abavuye ku rugerero (demobilized soldiers)

Note: Frw = Rwandan franc

Source: various *Ubudehe* return forms from cellules

begun to influence systematically the content of *Imihigos* (performance contracts) at cellule, sector, and district level, with district officials being asked to account for variations if data showed that poverty levels were increasing. In many cases, sector-level agronomists were assigned the role of programme monitoring given their close proximity to villages.

National sector policy design

At the national level, *Ubudehe's* protagonists at the Ministry of Local Government (MINALOC) have persistently tried, despite the lack of capacity in terms of manpower and resources, to demonstrate the aggregative potential of the wealth of data available from the social maps. This persistence has in some instances yielded fruit. The Ministry of Agriculture, for instance, has used the *Ubudehe* data to identify poor and marginalized households who could benefit from livestock restocking programmes. Most recently the data generated from the social maps has received attention from the Ministry of Health, which was lacking data on how to identify poor and marginalized households to benefit from free health insurance and to identify those households that ought to be paying into the health insurance kitty. After carrying out pilots and validating the authenticity of *Ubudehe* data in specific districts (see Figure 4.1), the Ministry of Health requested the nationwide data to enable it to offer free health insurance to the poor and marginalized categories of households. The *Ubudehe* secretariat did not have the resources or manpower to meet this request. As a result, in December 2010 the Ministry of Health in collaboration with the National Institute of Statistics (NISR) funded the Ubudehe Secretariat to create a national database from the citizen-generated data (MINALOC, 2010). At the time of writing this chapter, data collection was underway.

The Vison Umurenge Programme

During this period, the government also conceived the Vision Umurenge Programme, a targeted economic programme aimed at spurring rural economic growth and reducing poverty. As part of a pilot programme of experimentation, the programme would use citizen-generated data from villages in pilot sectors in each district (see, for example, the case of Busengo Sector in Figure 4.2). It aimed to target community members who could benefit from its three programme components of Direct Support, Public Works, and Financial Services. The Direct Support component would provide unconditional cash transfers to the neediest and most vulnerable households unable to work due to disabilities or other vulnerabilities. The Public Works component would provide employment to those individuals from the poorest and landless households who were able to work.

The financial services component would offer low-interest loans to individuals and groups in villages to promote economic growth. The Vision Umurenge Programme would rely on *Ubudehe* data for identifying beneficiary households and rely on the fund transfer systems developed by *Ubudehe* transferring resources directly to village banks. The Vision Umurenge Programme acted as an additional indirect source of funds for *Ubudehe*-type activities specifically addressing issues of marginalization affecting poorer members of the community. Since inception in 2007 to date, it has provided an additional 22 million euros for pilot experiments.

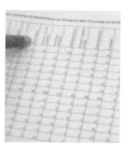

(top left to right): Fidele Kayira and Francis Karake, Ubudehe Master Trainers, examining village maps in MINALOC, Kigali; Francis (l) and Fidele (r) demonstrate map data to Laetitia Nkunda (CDF Director); tabulated data listing social categories in each village generated from village social maps.

(bottom left to right): Data obtained from a village in this example shows that 67 households (first two socio-economic categories) qualify for free health insurance; villages then provide detailed information about the dependants of each household who will get free health insurance cards; a vulnerable household in Gakenke district that benefited from free health insurance cards after being identified through social map data.

Figure 4.1 *Ubudehe* data used by the Ministry of Health following persistent influence by *Ubudehe* protagonists

Photos: A. Shah, 2006 and 2010. Consent obtained

Interestingly, regular updating of the social maps has enabled participatory monitoring of the performance and impact of the Vision Umurenge Programme. In the case of Busengo Sector, for example, social maps updated immediately after the programme intervention revealed positive shifts in people's socio-economic status from one category to another. However, when the social map was updated in 2010, it revealed that the changes in people's socio-economic status were not as dramatic as initially thought. This has led to district officials going back to the drawing board to examine why the effects of the social protection programme have not been sustained. Figure 4.3 demonstrates how social map data generated from Mugunga Village in the Busengo Sector can be analysed to demonstrate changes in people's lives. It also highlights the fact that data from social maps is easy to generate, and one does not need to wait for a lengthy evaluation process, especially in the case of programmes where much damage is being done, to recognize that policies may not necessarily be having the imagined impact.

(left to right): The Executive Secretary of Busengo Sector shows the importance of the *Ubudehe* social map in identifying marginalized and vulnerable households; list of households to benefit under the VUP generated from the village social map; residents of Busengo Sector claiming payments from the Direct Support and Public Works scheme of VUP.

Figure 4.2 Using *Ubudehe* data to offer targeted social protection to marginalized and vulnerable households under the VUP

Photos: A. Shah, 2010. Consent obtained

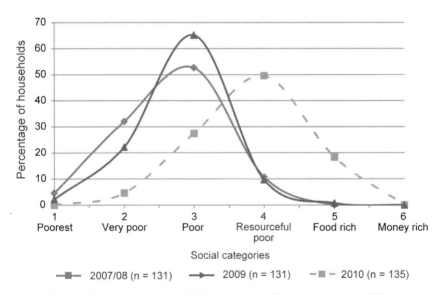

Figure 4.3 Analysis of participatory trend statistics in Mugunga Village, Busengo Sector

Source: analysed from village social map and cross-checked with village facilitator data and *Ubudehe* records

Conclusion

Ubudehe is original in both its design and instruments (Uvin et al., 2003). While still evolving in form, the story of *Ubudehe* so far suggests that it has contributed to democratization in Rwanda through the introduction of elements of village-level participatory democracy and through a less tangible impact on a broader shift from an 'obedience culture' to a 'citizenship culture' in the country.

Of particular significance to the theme of participatory statistics explored in this book, the *Ubudehe* experience in Rwanda has demonstrated how participatory numbers can be collected and taken to scale in an efficient and timely way. The willingness of district administrations and sector ministries alike to recognize the validity and utility of this national data set signals the extraordinary potential that exists for participatory processes that encourage democratic transformation to provide robust evidence for progressive policymaking. And this is only the beginning. With continued local mapping and well-being analysis, allied with persistent advocacy with policymakers and technocrats, the 'win–win' potential of participatory statistics in Rwanda remains high.

References

Chambers, R. (1997) *Whose Reality Counts? Putting the First Last*, Practical Action Publishing, Rugby.

Checkland, P. (1989) 'Soft systems methodology', in J. Rosenhead (ed.), *Rational Analysis for a Problematic World*, John Wiley and Sons, Chichester.

Gandhi, M. and Parel, A. (eds) (1997) *Hind Swaraj and Other Writings*, Cambridge University Press, Cambridge.

Joseph, S. (2006) 'Ministry of Local Government (MINALOC): creating spaces for citizen participation', unpublished paper, MINALOC, Kigali.

Korten, D. (1980) 'Community organization and rural development, a learning processes approach', *Public Administration Review* 40(5): 480–511.

Ministry of Economics and Finance (MINECOFIN) (2003) 'Ubudehe mu Kurwanya Ubukene, Ubudehe to Fight Poverty', Concept Note, Government of Rwanda, MINECOFIN, Kigali.

Ministry of Local Government (MINALOC) (2006) 'Creating spaces for citizen participation', in *Self Governance, Poverty Analysis, Local Problem Solving, Sector / District Planning*, MINALOC, Kigali.

Ostrom, E. (1990) *Governing the Commons*, Cambridge University Press, Cambridge.

Ostrom, V. (1997) *The Meaning of Democracy and the Vulnerability of Democracies: A Response to Tocqueville's Challenge*, University of Michigan Press, Ann Arbor.

Republic of Rwanda (RoR) (1999) 'Report on the reflection meetings held in the Office of the President of the Republic from May 1998 to March 1999', Office of the President of the Republic, Kigali.

Shah, A. (2011) 'The paradox of "hidden democracy" in Rwanda: The citizens' experience of Ubudehe', unpublished thesis, Department of International Development, University of Oxford, Oxford.

Tocqueville, A. (2002) *Democracy in America*, A Penn State Electronic Classics Series Publication, Pennsylvania State University. Available from: www2. hn.psu.edu/faculty/jmanis/toqueville/dem-in-america1.pdf [accessed 19 September 2012].

Uphoff, N. (1996) *Learning from Gal Oya. Possibilities for Participatory Development and Post-Newtonian Social Science*, IT Publications, London.

Uvin, P. and Nyirankundabera, J. (2003) 'Le projet ubudehe: une reflexion et evaluation prospectives', provisional version, 13 June.

About the author

Ashish Shah is a Kenyan citizen, currently completing his doctorate at the Department of International Development, University of Oxford. His research compares citizen experiences of democracy and voice in Rwanda and Malawi. Ashish has over 10 years of experience working with two international NGOs and he is deeply passionate about how governments, NGOs, and donors can improve their accountability to the citizens they claim to work for, and how citizens can gain more strategic 'voice' through participatory numbers.

Chapter 5

Generating numbers with local governments for decentralized health sector policy in the Philippines

Rose Marie R. Nierras

Participatory statistics have been generated and standardized for regional or national policymaking in many different policy contexts and sectors. This chapter describes how, during the 1990s in the Philippines, participatory statistics generated on health outcomes provided the data necessary for policymaking in a context of decentralized governance. Through participatory diagnostic workshops, grass-roots health workers classified and mapped diseases, producing statistics at variance with official statistics but which officials came to accept. These participatory statistics were used to identify priority actions which led, in the space of a few months, to a sharp decrease in mortality. This chapter attempts to capture part of the story of the decentralization experience in Cotabato Province in the Philippines and shows how the participatory process of generating numbers for public policy grounded participatory local governance in this context. Local governments were assisted to understand better what their new mandates under a decentralized system of public administration were, what citizens expected, and how to make that transaction happen. At the same time, citizens experienced how to raise their voices more effectively and demand more responsive governance, while at the same time understanding the limitations local governments face in carrying out their functions.

Decentralization and local governance in the Philippines

Decentralization in the Philippines was mandated by Republic Act No. 7160, otherwise known as the Local Government Code of 1991. This Code mandated the complete transfer of responsibilities for the delivery of basic services, personnel, and budgets for health, social welfare, and development, and agriculture from the national government to the local governments. In the health sector, the national government's Department of Health retained technical and regulatory authority in all matters of public health and administrative control over regional and specialized hospitals. Beyond this, decentralization vested local governments with administrative authority over health care provision, including the design and implementation of health programmes, the management of public health personnel and assets, and the appropriation of budgets for public health (see Table 5.1).

http://dx.doi.org/10.3362/9781780447711/005

Table 5.1 Levels of administrative authority and persons responsible within local governments for the health sector by type of local government unit

Local government unit type	Authority over health care provision	Persons responsible within the local government
Provinces Highly urbanized/ chartered cities	Hospital-based health care (district and provincial hospitals) and technical assistance to public health care programmes for all lower-level local governments	Governor for Provinces (elected) Mayor for Cities (elected) Provincial/City Health Officer and Provincial/ City Health Officer Staff (devolved)
Municipalities Component cities	Public health care programmes	Mayor (elected) Municipal Health Officer, Public Health Nurse, Midwives (devolved)
Barangays (villages)	Primary health care programmes	Barangay Chairperson (elected) Barangay Health Worker (volunteers)

Source: author compiled from Republic Act 7160

In addition, the Local Government Code made very clear provision for citizen participation through 'Local Special Bodies'. For the health sector, all levels of local government, with the exception of *barangays* (villages), were mandated to organize and constitute Local Health Boards to serve as an advisory body to the local health offices, recommend the annual health budgets to the local chief executive, and function as the grievance committee for all health personnel within the local health offices. As mandated, the composition of the Local Health Boards included the Local Chief Executive, the Head of the local health office, the Chair of the Committee on Health of the local legislature, a representative from the Department of Health, and representatives from the non-government sector.

Like most major administrative reform measures, the decentralization of the health sector was far from smooth. Most elected local chief executives were wary about taking on the responsibilities for the provision of health services. Provincial governors were reluctant to take on the responsibilities for the maintenance and management of public hospitals, particularly in the light of the huge costs this entailed. Municipal and city mayors were generally hesitant about managing the public health programmes, especially since few had medical backgrounds themselves. It did not help that the public health workers had traditionally been highly organized as a sector. The professional organizations of public health workers openly campaigned against the implementation of the Local Government Code and many resisted the idea of having to report to administrative authorities (governors and mayors) they considered to be 'less educationally prepared' to supervise their work.

The Cotabato experience with health sector decentralization

The Province of Cotabato is located in central Mindanao, the southernmost island of the Philippines. It has a land size of about 565,000 hectares, and in 1996 had a population of about 600,000 unevenly residing within the 18 municipalities of the province. The technical transition to a devolved health service in Cotabato involved a transfer of administrative authority over the public health personnel and the transfer of funds from the national government directly to the local governments. How the Cotabato local governments managed these resources was an altogether different story. One anecdote perhaps best describes the situation. Since the implementation of the Local Government Code, the Governor expressed concern that the province had consistently appropriated a significant amount of money for the Leprosy Control Program despite the absence of any incidence of leprosy in the province. Every year from 1993 to 1996, resources were appropriated for the Leprosy Control Program and had to be realigned for other purposes. The Provincial Health Officer, who was an openly staunch advocate of the 'recentralization' of the health sector, continued to do so on the argument that 'this was on the directive of the national government' (Associates in Rural Development, 1993b). The elected mayors of the 18 municipalities of the province all continued to express the need for help in the management of public health programmes. And, in addition, they repeatedly asked for direct assistance in the form of free hospitalization in public hospitals for sick constituents.

Hence for the province of Cotabato, the challenge of decentralization was all about 'localizing' the public health sector. Two things are implied by this need to localize. Firstly, it meant building a shared understanding among local stakeholders of what public health policies and programmes were all about. And secondly, it meant planning and implementing programmes – independently of the Department of Health – in a manner that allowed local governments to be more responsive to local health needs.

In the second semester of 1995, the Governance and Local Democracy (GOLD) Project was introduced in the province. The GOLD Project was designed by the United States Agency for International Development (USAID) to bring about more responsive democratic institutions with greater citizen participation in local governance. The project hoped to achieve this through a strategy of assisted self-reliance and the provision of technical assistance to local governments and their communities on a demand-driven basis. Implemented and managed by the Associates in Rural Development (Tetra Tech ARD), the GOLD Project supported local governments with technical assistance in areas of work that they themselves identified and prioritized. ARD's approach to the provision of technical assistance accorded a heavy premium to facilitated processes, with different stakeholders involved in and affected by the issues technical assistance addressed.[1] For the province of Cotabato, technical assistance in the management of the public health sector became one of the priorities put forward to the Project by both the local governments and the citizens alike. And it was with technical assistance from this Project that the province was able to pursue many of the activities that are discussed in this chapter.

A participatory planning methodology: the Health Sector Review workshop

Workshop objectives and participants

As a first step in strengthening participation in health sector decision making, key stakeholders from local governments and civil society organizations working in the health sector of the province convened a 'Health Sector Review workshop'. The purpose of the diagnostic workshop was to identify the local health needs, and match these more effectively with the (limited) public health resources across all local government levels in the province. Stakeholders hoped that the workshop would help to 'de-mystify' the health sector for non-health personnel of local governments and their civil society partners.

The Health Sector Review workshop involved the health personnel of the provincial, municipal, and *barangay* local governments, their Local Health Boards, and a number of local chief executives from these local governments. In addition, the volunteer *Barangay* Health Workers ('barefoot health workers') and civil society groups involved in community health programmes were asked to join the workshop. The Director of the Local Government Assistance and Monitoring Service of the Department of Health, who was concurrently serving as Director of the Department's Health Intelligence Service, was also invited to participate. The workshop was held on 21–22 May 1996.

The workshop was designed in two parts. The first part engaged the participants in an exercise to establish 'snapshots' of the current 'demands for' and available 'supply of' public health services in the province. To complete a picture of the demand for health services, the participants put together their data on the leading causes of morbidity and mortality in the province. Generating the snapshot of supply involved them working through the public health resources that were available. This was then followed by an analysis of their data and on which basis they identified ways to better apply their limited resources.

Health mapping exercise: data aggregation for analysis

Workshop participants started by establishing the incidence and causes of morbidity and mortality. Municipal data was pooled from the midwives' records, which in turn was drawn directly from the *Barangay* Health Workers' household records. Data from these household records were aggregated at the municipal level, and this served as the basis for the provincial incidence totals (see Tables 5.2 and 5.3).

Table 5.2 Participatory analysis of the top five leading causes of mortality in municipalities represented

Cause	No. of municipalities in which cause ranks in top five	Rank order of cause based on provincial data
PTB	9	2
Cardiovascular disease/ heart	8	6
Pneumonia	5	8
Violence (all forms)	5	4
Accidents	5	5
Hypertension	4	1
Senility	4	3
Cancers	–	7

Source: Cotabato Heath Sector Review Workshop Report

Table 5.3 Participatory analysis of the top five leading causes of morbidity in municipalities represented

Cause	No. of municipalities in which cause ranks in top five	Rank order of cause based on provincial data
URTI/ARI/bronchitis	11	1, 2
Diarrhoea	5	3
Pneumonia	4	–
GI disorder	3	–
Malnutrition	3	5
Skin diseases	3	–
Anaemia	1	4

Source: Cotabato Heath Sector Review Workshop Report

At this early stage in the workshop, it was already apparent that the data being generated were at variance with the official records at the provincial level, which were regularly passed on to the Department of Health's Field Health Surveillance and Information System ('Information System'). That the Director from the Department of Health in charge of this Information System was a participant at the workshop was purely coincidental, but this was an opportunity not lost on the participants. They questioned the basis for the provincial data reported by the national Information System, and commented on how 'poorly' it depicted the health status of the province. After much discussion, the workshop participants decided to completely ignore the statistics presented by the Information System, which had been traditionally relied on for health planning purposes, and to proceed on the basis of the data that they had put together.

Participants compared incidence figures for each of the causes of morbidity and mortality across municipalities within the province and defined what they considered to be 'high', 'average', and 'low' incidence. This determination was made on the basis of the numbers they had generated and available official health records over the last five years. Once completed, they compared the incidence figures of the causes of morbidity and mortality with the national averages. Interestingly, what the national figures indicated to be 'average' for each of these causes, the workshop participants had decided among themselves to be 'high'.

Participants then indicated the incidence levels for each of the ten leading causes of mortality and morbidity in their municipality by shading in their area in each of the 'morbidity maps' and 'mortality maps' using pre-agreed colours. Figure 5.1 illustrates a mortality map produced at the workshop. These 20 maps, one each for the leading causes of mortality and morbidity, translated their data into a visual form that helped to facilitate further discussion and analysis. Participants clustered around the different maps in the hall and discussions started on how municipalities compared with one another, reasons for how each one fared, and practical ways by which incidence was held in check. Diagnostic discussions covered the causes of morbidity and mortality, and the relationships between the two. Discussions led to the realization that, in all but one municipality, the data suggested that the transition from communicable to degenerative diseases and causes of death was beginning to manifest in the province.

Generating the morbidity and mortality maps was only one part of the data they were aggregating. The other part involved generating the 'supply' maps – those that provided the data on the public health resources of the province. Using a similar process, the participants first generated the numbers on health personnel and facilities by municipality. These were then compared to the technical standards set by the Department of Health on ratios of health personnel to population and acceptable coverage areas for public hospitals. On this basis, the participants generated separate maps for public health personnel and public health facilities, this time indicating whether the local governments were within the technical standards set by the Department of Health. Participants produced these supply maps on plastic film, to the same scale as the mortality and morbidity maps. This allowed participants to view these health resource maps as an overlay to the morbidity and mortality maps when they were later asked to do more detailed analyses for each of the causes of morbidity and mortality.

To complete the picture of the available public health resources, participants analysed the national health budget for the year to determine the 'share' of the province. To this figure, the participants added the provincial and municipal health budgets for the same year. This allowed them to calculate the average *per capita* investment that public health budgets from all sources afforded. This exercise was an eye-opener for all the participants at the workshop. Even the public health personnel present had not fully appreciated how severely limited – in real *per capita* terms – the public health budgets were.

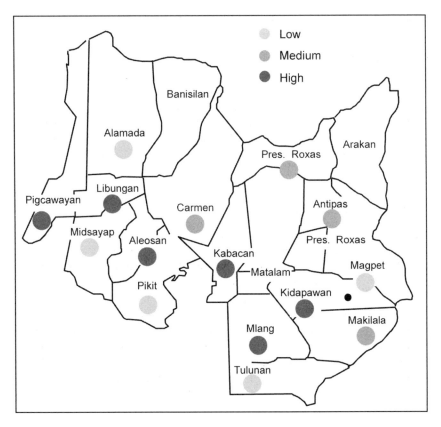

Figure 5.1 PTB mortality map, Cotabato Province

Source: Cotabato Heath Sector Review Workshop Report

Data analysis for action

Once all the maps were completed, the participants then self-selected into 20 'break out' groups, each one assigned to discuss and analyse one map, or one cause of morbidity or mortality. They considered the following: what brought about the leading cause of the morbidity or mortality they had selected, what measures were already being taken in ongoing programmes, what other initiatives could realistically be taken, and how these suggestions could be taken forward. They reflected on the current supply of public health resources available using the supply maps they had generated. There were reports from all groups in a final plenary session at which even more discussions took place. The two-day workshop ended with the participants agreeing on next steps for taking forward what they had all started.

Actions from the Health Sector Review workshop

The foregoing description of the Health Sector Review workshop process provides an idea of how the creative application of participatory approaches to generating numbers has helped stakeholders within the province better appreciate their own health situation. Critically, the participatory mapping and diagnostic discussions prompted a number of policy actions in the local health system. These actions happened at the different levels of local government. And in all instances, they took place as a joint effort between the local governments and key civil society partners. A few of these are described briefly below.

The Provincial Traffic Code

The workshop established that the third leading cause of mortality in the province was road accidents. When the available public health resources were looked into, it was further established that none of the public health personnel was a specialist in the trauma field necessary to deal with such situations. In addition, the medical equipment needed was not available. Clearly, the public health system was in no position to respond. So the members of the Committee on Health of the provincial legislature who were present at the workshop immediately worked to pass legislation establishing speed limits on the national highways running through the provincial boundaries. Within six months of the passage of the Provincial Traffic Code, the incidence of mortality due to road accidents had dropped significantly.

Accessing ambulances

At the workshop, the capital municipality of Kidapawan repeatedly registered the highest number of casualties. When this was looked into, it was established that the high mortality rate in the municipality was largely accounted for by deaths at the Provincial Hospital. And on closer inspection of their data, a large number of these deaths were patients from the outer municipalities of the province. More importantly, many of these deaths took place within the first 24 hours of confinement, the period within which hospitals could not be held liable for casualties. This indicated that seriously ill patients were not availing of in-patient care services from the district hospitals closer to them. And part of the reason for this was that most district hospitals had limited ambulance facilities, if at all, to be able to respond to call-outs from the seriously ill. While the participants agreed that the long-term solution was to make the referral systems for hospitals work, it was also thought useful to help all municipalities get access to an ambulance so the municipal governments could help transport patients to the closest district hospital. By December 2000, ambulances had been accessed from the Philippine Charity Sweepstakes for all municipalities.

Responding to the emerging changes in disease patterns

The morbidity and mortality maps generated at the workshop had suggested that the shift from communicable to degenerative diseases as causes of death had begun to manifest as a trend throughout the province. The entire public health system of the country was heavily oriented to communicable diseases. While local governments now recognized the need to begin making the investments in strengthening its capacities to administer to degenerative diseases, resources were extremely limited.

To get beyond this constraint, the Cotabato provincial government decided to undertake revenue enhancement and cost recovery measures from the operations of the public hospitals.[2] In the first year of introducing these measures, the Provincial Hospital generated the equivalent of 20 per cent of its total operating budget for the year. Five years later, these measures had delivered the equivalent of 60 per cent of its operating budget for that year (Governance and Local Democracy Project, 2001b). A good proportion of these resources was subsequently reinvested in the training of public health personnel and in the upgrading of facilities at public hospitals throughout the province. Other initiatives along these lines were more easily organized. For instance, a few months after the workshop, the province had organized and set up a Diabetes Clinic within the premises of the Provincial Hospital. Diabetic patients were recruited to help in educating patients newly diagnosed with the disease. In addition, the Clinic provided regular medical consultations for all members and organized bulk purchases of maintenance medications at cheaper prices.

Municipal Health Sector Review workshops

Health Sector Review workshops were organized and conducted on the request of the municipal teams present at the provincial workshop. Technical assistance for these workshops, conducted in 9 out of the 18 municipalities, was also provided from the GOLD Project. All of these workshops were facilitated by persons present at the provincial workshop, who were then trained as facilitators. The facilitating teams included personnel from the provincial government and representatives from civil society organizations. The process flow for these workshops was slightly modified so that the municipal workshops could utilize all the outputs that had been generated at the provincial workshop. Having the processes repeated at the municipal level also allowed more stakeholders within the municipalities to benefit from participating in them.

Municipal and Barangay health planning and budgeting workshops

The conduct of Municipal Health Sector Review workshops immediately led to actions around health planning and budgeting exercises of the municipal and *barangay* governments. These health planning and budgeting exercises, which also involved the use of participatory approaches for generating numbers, were conducted in all of the nine municipalities that had Municipal Health Sector Review workshops, and in at least 25 per cent of the *barangays* in each municipality.

In all of the Health Sector Review workshops conducted, participants had repeatedly identified that what was needed to prevent the incidence of some of the most common causes of morbidity was a combination of safe water, nutritious food, and basic health education. Significantly, none of these had traditionally been considered as 'health expenditures'. However, in the majority of subsequent health planning and budgeting exercises, there were increased appropriations for activities in these areas. And most importantly, the local governments had broken the habit of simply applying the '10 per cent over last year's targets and 10 per cent over last year's budget' formula to health planning and budgeting.

Appreciating the energizing effect of the Health Sector Review workshops on the nine municipalities that initially decided to conduct these, the province allocated the funds necessary to support similar exercises in the other nine municipalities of the province.

Establishing new ways of doing things

The conduct of the Health Sector Review workshops had effectively introduced to local governments in the province new participatory ways by which they could go about exercising their mandates. Because the workshop involved the volunteer *Barangay* Health Workers and representatives from civil society organizations, the local governments continued to seek their participation in all the actions described above. But their participation was also sought in other aspects of public health work. Workshops with citizens and communities had begun to be more widely accepted as the desired standard by government, and the civil society groups and communities began to expect their local governments to be constantly organizing participatory events.

Emerging lessons and issues

There are many lessons that can be drawn from the Cotabato experiences with their Health Sector Review workshops and subsequent participatory exercises. There are a few worth highlighting as follows:

Design of the workshop

The design of the Health Sector Review workshop was critical to subsequent successes in deliberative decision making and follow-up actions. Workshop design was a joint effort between technical experts in public health and process facilitators based on expressed stakeholder objectives. With these in mind, it was possible for the team to put together a simple process that would engage the participatory generation of statistics as part of a diagnostic process that would enable the participants to find immediate and practical use for their data for their public health policies and programmes.

The diagnostic process enabled participants to contextualize, analyse, and act on their data. Hence data generation was immediately followed by exercises that involved comparing the data generated with other data sets. After these comparisons were made, the data generated by the participants were revisited and analysed. This analysis was directed towards the identification of 'doable' actions that the local governments and their communities could then take forward.

Preparation by participants

The preparatory work that the participants themselves had to complete before the workshop was just as critical. Participants were asked to bring the health records and budgets of their local governments for the current year, as well as those for the past five preceding years. For the *Barangay* Health Workers, this was particularly a challenge. There was one *Barangay* Health Worker for every 30–50 households. Given the population of the province, it was unlikely that all these volunteer Health Workers could be accommodated at the workshop. So the workshop coordinators decided that only the officers of the federations of *Barangay* Health Workers in each municipality would be invited. This meant that those officers invited had to aggregate the household records of all the Health Workers in their villages and municipalities in advance of the workshop.

Facilitation of the workshop

The workshop process involved close collaboration between the facilitators and technical experts. The facilitator led the participants through the workshop, with public health experts available to intervene for clarification on technical questions and to support participants in their analytical work. Subsequent Municipal Health Sector Review workshops were facilitated by teams composed of local government and civil society facilitators. They were initially trained in the facilitating methods employed. But they were also involved in the modification of the workshop design to suit its application at the municipal level. Discussions on the design revision allowed the chance for the facilitators from local government health offices to appreciate process considerations. Through participating in these discussions on process design, civil society facilitators could be sensitized to the technical aspects of public health issues and concerns, and contribute to identifying the best ways of handling these in the process.

Conclusion: from participatory statistics to participatory governance

This paper considered the experiences of the Province of Cotabato in using participatory approaches to generate numbers for public policy in the health sector. The Health Sector Review workshop in Cotabato Province was the start of a larger 'cascading' process of follow-up workshops for local governments and their communities in the Province. Those referred to in this paper include the workshops to identify revenue enhancement and cost recovery measures for the Provincial Hospital, and the municipal and *barangay* health planning and budgeting exercises. Within each of these processes, the participatory generation of statistics aided diagnostic analysis, policy, and planning discussions.

The Cotabato workshop was also conducted in the context of improving local government performance of decentralized mandates in the provision of public health services. To this end, it was important that the process involved stakeholders from local government, civil society groups, and the communities themselves. Exercises with participatory statistics very quickly situated local government officials and citizens 'on the same page'. Discussions and analysis of these numbers also served as effective avenues for dialogue, negotiation, and exchange.

Clearly generating statistics can be an effective tool for participatory local governance. But its application has to be carefully thought out and planned for. There can be a tendency to accord the premium on the exercise of generating the numbers at the expense of losing sight of the larger purposes for which the numbers can and should serve.

Finally, the issue of 'who participates?' and 'who is excluded?' should also be the subject of continuing critical reflection, especially as participatory exercises gain traction at higher levels of government. The participation of *Barangay* Health Workers at the Provincial Health Sector Review workshop was limited. This was equally true for other public health personnel like midwives and nurses. The same questions also have to be raised for civil society representation: which civil society organizations should have been invited, and can these civil society organizations be assumed to represent all sectors of the communities? Yet despite the 'limited' participation, this case demonstrates that diagnostic workshops utilizing participatory statistics can provide meaningful spaces for citizen participation and strengthened local governance of public resources.

Notes

1   One of the hallmarks of the GOLD Project was its wide application of the 'Technologies of Participation' to enable the facilitated management of various project issues. Participatory methods were employed to provide technical assistance and support to local governments in a wide range of governance sectors (health, environment, local planning and budgeting,

local investment planning and design, health, social services delivery, and organizational and systems development) and issues. In the course of its implementation, the GOLD Project developed an extensive application of facilitated processes relevant to strengthening local governments, wrote up manuals for those processes that could be more widely adopted, and trained a cadre of over 3,000 process facilitators from local governments and partner civil society groups.

2   How these measures were identified is another story, beyond the scope of this chapter, about practical applications of participatory approaches to generating numbers not too dissimilar from the Health Sector Review workshop earlier discussed.

Bibliography

Amado Diaz Development Foundation (2000) (unpublished) 'A narrative report on the Governance and Local Democracy Project Technical Assistance in the Province of Cotabato', Amado Diaz Development Foundation, Midsayap, Cotabato, Philippines.

Ateneo School of Government (2000) 'Synopsis of findings', Tenth Rapid Field Appraisal of the Status of Decentralization: The Local Perspective, GOLD Project, Makati, Philippines.

Bulosan, Luce S. (2000) (unpublished) 'Eight years of tracking decentralization on the Philippines: a meta-synopsis of the ten rapid field appraisals on decentralization', GOLD Project, Makati, Philippines.

Evelio, B. (Javier Foundation) (1995) 'Synopsis of findings', Fifth Rapid Field Appraisal of the Status of Decentralization: The Local Perspective, GOLD Project, Makati, Philippines.

Governance and Local Democracy Project (2000) 'Measuring public hospital performance', Local Governance Technical Notes, Public Hospitals, 2, GOLD Project, Makati, Philippines.

Governance and Local Democracy Project (2001a) 'Situating public hospitals in the health system', Local Governance Technical Notes, Public Hospitals, 1, GOLD Project, Makati, Philippines.

Governance and Local Democracy Project (2001b) 'Generating revenues from local government hospitals', Local Governance Technical Notes, Public Hospitals, 3, GOLD Project, Makati, Philippines.

Nierras, Rose Marie R. (2000) 'Decentralized capacity building: the experience of the Governance and Local Democracy (GOLD) Project', Local Autonomy Paper Series No. 4, GOLD Project, Makati, Philippines.

Perez, J.A. III (1998) 'A promising start: the first five years of devolution of the Philippine public health system', Occasional Paper No. 98-04, GOLD Project, Makati, Philippines.

Tetra Tech ARD (1992) 'Synopsis of findings', First Rapid Field Appraisal of the Status of Decentralization, Local Development Assistance Program, Makati, Philippines.

Tetra Tech ARD (1993a) 'Synopsis of findings', Second Rapid Field Appraisal of the Status of Decentralization: the Local Perspective, Local Development Assistance Program, Makati, Philippines.

Tetra Tech ARD (1993b) 'Synopsis of findings', Third Rapid Field Appraisal of the Status of Decentralization: The Local Perspective, Local Development Assistance Program, Makati, Philippines.

Tetra Tech ARD (1994) 'Synopsis of findings', Fourth Rapid Field Appraisal of the Status of Decentralization: The Local Perspective, Local Development Assistance Program, Makati, Philippines.

Tetra Tech ARD (1996) 'Synopsis of findings', Sixth Rapid Field Appraisal of the Status of Decentralization: The Local Perspective, Governance and Local Democracy (GOLD) Project, Makati, Philippines.

Tetra Tech ARD (1997) 'Synopsis of findings', Seventh Rapid Field Appraisal of the Status of Decentralization: The Local Perspective, GOLD Project, Makati, Philippines.

Tetra Tech ARD (1998b) 'Synopsis of findings', Eighth Rapid Field Appraisal of the Status of Decentralization: The Local Perspective, GOLD Project, Makati, Philippines.

Tetra Tech ARD (1999a) 'Synopsis of findings', Ninth Rapid Field Appraisal of the Status of Decentralization: The Local Perspective, GOLD Project, Makati, Philippines.

About the author

Rose Marie R. Nierras is the Director of Operations at the International Budget Partnership in Washington, DC, where she is responsible for strengthening organizational systems, including the monitoring and evaluation of its work with partners all over the world. She previously led Plan International's youth and governance programme from Plan UK and coordinated LogoLink, a global learning network of civil society organizations on participatory local governance. Rose was also part of the GOLD Project team in the Philippines, initially as its Participation Development Specialist and then later as its Deputy Chief of Party for Capacity Building.

Chapter 6

From fragility to resilience: participatory community mapping, strategic planning, and knowledge management in Sudan

Margunn Indreboe Alshaikh

Sudan is faced with a new reality after the secession of South Sudan. External and internal pressures are exacerbating a fragile post-CPA[1] context as the government attempts to secure progress towards sustainable peace and economic growth. With the loss of oil revenues and continued regional instability, the need for a grounded process of prioritization in resource distribution, service delivery, and provision of security is ever more apparent. Through a collaboration with UNDP's Crisis and Recovery Mapping and Analysis (CRMA) project, State Departments of Planning across Sudan have been able to create an evidence base for strategic planning using novel technologies and participatory approaches ensuring direct engagement by communities throughout the process. Community engagement has involved state- and locality-level Crisis and Recovery Risk Mapping (CRM), participatory analysis, as well as identification and design of priority interventions. Using this informa-tion, the State Departments have produced stakeholder-inclusive and multi-sectoral analyses that lay the foundations for conflict-sensitive, evidence-based strategic planning and decision making. Through this work, positive and reinforcing rela-tions have been fostered between state and society, increasing dialogue, shaping joint visions of the future, and building the capacity of the state to respond to the demands made by the diverse communities of Sudan. Creating a culture of knowledge and knowledge management within the state has meant that, even in a context of fragility, it has been possible to build elements of resilience that can assist the country in managing its resources more effectively and thereby to over-come some of the factors of instability and tension that have marked much of its recent history.

> Effective states matter for development, and the prospects for moving from fragility to resilience depend on the capability, accountability and responsiveness of the state and its relationship with society. (OECD, 2011)

July 2011 saw the birth of two new nations, South Sudan and Sudan. Sudan, as well as its new southern neighbour, is now grappling with a new national reality, following decades of war and an uneasy transition period guided by the

http://dx.doi.org/10.3362/9781780447711/006

Comprehensive Peace Agreement (CPA) of 2005. With the independence of South Sudan, Sudan lost around 75 per cent of its oil revenues and is currently facing soaring inflation rates and severe budget deficits. With armed uprisings in what are now the new southern states of South Kordofan and Blue Nile, the unresolved status of Abyei and continued conflict in the western region of Darfur, as well as persistent challenges of poverty, food insecurity, and environmental degradation in much of the east and the north, the national government faces serious challenges in terms of ensuring stability, development, and prosperity for its people. Accordingly, characteristics of fragility will continue to impact the national context for some time to come. Regardless of the uncertainties facing the immediate future of Sudan, there is a constant and urgent need for a solid evidence base on which to design government policies and develop plans for institutionalized arrangements to effectively manage conflict, negotiate access to resources, and produce and distribute public goods. Enriching this evidence base with direct inputs from a broad cross-section of society fosters constructive state–society relations and interaction, as resources are targeted strategically and the state is able to build consensus through systematic consultations.

Since 2008, UNDP's Crisis and Recovery Mapping and Analysis (CRMA) project has supported the State Departments of Planning in Eastern Sudan, Blue Nile, and South Kordofan states, as well as in Darfur, to create an up-to-date evidence base for strategic planning using new technologies and participatory methodologies. Initially the CRMA was designed as a targeting mechanism for UNDP community security interventions. Working with local communities in the pilot state of South Kordofan throughout the risk mapping process, and with the interest that the information generated among both international and national actors, it was soon realized that CRMA should cast its net wider than focusing solely on conflict issues in order to help fill the glaring information gap for actors in the recovery and development field. With shifting dynamics across time and space, the net of fragility and conflictivity in Sudan extends to issues as wide ranging as access to basic services, gender, modernization, environment, natural resource management, and livelihoods. Through continuous engagement and dialogue between state and society, one can start to build a greater contextual understanding, negotiate visions for the future, and thereby foster increased capacity and responsiveness to manage the diverse factors causing fragility. This article looks closer at the methodology developed by the CRMA project and explores how it has come to support both state- and peacebuilding through its participatory processes in a fragile setting.

Fragility and statebuilding

The process of statebuilding faces particular challenges in fragile contexts, which in turn has implications for communities in terms of ensuring their basic security, livelihoods, and well-being. There is nothing linear or short term about this process, and actors are often confronted with multiple, and sometimes contradicting, priorities and objectives. State fragility can be defined as the lack of capacity to perform basic state functions, such as a) organizational, institutional, and financial capacity to carry out key functions of governing a population and a territory; and b) the state's ability to develop mutually constructive and reinforcing relations with society.

A characteristic of many states in fragile situations is that weak governance and continuous internal tensions and conflict become routine. Institutional structures and processes suffer from high turnover of staff, weak institutional memory, and limited capacity to implement and enforce plans and policies. Power is divided amongst political and economic elites, many of whom may have vested interests in undermining the development of a resilient state, as this could threaten their own power bases and patronage networks through which their accountability is defined.

In many parts of the world, building a resilient state has often been the product of a long history of intense interaction, negotiation, tension, and conflict between and among different state and societal actors, with the outcome that people have accepted the state as legitimately vested with the authority to make and enforce binding decisions for society as a whole (OECD, 2010). Statebuilding is thus inherently an endogenous process, and external actors can only play a limited role in supporting it (World Bank and UNDP, 2010). Key to this issue is gaining an in-depth understanding of the political, historical, cultural, economic, institutional, and social context that is causing fragility. The ability to maintain stability, foster reconciliation, and encourage recovery and growth necessitates an in-depth understanding of the context, fluidity of relationships and the social fabric, alternative structures of power, and the possible pressure points in any given community. At the heart of these processes of change is, thus, fostering constructive state–society relations through a common understanding of the context, and the different perspectives within, and in turn channelling this knowledge and direct engagement into policymaking and planning processes at all levels of government.

The role of information

Creating an evidence base emerges as a key priority for any institution wishing to respond effectively to needs for security, service delivery, recovery, and development. In post-conflict and fragile situations, the existing evidence base may be particularly weak, as authorities have not had the capacity or possibility to conduct national or sectoral updates, surveys and assessments, periodic censuses, or even rescue historical records from war-torn offices. Similarly, institutional memory may be weak, as populations have been displaced, government staff dismissed or rotated, and government offices periodically closed down. Furthermore, existing records of public facilities may no longer reflect the current reality, as buildings may have been destroyed, supply lines interrupted, and services discontinued. Pre-conflict surveys and baselines are thus of limited value when targeting interventions for recovery and development.

In an attempt to overcome these information challenges in Sudan, the idea of creating a common information management platform for international and national institutions was developed in 2008. With the support of its counterparts, the CRMA team set out to compile and share geo-referenced, public data from international and national actors alike, across all sectors. Data sets collected range from hydrology, soil types, and land cover to demography, distribution of basic services, and an overview of key implementing actors and their interventions. In planning and programming for crisis and recovery purposes, more often than not, multiple actors work in the same sector and geographic areas. Nevertheless, data collection and analysis are often carried out in silos with minimal engagement and interoperability across actors. As data compiled through CRMA is geo-referenced, this allows institutions to quickly gain an overview of the context in which they are working and thereby design their interventions according to a common evidence base, avoiding duplication of efforts. Easy visualization of key data sets allows institutions to analyse baseline and contextual data with their own internal data. Such visualization facilitates analysis, targeting, and planning in what are often complex and rapidly changing contexts.

By 2012, this initiative has led to the establishment of an Information Management Working Group (IMWG) of all core UN agencies and will soon expand to also include international NGOs. Building on the work of the CRMA, the IMWG platform has chosen a GIS-based system and a Digital Atlas as its primary data-sharing and dissemination tool. Members sign an official information-sharing protocol and the data is updated and published on a quarterly basis. The Digital Atlas interface is further complemented by a resource library containing the most recent state situation analyses and strategic plans as key reference documents. Alongside this IMWG, there is a government-led initiative to establish a national information management network that can lead on standardization of data collection, management, and sharing efforts across government structures at federal and state levels. Importantly, this network can act as an interlocutor with the IMWG, and ensure that information resources from all across Sudan are shared and channelled through to the relevant policy- and decision-making departments and offices of the federal government system.

The role of community mapping

Given the challenges surrounding the availability, coverage, and validity of baseline data in post-conflict Sudan, CRMA designed a Crisis and Recovery Risk Mapping (CRM) process at community level in order to fill the information gap with data and inputs from the grass-roots level. The main objective of the CRM process is to gather information on community perceptions and experiences of risks and challenges related to accessing essential resources like water, land, and basic services; ecological hazards- and livelihoods-related issues; as well as experiences with personal security issues including small arms proliferation, counterproductive behaviours, and rule of law deficits.

When talking about collecting 'community perceptions' we need to be aware that community is defined in the most basic sense as people who share a certain geographic space whose boundaries have artificially been constructed by political authorities as a 'locality' – the most local level of governance in the three-tiered federal system of Sudan. In other words, the data collection method is organized on a locality-by-locality basis, with an introductory CRM workshop also at state level. However, participants in the CRM process may define themselves as belonging to several different communities in terms of kinship, tribe, religion, social relations, geographic homesteads, livelihood groups, and so forth. The key to the CRM approach in terms of capturing community perceptions is thus to gather representatives from the various groups that share in their day-to-day life the geographic space of a locality. Given the diversity of Sudan, CRMA has set out a list of possible groups that through its local government partners should be invited to participate in the data collection and analysis process:

- locality administration
- tribal leaders
- religious leaders
- representatives of political groups (not already represented in the locality administration)
- representatives of civil society (farmers' unions, pastoralists' unions, fisheries' unions, youth and women's organizations, and other relevant representatives).

Further, there needs to be a gender and age balance amongst the participants. Following these guidelines, it is the responsibility of the locality administration and State Department of Planning[2] focal points to extend invitations to particular individuals and thereby ensure a balanced representation of the locality population at the workshops. Each CRM workshop gathers around 25 to 35 participants over the course of two days and is facilitated by at least two CRM staff members and two national counterparts from the State Departments of Planning who are familiar with the CRM process and methodology.

During the CRM process, perceptions and experiences are recorded through lengthy discussions in plenary fora, risk mapping, mind mapping, and focus group exercises. Following an introductory presentation by the CRM team on the project background, process, purpose, and goal, participants are given an opportunity to ask questions and to raise issues they consider critical to consider over the two days. Facilitators assist in noting down the issues that are brainstormed by the plenary, and based on an initial plenary discussion, participants reach a consensus on the ten most critical risks and challenges facing their communities, which in turn provide the order of the day for the risk-mapping exercise (see Box 6.1). Following this initial brainstorming and prioritization exercise, participants are divided into smaller groups of five to seven people and gathered around a large map. An attempt is made to have a balanced representation in terms of gender, age, livelihood, and geographic spread in each group. However, due to cultural or local conflictivity issues, dedicated women's groups, tribal leaders, or other are also accommodated upon request to ensure an open and frank discussion. Throughout the day, each group goes through the list of ten critical issues, discusses them, and assigns each risk discussed symbols on the map as well as detailed descriptions on a dedicated data collection sheet. Each risk is thereby explained in terms of geographic location, context and impact, extent, timeframe/periodicity, actors/affected populations, severity, and likelihood. Together with the CRM team, the risks are then assigned indicators and fed into an overall Human Security Framework in the CRM database designed specifically for this purpose.

Box 6.1 Ten critical issues from Nyala Locality, South Darfur (October 2011)

 1 Water
 2 Security
 3 Infrastructure
 4 Environment and sanitation
 5 Displacement
 6 Poverty and unemployment
 7 State resources (economic, capacity, etc.)
 8 Education and health
 9 Agriculture
10 Urban planning

Alongside integrating risk data into the CRM database, day two of the workshop is dedicated to focus group discussions in which three or four broader topics which have emerged throughout the process are discussed in more detail, and linkages between the different risks are identified and analysed in terms of the overall impact on their communities. Mind maps, problem trees, and summary presentations to the plenary are used. The information from these exercises is transcribed and included as annexes in the State Situation Analyses. Information from the CRM process is also recorded through workshop reports in which facilitators are given the chance to reflect on the participation, discussions, and dynamics that emerged over the two days, particularly when dealing with sensitive issues that do not easily lend themselves to plenary discussions. There are cases when sensitive and conflictive issues are silenced by participants who enjoy a certain amount of leverage and power in the communities. In order to overcome such challenges, facilitators have made available an 'issue box' into which participants can slip notes or comments that they would like to communicate but not discuss. The 'issue box' also gives participants a chance to continue the discussion of critical issues at home with their family and friends, and return with report cards for submission on day two of the workshop. These issues are duly recorded and addressed through the analysis process.

Mapping crisis and recovery risks in Azum locality, West Darfur (June 2011)

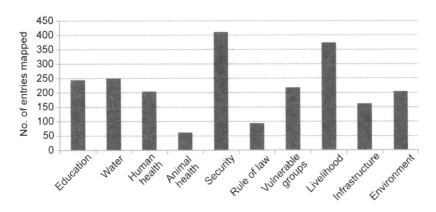

Figure 6.1 Thematic distribution of crisis and recovery risks in West Darfur

A map of the war-affected communities of Eastern Sudan provides a good example of how multiple information sources, coupled with CRM data, enables quick analysis and a foundation for targeting interventions in a conflict-sensitive manner (see Figure 6.2). The border areas of Red Sea and Kassala states with Eritrea have suffered from decades of cyclical conflicts, continued marginalization, and isolation, leaving the populations disenfranchised and vulnerable

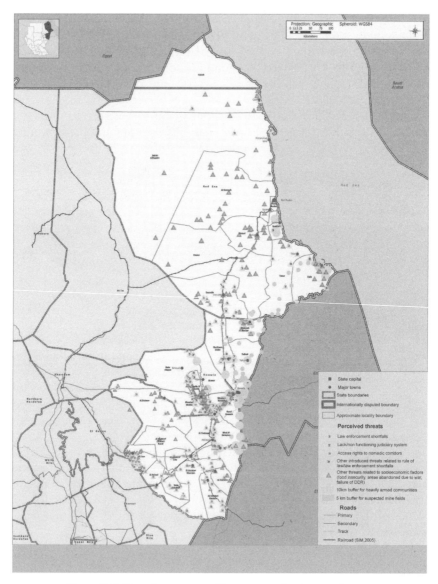

Figure 6.2 Mapping post-conflict recovery in Eastern Sudan

Note: The names and boundaries on this map do not imply official endorsement or acceptance by the Government of Sudan or the UN.

Source: processed by TRMA/UNDP for the Sudan Information Management Working Group

to any external or internal shocks. The presence of mines,[3] widespread access to small arms,[4] illegal trade, and cross-border movements, coupled with insufficient police presence and rule of law[5] institutions displayed in the map layers, continue to destabilize these localities and warrant particular attention. Investment and service delivery are needed not only to ensure the recovery of the most conflict-affected areas, but also to stabilize surrounding areas that are experiencing added pressure on already limited resources as a result of internal displacement and the search for livelihood opportunities and protection by those most heavily affected by conflict. The distribution of livelihoods[6] and rule of law[7] risks in a buffer around these communities in Eastern Sudan provides an indicative visualization of the complexity of issues and their relationships in a post-conflict setting. The strategy of marginalization has not only affected the targeted communities, but endangered the stability of the region as a whole as conflicts continue to erupt. To break the cycle of conflicts and relieve the pressure on surrounding areas, a minimum level of investment and service delivery is required for the conflict-affected communities along the international border.

Participatory analysis

The data analysis approach used is based on grounded theory, which is founded on the principle that theories should be derived from data, rather than having theories drive how data is conceptualized and analysed. This inductive approach means that important themes are grounded in the data itself instead of developed from a pre-existing framework. The aim of this approach is to explain a phenomenon – in this case perceptions of risks and challenges to communities – by identifying key characteristics, relationships, and processes involved. This approach is particularly useful in post-conflict settings where contexts, relationships, and actors frequently change over time and space, above all in such a vast and diverse country as Sudan, rendering rigid analytical approaches difficult to use.

The participatory analysis of community perceptions of risks and challenges serves two main purposes. First, it can help to identify priority areas for intervention in all the sectors covered by the risk indicators. For example, where an actor is interested in areas that are prone to conflict and have a lack of water services, CRM data can identify locations where communities report tensions between groups and problems with access to water. Second, since all inputs are geo-located at the village level, it can provide contextual information about a specific location of interest to actors that is more detailed than most situation analyses. Additionally, it can provide a way to check how the objective situation on the ground compares to the subjective perceptions of communities. This means that both positive and inverse correlations with quantitative/baseline data are of interest during the analysis phase. There are many contexts in which lack of access to basic services appears a critical risk, whereas quantitative data from ministries and organizations would show a relatively adequate presence of services. The key question to answer in such settings is thus why the subjective reality of local communities differs from that which can be deduced from official records. The reasons are manifold, but crucial for policy and planning processes to identify and consider. There may be shortfalls in operational capacities or access, it may be an issue of pockets of poverty and cost recovery practices, cultural practices, and social inhibitions that prevent certain sections of the population from taking advantage of the services, and so on. Positive and inverse correlations between CRM data and other quantitative/baseline data thus require careful and particular analysis, which can greatly enrich the ability of decision makers to target and design appropriate investments and interventions in fragile settings.

The analysis process is undertaken with the aim to produce a joint Government–UNDP State Situation Analysis with clear policy and strategic planning recommendations grounded in the data. A small team comprised of a Sudanese analysis expert, local government, and civil society representatives takes the lead in analysing the data, conducting (semi-)structured interviews, focus groups, workshops, and field visits to further discuss the data and provide additional nuances to the emerging themes. The CRMA team sets out principles and guidelines for the analysis phase and its methodology, but leaves the detailed process and content design to the analysis team, assuring local ownership throughout. The principles set out focus on four key concepts:

Mixed methods. The purpose of employing a mixed-methods approach is to enable participants to engage with the data and contextualize it in several different ways to ensure rigorous evaluation and triangulation, eliciting multiple perspectives and aspects of the complex issues and questions that arise.

Participatory and consultative. A key outcome of the analysis process is to foster a common understanding of local dynamics and contexts, and as key stakeholders feel they are integral to the analysis process, the analysis product becomes a local product endowed with a strong sense of ownership and significance.

Conflict-responsive. CRMA strives to look at the multi-faceted nature of the issues at hand, analysing each aspect and developing recommendations that could have a stabilizing and transformative impact on the local high-risk communities and vulnerable groups which in traditional sectoral analysis and strategic planning processes may be overlooked.

Evidence-based. The CRMA indicators used throughout the mapping process are derived from the data collected and are designed to allow space for contextual variances and analysis of specific angles and issues pertinent to its partners according to their particular needs. The focus on data and direct inputs from participants is maintained throughout the analysis and planning processes.

The State Situation Analysis covers all basic sectors and baseline data before it delves into the core issues for policy and planning. Based on the joint Government of Sudan and UN Development Assistance Framework (UNDAF), issues are analysed and recommendations are grouped under four key outcomes: peacebuilding; governance and rule of law; livelihoods and productive sectors; and basic services. These State Situation Analyses are published as official government documents, and provide the platform for dialogue and conflict-sensitive evidence-based planning for recovery and development both internally in the government through their five-year strategic planning processes and with their international partners. With close engagement throughout the process, State Departments of Planning gain an unprecedented insight into the complexity of dynamics and perceptions in a society affected by instability and crisis. Feeding this knowledge into formal state policy and planning processes has greatly enhanced the government's capacity to respond to and interact with its communities, and offers a foundation for shaping a common vision for the future.

A platform for conflict prevention and peacebuilding

Beyond collecting grass-roots information of community perceptions, the community mapping and analysis processes provide an important opportunity for diverse communities to come together in the aftermath of crisis to discuss challenges, differing perceptions of the situation, and ways to tackle the detrimental impact it has had on their lives. The process fosters an open dialogue in a secure setting where opinions are heard and valued rather than silenced and criticized.

In South Kordofan, UNDP has built on this approach to tailor its support to conflict prevention and peacebuilding through the government-led Reconciliation and Peaceful Co-existence Mechanism (RPCM). The CRM data provides the foundation for a conflict early warning system, and enables responders to identify potential hot-spots and engage communities in a discussion on priority responses and reconciliation processes that can prevent renewed outbreak or escalation of conflicts and foster peaceful co-existence. In close collaboration with CRMA, the Conflict Reduction Programme (CRP) accompanies the RPCM members through the process of creating the evidence base, analysing data, and designing peace processes and identifying peace dividends together with conflict-affected communities. Providing the quality assurance of the process itself, CRP is enabling a local institution to effectively mediate and respond to conflicts at the community level in a participatory and inclusive manner. Building the capacity of both the RPCM and communities to openly discuss core issues, and design and monitor responses, the CRP is building resilience among its partners in a fragile period of transformation towards peace and stability. Tying the evidence base and an early warning system to early responses ensures data is turned into actionable knowledge and impact on the ground. The process builds trust and confidence amongst

Creating a common vision among Sirer and Batran communities
in Dabker, South Kordofan (2011)

the participants and fosters a sense of purpose, moving away from the notion
of local communities as beneficiaries and victims towards becoming active
responders, with a clear stake in the success of the interventions identified.
Involving communities in targeting, design, and monitoring processes paves
the way for effective impact assessment and capacity development processes
in peacebuilding and statebuilding interventions that hitherto have not
received sufficient attention.

Strategic planning and statebuilding

Though statebuilding was not a primary focus of the government collaboration with CRMA, the community mapping and analysis process enables an
inclusive state–society relationship by supporting communities in their efforts
to articulate their needs and perceptions, facilitating dialogue across different
groups of society as well as with state institutions. The overall objective of this
process of data collection, management, and analysis is to help enable federal
and state institutions to develop policies and strategic plans that are more
inclusive and responsive, as well as monitor their distribution of resources
and services based on a solid evidence base and a participatory approach. It
is important to understand that just as all key political leaders need to be
involved, so do groups that can speak for different levels and sections of
society, geographic regions, political backgrounds, ethnic identities, and livelihoods groups for the governance process to be viable and resilient in the long
term. Only with embedded and active support from society will the process of
formal governance be regarded as legitimate.

Core strategic priorities for any government tend to centre on provision of incentives for the productive sector, support to rural livelihoods and infrastructure, support to job creation, and targeted vocational training. However, in post-conflict settings, with low revenue bases, governments are forced to make difficult prioritizations in terms of sectoral targeting and geographic focus. With the participation of communities through mapping and analysis of key risks and challenges, state actors are able to identify interventions that target the most vulnerable populations and critical issues to avoid exacerbating inequalities and factors of instability that could undermine the recovery and development process. Communities themselves are involved in making the strategic prioritization, gaining an understanding of the complexity of the situation, and state actors have the opportunity to negotiate expectations and thereby avert the risk of falling short in their social contract. Being able to maximize the impact of scarce government resources, the government can make sure it meets the most urgent needs as prioritized by the population. This is the essence of conflict-sensitive planning.

In 2009 and 2010, the state governments of East Sudan embarked on mid-term reviews of their five-year State Strategic Plans (2007–11), with the participation of all key line ministries as well as private sector, civil society, and international partners. With a thorough performance review and an updated community mapping and situation analysis, the state governments were better able to identify key strategic priorities for the remaining planning period, with the recovery of war-affected communities emerging as a key strategic priority after decades of marginalization and isolation. This process has thus positioned these actors at the forefront of evidence-based, conflict-sensitive strategic planning in Sudan. As the planning for the next five-year period (2012–16) is underway, these state governments have also embarked on an ambitious capacity development process, consolidating their experiences and lessons learned in knowledge management and strategic planning over the last few years.

Knowledge management

An inherent risk in participatory analysis and planning processes, if not appropriately managed, is that expectations are raised vis-à-vis the state, and the latter may fall short in its capacity to respond to the demands from communities for provision of security and basic services, distribution of resources, and diversified livelihoods opportunities. Falling short of society's expectations, the state endangers its fragile legitimacy and risks reversing the progress made towards creating constructive state–society relations. Appropriate and institutionalized knowledge management can aid the government in overcoming these challenges by ensuring that data and inputs collected from the grass-roots level are turned into actionable knowledge and disseminated to all relevant stakeholders and decision makers, as well as back again to the communities. Making use of a range of analytical tools and technology, the government is thus able to make strategic choices and decisions, confident that the evidence base on which they draw is solid and up to date. Developing such a 'culture of knowledge' is a lengthy process and requires strong buy-in across all departments and levels of government. However, it can deliver lasting results, as the government proves responsive to key demands placed upon it, eager to maximize on its capacities and able to make the strategic choices that in the long run will ensure its survival and resilience through challenging and transformative periods.

Despite national efforts to move towards e-government systems, Sudan faces serious challenges with regards to institutionalizing the use of information and knowledge management support. With limited capacity amongst civil servants in information management and modern information technologies, unreliable power supplies, areas of the country still without mobile network coverage, and limited resources to spend on infrastructure and software, the road ahead is steep. Yet progress has been made, particularly on the infrastructure front. Though knowledge management covers a much broader area of practice, focus even at a global level has tended to be dominated by aspects surrounding technology. Capitalizing on the success of the community mapping, analysis, and strategic planning processes seen at state level, the focus of CRMA's collaboration with government counterparts, however, is on people and processes, viewing technology as a crucial enabler and not a solution by itself. Fostering a knowledge-based culture, capacity development efforts are aimed at increasing the ability of people to use their knowledge within the organization and improve processes and institutional structures that facilitate knowledge production, sharing, and utilization.

Beyond the work of the Information Management Working Group and their efforts at ensuring a consolidated and up-to-date evidence base available to all actors working on recovery and development in Sudan, the CRMA project has designed, alongside its process accompaniment approach, an ambitious knowledge management for strategic planning course. This course has been tailored for key civil servants at state and national level that are tasked with elements of data collection, data analysis, and strategic planning in their day-to-day jobs. The course modules are based on the lessons learned from the joint collaboration between CRMA and State Departments of Planning over the past few years, including modules on the facilitation of crisis and recovery risk mapping and use of GPS and GIS for data aggregation and analysis.

Through these modules, civil servants and specialists are given the basic skills to create, maintain, share, and analyse baseline and CRM data for strategic planning. Taking a systems and grounded approach, applying the skills and knowledge in day-to-day tasks within the departments and institutions, the aim over the next couple of years is to institutionalize a solid and sustainable knowledge management system that can enhance decision- and policy-making processes at state and national levels.

It is important that in a context of fragility one does not only focus on risks and challenges, but also strengths and opportunities. Working through local actors such as the State Departments of Planning and South Kordofan's Reconciliation and Peaceful Co-existence Mechanism, enhancing their institutional capacities provides a crucial entry point for this. There is both political buy-in and a window of opportunity for focusing on knowledge management and sustained capacity development in the public administration of Sudan.

Conclusion: towards state and community resilience

> A resilient society requires a state with the capacity to predict, manage and respond to crisis in an equitable manner. But it also entails a society that can persevere and rebound from stresses with a modicum of self-sufficiency. (UNDP, 2012)

Accompanying state governments through a data collection, analysis, and strategic planning process, employing novel technologies and participatory methodologies, UNDP's CRMA project has had the opportunity to support the strengthening of government capacities and foster new relationships between state and society. This process has created a platform for resilience in a context of fragility, with an up-to-date evidence base and direct engagement of communities in processes of strategic prioritization of public resources and government decision making. Enabling communities to articulate and prioritize demands and assisting governments turning data into actionable knowledge, previously troubled relations between states and society have turned constructive and reinforcing. Building on the successes from Eastern Sudan and South Kordofan, this is paving the way for a new phase of UN and international community engagement with government authorities and public institutions also in the troubled region of Darfur.

Nevertheless, with limited capacities and resources at hand, state institutions still face challenges in their ability to maintain a solid knowledge management system, updating and channelling information to the appropriate policy and decision makers in a timely manner. As the process becomes ever more inclusive, demands on state responsiveness increase and capacities need to be in place in order to manage these demands and prioritize responses that do not endanger the legitimacy achieved to date. Pooling information resources, creating institutional memory, fostering synergies, and collaboration across departments and levels of government in an effort to develop a culture of knowledge through evidence-based decision making and planning are all key to improving the capacity of the government to better manage its state–society relations. Building on current systems and capacities, further support to a robust knowledge management system and culture is required at national, state, and local levels to ensure both communities and the state build the resilience needed to manage the transitions that since July 2011 are facing a new Sudan.

Notes

1   Comprehensive Peace Agreement signed between the Sudan People's Liberation Movement/Army and the Government of the Republic of Sudan, 9 January 2005.
2   These departments fall under the state ministries of finance, and the Ministry of Finance and National Economy at federal level.
3   5km buffers for suspected minefields are displayed as orange circles.
4   10km buffers for heavily armed communities are displayed as green circles.
5   Law enforcement shortfalls, cross-border and illegal trade are displayed as yellow triangles.
6   Livelihoods risks are displayed as grey triangles, including food insecurity, areas abandoned due to war, lack of DDR, and lack of employment opportunities.
7   Rule of law risks are displayed as yellow triangles, including law enforcement shortfalls, illegal trade, and banditry.

References

OECD (2010) *The State's Legitimacy in Fragile Situations: Unpacking Complexity*, Conflict and Fragility Series, OECD Publishing. Available from: www.oecd.org/development/conflictandfragility/44794487.pdf [accessed 19 September 2012].

OECD (2011) *Supporting Statebuilding in Situations of Conflict and Fragility: Policy Guidance*, DAC Guidelines and Reference Series, OECD Publishing <http://dx.doi.org/10.1787/9789264074989-en>.

United Nations Development Programme (UNDP) (2012) *Governance for Peace: Securing the Social Contract*, United Nations Publications, New York.

World Bank and UNDP (2010) *State-building, Key Concepts and Operational Implications in Two Fragile States: The Case of Sierra Leone and Liberia*, The World Bank, Washington, DC, and UNDP, New York and Geneva.

About the author

Margunn Indreboe Alshaikh is the Replication and Policy Coordinator for UNDP CRMA in Sudan, where she focuses on crisis mapping, conflict early warning, and the use of participatory methods for analysis and strategic planning. Prior to joining CRMA in 2007, she worked for the Royal Norwegian Embassy to Sudan, the UN Regional Information Centre in Brussels, and various international communications and policy research institutions.

Part II

Who counts reality? Participatory statistics in monitoring and evaluation

Chapter 7

Accountability downwards, count-ability upwards: quantifying empowerment outcomes in Bangladesh

Dee Jupp with Sohel Ibn Ali

This chapter describes the process of participatory self-evaluation of empowerment within a social movement in Bangladesh that was receiving donor project funding. Empowerment and changed relationships are recognized by donors as important outcomes of development assistance, but there have been few successful attempts to quantify these. The approach described in this chapter generated robust and valid quantitative measures from a participatory self-assessment process. This process and the data generated met the diverse needs of both primary and secondary stakeholders. Primary stakeholders – the social movement members – defined their own meaningful interpretations of empowerment and reviewed their own progress in a process which was purely for themselves and was in itself empowering. Further quantification and aggregation happened outside this community-level process and therefore did not distort the ground reality. It used an elegant method which weighted and aggregated the empowerment data to show distributions, trends, and correlations that satisfied the demands of results-based management of programme implementers and donors alike.

Background

Donors recognize the importance of measuring changes in processes and relationships, such as empowerment, governance, and accountability. However, donor and government agencies are more used to measuring observable outcomes using metrics such as an increase in household income or in school attendance. Evaluating changing behaviour and relationships – some of which are linked to these observable outcomes – enables donors and governments to understand complex change processes and their contribution to (predicted and unpredicted) outcomes. Scoring of qualitative changes in relationships, generated through participatory processes, creates space and legitimacy in project monitoring frameworks for these difficult-to-measure elements, while opening the door to in-depth participatory diagnostic analysis. Importantly, the use of quantification can be very effective in opening up policy space for discussing non-monetary impacts and linking this discussion to a broader

http://dx.doi.org/10.3362/9781780447711/007

policy debate that incorporates process issues of governance, empowerment, social inclusion, and so on.

Demonstrating empowerment has several challenges, as it is both a contested concept and a moving target. It comprises complex, interrelated elements embracing values, knowledge, behaviour, and relationships. The empowerment process is non-linear and depends largely on experience gained from opportunities to exercise rights which are inherently context specific. So, for example people may become socially empowered but have limited political empowerment in one context, but may become relatively politically empowered with limited social empowerment in another. The non-linear and context-specific nature of empowerment poses a challenge for conventional monitoring, which generally assumes a linear progression and defines normative milestones to be attained. The approach presented here embraces the idea that different aspects of empowerment may be achieved asymmetrically and at a different pace in different contexts, by recognizing and quantifying all positive changes.

The clash of social movement ideology and donor demands in Bangladesh

In the late 1990s, a long-standing social movement in Bangladesh attracted donor interest. This interest stemmed in part from the aid industry's increasing disenchantment with structuralism and a stated intent to seek more people-centred and rights-based approaches for aid support. This movement was an indigenous grass-roots organization, which was dealing head-on with rights abuses and the struggle to secure rights to *khas* land – government land intended to be redistributed for the use of poor people (see Box 7.1). It was just the sort of organization donors were looking for. However, the procedures to enable donors to channel funds to such an organization placed demands to prove value for money on the essentially informal organization which, as a people's movement, it had hitherto felt unnecessary.

But herein lay the dilemma. Most of the donors were interested in the movement because it tackled land rights issues, and there was a clear correlation between land acquisition and economic advancement through productive use of the acquired land. The correlation provided a level of comfort and a means to appease bureaucrats still ill at ease with the notion that rights-based programmes were largely considered to have 'non-quantifiable' outcomes. The movement's land rights programme could, they suggested, be measured through conventional economic rates of return. But (and this is an important 'but') not all the movement's groups got access to land and this did not seem to affect the enthusiasm with which groups continued to meet and be active. Belonging to the movement was apparently *important irrespective of gains made in land acquisition.*

Box 7.1 A short history of the social movement

The movement described itself as an organization of the landless poor and started its activities as a youth organization supported by freedom fighters and social workers more than 35 years ago. Originally in essence a cultural and leisure group, it gradually started to undertake voluntary activities within the community. The movement's very first success was to raise funds to buy land to make a simple walkway access to the main road when it had been prohibited by the landowner. It then became involved in monitoring other injustices and won a local media prize for bringing legal action against people hijacking electricity. Inspired by these successes they started to focus more on development activities, including fish cultivation and establishing a rice mill.

However, movement members felt that the rich continued to benefit from their success rather than the poor. To redress this they stepped up their fight against injustice and, following registration with the Ministry of Social Welfare, started mobilization activities in 1983. Local research indicated that several hundred acres of *khas* land had been appropriated by wealthy landowners. The fledgling movement identified this *khas* land issue as a vital one to establish the rights of the poor. The ensuing struggles were confrontational and resulted in deaths and imprisonment, as well as continuing harassment.

Subsequently, the movement continued to champion the rights of the poor to *khas* land and other *khas* resources, such as water bodies, and to mobilize groups to realize their entitlements. It spread rapidly to cover 22 of the 64 districts in Bangladesh, with over 543,000 members. By June 2007, it had recovered nearly 100,000 acres of *khas* land and water bodies.

In fact, less than one third of the groups acquired *khas* resources, and yet they still met together without external assistance or insistence week in week out and had done so for up to 20 years. Why were they doing this? What benefits were being derived? Nobody living in poverty with the exigencies this state imposes would give up valuable time to meet if there weren't important benefits. It was clear that neither the donors nor the organization itself knew what these benefits really were. Calculation of a rate of return on donors' investment, which relied solely on the acquisition of *khas* resources and the economic benefits accrued through its productive use, would clearly be a gross underestimate of the value of the membership of the movement.

A consultancy team, comprising participation facilitators and members of the movement's own management staff, took on the challenge of trying to understand what the motivations of the movement members might be, with a view to developing better ways to measure these benefits. The authors, Dee Jupp and Sohel Ibn Ali, were the team leader and the movement's Head of Advocacy respectively at the time.

This feisty movement did not want to be tied down to predictable outcomes as dictated by log frames and project documents. Its ideology was predicated on members finding their own causes to protest about and change, as well as responding to context-specific challenges for mutual support. It felt it could demonstrate impact by collating these diverse positive changes and presenting this to the donors. But with the substantial amount of investment being made by donors, this was not considered good enough.

Finding a middle ground

It was clear that all those other benefits beyond agricultural productivity would have to be quantified within a conventional monitoring system. From the outset, the movement insisted that the monitoring system should be driven by its members and should be intrinsically useful for them. It fiercely resisted being categorized as a non-government organization or a project with targets. It was only too aware that change happened as a result of a constellation of factors at the local level, and was driven primarily by the response of its members to those constellations and not by external interventions.

The answer proposed in the terms of reference developed by the donor for the consultancy team was to undertake a 'participatory grass-roots review'. This was expected to 'provide insights as to how to assess quality issues over the coming years of expansion'.[1] The donor was, in effect, saying that the complexity of the context-specific nature of the movement's empowerment was impossible to quantify and proposing returning to the 'second best' option of capturing broad qualitative data to illustrate the diversity of these changes. These would draw on case studies and stories that would supplement what was considered to be the more robust economic data, derived from productive land use. The principles for the monitoring and evaluation system were recommended to be 'focused learning rather than quantitative targets'.

The participatory grass-roots review took place in 2003. It used participatory rural appraisal (PRA) techniques and 'listening study' insights into what movement members saw as the diverse and broad benefits of membership. These insights heralded the beginnings of identifying indicators and change processes. The rich and diverse insights resulting from this led the team to consider other methods to facilitate understanding what empowerment meant to the people being empowered, including participatory drama.

People's own analysis of empowerment

The consultancy work moved beyond the original mandate of a participatory grass-roots review. The following illustrates one of the many processes the consultancy team facilitated to help people analyse their own 'take' on empowerment. We asked three groups of women and three groups of men in quite different locations in rural Bangladesh to develop dramas to tell the story of their social movement. Each group was asked to prepare three scenes:

the first illustrating life before association with the movement, the second illustrating the current situation, and the third depicting their aspirations for the near future (around 2–3 years). Apart from this framework, the groups were given no other guidance, hints, or input: nothing from us. We went away and left them entirely on their own to 'come up with something'. The intention was to enable the groups to express themselves *freely* and *spontaneously*.

After an hour or so, the groups were ready to perform their dramas. Their performances were recorded unobtrusively by a locally hired videographer. The dramas were remarkable. In fact, when later shown to support staff of the movement, there was almost disbelief. Each drama portrayed clear and unambiguous examples of what empowerment meant for the group members. The stories were based on real experiences rather than regurgitated rhetoric, and were peppered with perspectives that had never occurred to the staff (so, by inference, could not have been influenced by the staff). Each drama was nuanced to the group's own understanding and context for change. The following is a very brief summary of the group drama to illustrate their view of empowerment.

The women's perspective

Figure 7.1 Empowerment in three acts

Scene 1: Before joining the movement. At the homestead. The scene opens with the wife crouched awkwardly sweeping the yard; her head and face are covered by her sari. The mother-in-law enters and berates the wife for being lazy. She beats her. The husband returns from labouring and joins in the haranguing of the wife. She weeps, but gets on with preparing food. They sit down to eat with their two children; the husband and boy get fed preferentially. The wife eats, after everyone else has finished, whatever is left from the meal – just gravy and rice. Only the boy goes to school (but irregularly, as he has to tend the meagre livestock and collect firewood). The girl is told to stay and help with the chores and also goes to work in the house of the rich in order to be fed. The father discusses at length with the mother-in-law the arrangements to get the girl married as soon as possible to incur the least possible dowry costs. The father brings home gifts from the market for his beloved son and nothing for his wife and daughter.

Scene 2: The present situation (2007). At the homestead. The actors have changed into better clothes, look healthier (happier), and are working together. However, the wife is not well and the husband and mother-in-law insist that she rests and they take on her domestic chores. The wife is allowed to visit the doctor alone and money is available for her treatment. The children are going to school regularly and time is made for them to study after school. The chores are shared between them. The gifts from their father's trips to market are equally shared. Mealtimes are taken together and food also equally shared. The father will not agree to the early marriage of his daughter – she will get an education and then employment, 'he' says.

Scene 3: The future. The boy and girl are to get access to higher education. The parents feel that this way they will have the knowledge and confidence to fight corruption. The family expects them to come back to serve the community after they have qualified. The wife and husband continue to enjoy good relations inside and outside the home. They make economic decisions together and regard their relationship as friendship. The wife is considering standing for local elections, with her husband's encouragement. She will campaign for improvements to the road and plans to mobilize volunteers to rebuild and protect the culverts. The community is very supportive of her ideas.

The men's perspective

Scene 1: Before joining the movement. At the market. All the 'actors' wear shabby clothing and make it clear that they have nothing else. Their low status and appearance leads to them being ostracized from social gatherings. They are discussing the lack of work and the conditions in which they have to work on others' land. There is competition for jobs and only the most able-bodied get them. They are mostly paid with poor-quality rice and often the payments are delayed. They are invited to social gatherings to work all day with the promise of a good meal, but after a long day's work they do not actually get the special food promised. They feel humiliated and powerless. The rich landlord's son takes advantage of one of the labourer's daughters, as she works as a maid servant in his home. There is no means to seek justice. The local informal court panders only to the rich and metes out punishment to the poor. The scene ends with a violent confrontation between the workers and the land grabber.

Scene 2: The present situation (2007). The men are better clothed and not only work as daily labourers, but also on their own land. There are savings to be drawn on in times of crisis. Through the unity of the movement they take action to confront the issues of land grabbing and sexual harassment of the labourer's daughter and insist that the local court delivers justice. The impact of their action turns the tables on the traditional client–patron relations. They are now included in the local village court decision making and even convene the court themselves at times. They are proactive in promoting social values in the community and vigilant against early marriage, unlawful divorce, harassment, and criminal activity, discussing how to tackle these in their weekly meetings. They are invited to social gatherings as guests, not workers.

Scene 3: The future. The men are very active in the local court and local government, and continue to monitor corruption. They are actively promoting collective income-generating projects and using under-utilized resources productively. They are respected citizens to whom others turn for advice. Community relations are harmonious and families are living without harassment.

The women's group drama illustrated how social changes at home had to be made before economic and political opportunities could be explored. Look again at the middle photo: the 'man' is a woman dressed up as a man; an extraordinary sight in Bangladesh, and all the more so if one recalls how in the 1980s, interviews with women had to be conducted by women behind curtains and, as recently as the turn of the millennium, many women were forbidden to talk to men who were not their relatives. Yet, these women felt confident enough to devise their own drama, dress and behave as men, and perform in front of strangers!

The men's drama concentrated on the struggles for economic justice, which subsequently led to increasing opportunities for political participation. Their inclusion in village decision making was a result of changes in social capital accumulation and enabled them to have an influence on their individual and collective economic and political capital.

However, the real breakthrough was that through such dramas and the many other participatory discussions and debate facilitated, indicators could be identified that could be measured. Through repeated dramas and listening studies in different areas, more than 8,000 statements of qualitative change were generated.

From qualitative understanding to quantification

The process of translating these complex qualitative understandings of change into quantified indicators used in results-based management is completed in two distinct parts: the first is led by 'insiders' (movement members) themselves, and the second comprises collation and analysis of the insider-generated data by 'outsiders' (project managers and others). This division is important.

The process can be summarized in three stages. **Stage 1** is a process entirely driven by and for the movement members. They enthusiastically give time to their group-level self-assessments because they are important for their own learning, planning, and progress. No outsider (except a movement member from another group who helps guide them through the assessment) is involved, so the self-assessment is done in a trusted space where disclosure is regarded as benefiting the future of the group and shaping its future plans and demands from service providers. There are no gains to distorting information and no sense of competition between groups, as each group undertakes the reflection exercise for themselves. The process of evaluation is in itself empowering.

Stages 2 and 3 are primarily for the project staff and donors, and comprise data analysis and reporting. These are conducted away from the community by project staff in order to meet the demands of results-based management. The results of the self-assessments are collected with the permission of the groups, and are aggregated and processed to provide analysis for programme design, staff performance assessment, and to satisfy donors' need for reliable quantitative information. The data are categorized and weighted to enable trends, distributions, and correlations to be reviewed.

Stage 1: community-level assessments

The annual assessments conducted by movement members themselves involve scoring their individual and collective achievements against a series of carefully worded statements of change. These statements are generated through facilitation (by outsiders) of a variety of means of community expression, which includes drama (as described above), pictures, conversations, discussions, and storytelling. For example, more than 8,000 statements were collected from the original *participatory grass-roots review* (comprising conversations, drama, and PRA techniques) and were sorted in order to describe the processes, outputs, and outcomes of participation and empowerment.

Sifting through these 8,000 statements led the consultancy team to cluster similar and related ideas, and gradually, patterns emerged. Benefits seemed to fall naturally into four categories: (1) those to do with the groups' and individual group members' feelings of enhanced power expressed through their ability to present their own views and negotiate for their own ends in formal and informal decision making (*political empowerment*); (2) those to do with mutual support, trust, respect, and equity (*social empowerment*); (3) those to do with access to and use of resources (empowerment related to use and control of *economic and natural resources*); and (4) those to do with the group's own capability and independence (*capability and self-empowerment*). Gradually, the statements were condensed into a total of 132 indicator statements within these four categories. Care was taken to use the exact words used by movement members in the formulation of the indicators and not to overlay 'facilitator interpretation'. They were rigorously field checked to ensure they were meaningful for all movement members.

The four categories of indicators were further categorized by three levels of developmental progression: 1) awareness, 2) confidence and capability, and 3) effectiveness and self-sustaining (see Table 7.1). The following demonstrates how this was achieved, with some examples of statements generated under the political category (political capital accumulation / political empowerment).

Awareness
'All group members can describe the structure and function of the Union Parishad' (lowest tier of local government).

Confidence and capability
'Group makes regular contact with the Union Parishad.'
'Group asks their local elected members of the Union Parishad to raise issues on their behalf.'

Effectiveness and self-sustaining
'Group [directly] checks whether the Union Parishad-administered allocations for the poor are complied with, and does this without the assistance of a field officer.'

Table 7.1 Matrix showing distribution of indicators across categories

	Awareness (A)	Confidence and capability (CC)	Effectiveness and self-sustaining (ESS)
(Group) political development	17	13	14
(Group) social development	11	10	11
(Group) economic and natural resource development	9	8	10
(Group) capability	7	12	10

Source: Jupp et al., 2010

These matrices with the indicators written out in full and in easily digested local Bangla were reproduced on massive sheets of paper and provided to each of the groups. The groups meet to review the statements once every year. Sitting together at times which are convenient for them (the men tending to prefer the evening and the women the afternoon), they organize some snacks and make an occasion of the session. The review process takes about three hours and is facilitated by a movement member (the facilitator) from another group, who guides the process of scoring achievement with happy/unhappy faces.

The facilitator reads out each statement and the group discusses whether it applies to them or not. The facilitator encourages them to explore what the statement means and requires them to *present evidence* to help them to assess their own achievement. For instance, in discussing whether they have achieved the indicator, 'the position of women and girls in all group members' families is valued' (an 'awareness' level indicator of social development), examples were provided by each member. Such examples as 'we all eat together', 'both girls and boys have time set aside to do school homework', 'mothers don't only eat the fish head as they had to before', etc. lead to extensive discussion before, finally, the group members feel satisfied that they can assign a 'happy face' (meaning *yes, we have achieved this*) or an 'unhappy face' (meaning *no, we have not achieved this yet*) to the statement. Any reluctance to score a 'happy face' (e.g. even one group member feeling it had not been her experience) is automatically scored as an 'unhappy face'. Although a binary score is used in the approach described here, it would be possible to use ranked scores to provide more nuanced reflections of progress. The fact that all the group members have to put forward their opinion and provide evidence to support this encourages joint analysis and mutual support.

Stage 1 is what interests movement members and provides opportunities for their own reflections and learning on the processes of change they are experiencing and the effectiveness of the support provided by movement staff. And according to them, it provides important and further opportunities for empowerment. In other words, the process of self-evaluation in itself was empowering. The movement members have called the process *'protipholan'*, which means 'reflection' in Bangla. They lead Stage 1 of the process and are fully engaged with it. In a review of the process after several rounds of self-assessment, members said that the annual exercise of going through the series of compiled statements was very important for them. They scored their achievements, reflected, and learned. It was motivating, local, and 'theirs'. As the process was self-facilitated, there was no deference to outsiders. As there were no material benefits to be gained from exaggerating performance, scoring was realistic. The assessment process was regarded by group members as entirely for their own benefit and an important exercise, which as far as they were concerned was where it ended.

Each group's main motivation was to eventually be able to insert 'happy faces' in all the boxes. They took the exercise very seriously, and where there were 'unhappy faces', they reflected on what the group must do in the following year to improve on this. They developed annual action plans based on their analyses and scores. They regarded this reflection process as an important milestone each year and looked forward to it. It was not used to compare themselves with other groups or as a means to access resources, but purely as a self-assessment tool that encouraged reflection and defined future action.

Stage 2: data analysis

The data generated at community level was subject to analytical frameworks only later, *after* assessment, ensuring that outsider values and judgement did not influence the outcome. The programme used the Stage 1 community-level review of statements only with the agreement of the community. In Stage 2, managers aggregated and quantified data, and made deductions, leading to evaluation of the effectiveness for results-based management from a programme perspective. This part is what interested the project administration, implementers, and donors.

In this stage, qualitative information was quantified by assigning numerical values based on the number of fully realized empowerment statements (ones scored with 'happy faces'). Each positive assessment was then weighted depending on whether it represented the A (awareness), CC (confidence and capability), or ESS (effectiveness and self-sustaining) level of achievement.

The idea behind the weighting of these indicators was the recognition that certain indicators had greater value in terms of empowerment than others. It also allowed for the fact that different groups progressed at different rates. For example, a particular group might have faced a situation involving the denial of certain rights and taken action (confidence and capability), but might not know how to tackle other obstacles to rights realization (awareness). This group would score higher for its experience of an actual situation than a group which only achieved awareness. But its lack of knowledge in some areas would be evident from its scoring on other indicators. Indicators of awareness were not weighted, whereas indicators for confidence and capability were weighted with a factor of 2 and indicators for effectiveness and self-sustaining with a factor of 3.

An overall Group Development Index (GDI) was calculated that combined information from the four categories or indices (social, political, economic/ natural resource development, and capability). This was a composite numerical score which usefully accommodated multiple largely qualitative indicators. Thus GDIs were calculated for each group, and in several successive years this amounted to thousands of groups, thereby generating substantive statistics. Group GDIs were also aggregated by age of group, area office, geographic area, gender, or other variables (e.g. with/without other kinds of support, such as locally mobilized women's action support groups) in order to provide insights into the effectiveness of different elements of the support programme. The movement staff tracked the composite GDI as well as the individual indices from which these GDIs were derived. Not only did the GDI provide information about the pace and quality of development of groups (*process*), but it also provided a means of continuous *impact* monitoring, as many of the statements in the ESS column demonstrated behaviour change and agency by the groups (strong indicators of empowerment); outcomes rather than outputs (Earl et al., 2001). Furthermore, since all the indicators were derived directly from group members' own perspectives, most of which have been demonstrated by older groups as being realizable, this was truly a member-driven monitoring and evaluation approach.

Detail was obtained by tracking the scores of the four individual empowerment indices (social, economic/natural resources development, political, and capability). The statement review data was analysed across the *entire* data set – it was easy to do so since every group was undergoing the *protipholan* process – and this then offset any possible sampling bias. Figure 7.2 shows how the aggregated scores for all the groups by *empowerment index* could be compared from year to year, in this case showing improvements in all elements for both men and women groups between 2006 and 2007.

Figure 7.3 provides another example of how the quantitative data was used to make management decisions. It shows how the level of literacy was correlated to the achievement of GDI and spawned a programme of support for group literacy.

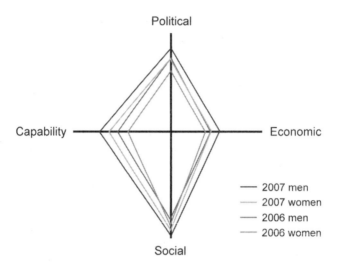

Figure 7.2 An example of quantifying qualitative changes

Source: Jupp et al., 2010

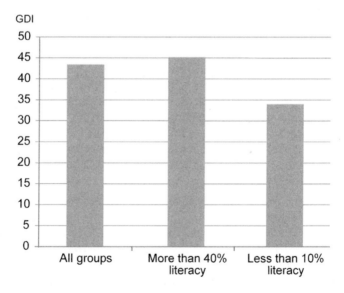

Figure 7.3 Literacy levels correlated with Group Development Index (GDI) achievement

Further examples are given in Jupp and Ibn Ali (2010) to illustrate the possibilities for analysis and programme adjustment that the member-generated data provided.

Stage 3: meeting reporting obligations

The GDI and component sectoral development indices provided robust evidence of enhanced empowerment over time. There were numerous ways that the programme provided quantitative evidence of change beyond the examples given in this short chapter. Over several years, incremental percentage changes were presented in reports to donors which satisfied their desire for numerical evidence. But perhaps more meaningful were the statements that were made to elaborate on these changes. Earlier reports to donors concentrated on outputs, such as the number of trainings provided, supplemented with unsubstantiated commentary. Reports were full of statements such as 'by awareness trainings the group members have been made aware of their rights, existing social system, social discrimination and exploitation and repression by influential (people) and have learnt to confront it. As a result they have become united and active against all forms of exploitation and oppression' (ex Annual Report, 2002). By contrast, the 2006 Annual Report was able to state, for example, 'that 79% of groups were able to access their full entitlements to primary education without the payment of any bribes' and 'more than 80% of groups meet regularly with the local government body while 30% independently checked that it properly utilised funds allocated for the poor'. Through elected representation of more than 3,500 group members onto various village committees, more than 76 per cent of groups could provide evidence that pro-poor decisions had been made by these committees.

As well as the quantification of the indices, and with little further effort, financial return of investments was also derived. For example, taking the issue of realization of primary school entitlements, children of families living in poverty in rural areas were entitled to government monthly stipends. There should have been no bribes paid to receive these, no costs for school-based coaching, no bribes for sitting exams or preparing transfer papers, and no additional school costs charged. Estimates of the savings made here and in other realms of experience (receiving social welfare benefits, health services, extension services, and so on), as well as the productive use of *khas* resources and group savings, were calculated to provide detailed financial return on investment data.

The group reflection process (Stage 1) enabled the collection of outcome data that previously could only be gathered through resource-intensive research studies and was quantified to meet the demands of donors. At last donors were getting answers to their question about the impact of the programme of empowerment: *'Empowered to do what?'*.

Conclusions

The approach discussed above demonstrates how participatory assessments can empower and transform relationships, and at the same time generate reliable and valid statistics for what were thought to be only qualitative dimensions of change. The evolution and application of the evaluation tool described in this chapter made it possible to use community-level generated information for the purposes of results-based management, in particular focusing on performance and achievement of outcomes and impact.

The introduction of such an approach was not without critics. However, Carlos Barahona, a professional statistician, provided helpful and balanced external critique of the method as it was developed, which challenged these criticisms and confirms that the method has exceptional rigour and validity. But still the consortium of donors supporting the movement took some persuading. One donor visited groups undergoing the *protipholan* and was able to see for herself the enthusiasm with which each indicator was debated and heard first-hand the powerful evidence that the group members shared to defend their decisions to score happy or unhappy faces, and became a powerful advocate of the process (and supported the publication of the approach).

The *protipholan* process cost only 5 per cent of project funds and contributed to achievement of the outcome of the programme by being an empowering process in itself. Significantly, greater credibility was still given to conventional external evaluation in the first instance. It was only when a major (and expensive!) external impact evaluation was conducted in 2007, which corroborated the data generated through the movement's own reflection process, that other donors began to accept the validity of the process. After several years, a donor who had complained before the introduction of *protipholan* – 'I know in my heart they are doing good work but not in my head' – confirmed that the method did adequately provide the numbers he needed to prove effectiveness. Once this breakthrough was achieved, the numbers generated in reports began to infiltrate discourse and influence decisions to continue funding as well as the design of other programmes for the extreme poor. Numbers gave a legitimacy to debates about what worked and what did not. People began to say that the numbers generated this way were actually more valid than through methods such as randomized control trials and conventional surveys.

The critique of many quantitative evaluations is that they produce 'countability' but not accountability. The approach described above is primarily one which privileges the need for accountability downwards over upward accountability. As the reflection and evaluation process was entirely driven by the group members themselves, it enabled the beneficiaries of the programme to hold the programme to account, make demands, and ask themselves 'how could we do this better?'. This is a self-perpetuating process irrespective of the input of donor funds and does not shy away from identifying failure. The outputs of this local process can be harnessed to provide the data required for programme learning towards developing more appropriate responses to the grass-roots needs, as well as upward accountability and assessment of value for money.

Acknowledgements

This chapter is modified from a paper originally published in *Sida Studies in Evaluation* 2010:1 (Jupp and Ibn Ali, 2010). We are grateful to Sida for granting permission to publish.

Note

1   Terms of Reference for Participatory Grassroots Review, DFID, 2003.

References

Earl, S., Carden, F., and Smutylo, T. (2001) *Outcome Mapping: Building Learning and Reflection into Development Programs*, International Development Research Centre, Ottawa. Available from: www.idrc.ca/EN/Resources/Publications/Pages/IDRCBookDetails.aspx?PublicationID=121 [accessed 19 September 2012].

Jupp D., with Ibn Ali, S. (2010) 'Measuring empowerment? Ask them', *Sida Studies in Evaluation* 2010:1, Sida, Stockholm. Available from: www.sida.se/Svenska/Om-oss/Publikationsdatabas/Publikationer/2010/juni/20101-Measuring-Empowerment-Ask-Them4/ [accessed 19 September 2012].

About the authors

Dee Jupp has been a social development consultant for more than 25 years. She has spent much of this time in Bangladesh and Jamaica, helping governments and civil society to adopt participatory approaches. Her recent work has focused on enhancing citizens' voice and understanding the perspectives of people living in poverty through Views of the Poor and Reality Check studies, which involve immersion in rural villages and slums. She was the team leader for the work with the Bangladesh social movement, which led to the development of the empowerment measurement approach described in this chapter.

Sohel Ibn Ali has worked for over a decade in development with NGOs, donor agencies, and consultancy firms. Currently, he works for the Swiss Agency for Development and Cooperation (SDC) as Programme Manager of their Local Governance Programme in Bangladesh. He specializes in rights-based social mobilization, gender equality mainstreaming, participatory monitoring and evaluation, local governance, decentralization, and pro-poor development.

Chapter 8

Community groups monitoring impact with participatory statistics in India: reflections from an international NGO collective

*Bernward Causemann, Eberhard Gohl,
Chinnapillai Rajathi, Abraham Susairaj,
Ganesh Tantry and Srividhya Tantry*

*This chapter reviews methodological innovations with participatory monitoring
and evaluation by an NGO collective of Northern and Southern NGOs, illustrating
its use with local communities in Karnataka state in India during the last six years.
The 'toolbox' designed by this NGO collective contains management tools for
NGOs, communities, and groups. The toolbox was used by local self-help groups
in communities in India to define, measure, monitor, review, and analyse progress
towards social, economic, and political targets, and to use this analysis as the basis
for empowering collective decision making – decision making that included the
most marginal group members. For the external NGO, the data collected allowed
for real-time monitoring against its own organizational logframe milestones
through 'people-centred', evaluative practice.*

The NGO-IDEAs initiative for participatory impact monitoring

In recent years, international discussion about the effectiveness of development assistance has motivated many development organizations, from large
donors to small NGOs, to look more closely at the outcomes and impacts of
their interventions. Specifically, NGOs feel challenged to reach optimal results
with their funds. The public who funds this work with donations increasingly
expects the projects to have relevant and demonstrable impact on the lives of
the people living in poverty or distress.

While many development projects contribute to important outcomes
and impacts, measuring and reporting at this level are frequently deficient.
Monitoring statistics give evidence on activities and outputs, but information
on outcomes and impacts is less focused, presented as rather vague, general
descriptions of change combined with impressive success stories of individuals. But is this sufficient? Have there been significant changes in people's
lives and for how many people? Who were the winners and losers? How much

http://dx.doi.org/10.3362/9781780447711/008

did the poorest and most excluded benefit? Can these changes be attributed to the NGO's interventions? NGOs increasingly have to answer such questions. But in day-to-day life, these questions do not chime with the most common research.

This chapter reflects on innovations with participatory research methods to answer challenging questions on impact, combining rigour and precision with explanatory depth. We reflect additionally on how this type of outcome and impact assessment is being increasingly integrated into ongoing monitoring and evaluation systems. This encourages an organizational culture of 'evaluative practice' in which organizations continually reflect on their contribution to broader change, rather than simply measuring performance against a predefined set of activities and outputs.

In the first part of this chapter we introduce the work of a North–South NGO collective on participatory impact monitoring methodology. We illustrate the implementation of this methodology in an NGO self-help group project in India, with a focus on participatory methods that elicit statistics. We finish by drawing out some general lessons for future applications of participatory statistics in impact monitoring.

An NGO collective with a participatory 'toolbox'

NGO-IDEAs (NGO Impact on Development, Empowerment and Actions) is a North–South collective of over 40 NGOs from Africa, Asia, and Germany working in the field of development cooperation. In two phases between 2004 and 2011, this collective identified and developed, in collaboration with local people in project communities, participatory methods for NGOs in assessing their effectiveness. The NGO-IDEAs experience is not, however, just another study evaluating the impact of NGOs' work. It combines research and development, knowledge management, learning and training, and advice and coaching to trigger a collective learning process for all partners involved.

NGO-IDEAs started in 2004 in South India by identifying good practices in monitoring and reporting of outcomes and impacts in savings and credit programmes. Several local NGO leaders in the collective promoted assessment of capacity building and empowerment impacts beyond a narrow concern with savings and credit performance as a focal point for participatory project management. With this commitment to measuring and reflecting on broader impacts, the collective identified a number of participatory tools to measure household well-being and institutional change.

The range of participatory tools and contexts for implementation expanded in the second phase of NGO-IDEAs (2009–11), as NGOs from many more countries and sectors actively participated in developing, testing, and refining the toolbox further (Gohl et al., 2011).[1] The tools are simple to use and participatory in application. They can be sequenced or used individually, and can be introduced to grass-roots organizations or used independently. Critically, the tools can measure change quantitatively, allowing both local and aggregated analysis. This quantified information prompts additional evaluative insights. The monitoring results encourage reflection on how the people's own action and other factors have contributed to change, and inform decisions based on the continuous monitoring of impacts. They can also be used for reporting where this is needed. The tools sensitize group members around poverty and social inclusion issues, and enable the poorest and most disadvantaged people to monitor their goal achievements and to improve their living standards and quality of life. The tools can be used for both short-term and long-term planning and monitoring.

A case study from India

One of the NGO collective partners that has experimented most comprehensively with the participatory toolbox for impact monitoring since 2005 is the Karwar Rural Women and Children Development Society (KRWCDS). Supported by Northern partners, this NGO works in Karnataka state with indigenous populations[2] in Joida district and with fishing communities in Karwar district with broad social justice and social sustainability goals. The NGO's main activities with these communities include awareness raising, organizational development and support to education, health, and agriculture. These projects aim especially at benefiting children, mainly from the poorest sectors of rural society. The NGO works through farmers' associations, self-help groups, and women's saving-and-credit groups, all meeting regularly to tackle social issues in their communities.

Initial poverty analysis with participatory wealth/well-being ranking

From 2006, KRWCDS applied participatory wealth/well-being ranking in the communities it worked with (Susairaj and Tantry, 2011). With KRWCDS facilitation, local groups developed their own criteria and sorted themselves into five poverty categories, from 'poorest' to 'rich'. This was an intensive community reflection and analysis process which enriched local understanding. The categorization also helped KRWCDS to become aware of various forms, meanings, and perspectives of rural poverty through open, shared reflections with the villagers.

Participatory wealth ranking was repeated by local groups in 47 villages in 2009 in order to assess the impact of a project that had recently closed. People could see for themselves how they had performed in terms of their own indicators. KRWCDS staff noted that people were generally impressed, and happy, to see for the first time such an improvement in their lives and in the lives of their neighbours in terms of clear indicators. The comparison of participatory wealth ranking analysis results (2006 and 2009) is presented in Figure 8.1.

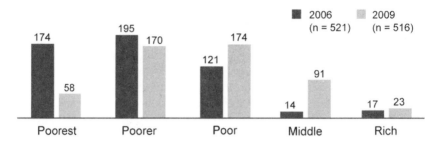

Figure 8.1 Changes in poverty status, 2006–09

A shift to participatory goal setting and monitoring

While participatory wealth ranking allows comparisons over longer periods, continuous monitoring of impact was conducted with two participatory planning tools from the NGO-IDEAs toolbox in which members of grass-roots organizations set their own goals: in SAGE[3] (situational analysis and goal establishment) they set goals for group members, that is, individuals and households. In PAG[4] (performance assessment by groups) they agreed on goals for the whole group. Using these tools, local people identified areas of expected improvements clustered into 'Attitude, Knowledge and Skills', 'Socio-Cultural', 'Economic', and 'Political'. This generated indicators for measuring and tracking changes in the percentage of local people reaching any of these goals.

The following description focuses on the use of SAGE. This tool was implemented every year, from 2006 to 2009, in the 47 villages, with answers scored on a simple binary of 'yes' or 'no' for each goal. Participants listed the goals set by the group members, row by row. In the next columns, the names of the members were listed and the well-being categories added. A women's association, for instance, identified goals of 'I immunized all my children equally' and 'I increased my knowledge about health issues'. Similarly, a men's farmers' association identified the goals of 'I know my land rights' and 'I increased my knowledge in organic agriculture'. Each member had to describe herself in terms of the goals set; unrealistic self-assessments were discussed and corrected by the group directly. That led to a lot of discussion. Peers gave fair and direct feedback, and suggestions on how people could improve. Social, business, and family issues were discussed in the process. People learned from the example of others and developed new strategies for themselves. This openness and feedback was possible because group members live in the same village and know each other well.

When all members had rated their goals, the 'yes' answers were immediately summed up, and the percentage of these was calculated. The group results were calculated in the rows, and the individual results in the columns. This allowed an immediate analysis with the group members.

With regard to the group performance, they asked:

- For which goals are we performing extraordinarily well? Why?
- For which goals are we lagging behind? Why?

With regard to the individual performance, they asked:

- Who is performing extraordinarily well? Why?
- Who is lagging behind? Why?

Additionally, group members could also identify, goal by goal, to what extent the members from the 'poorest' or 'poorer' categories as defined in participatory wealth ranking reached these goals. How did they perform compared with the average of the group? In some groups, these results were also compared with the last assessment, or with the initial assessment, depending on the time available in the meeting. For results to be used by group members, it was crucial to analyse things immediately rather than getting delayed feedback on the consolidated results.

While this was happening within community groups, the results of the assessment were used externally by the NGO KRWCDS to compare with the previous year's results and to support group action plans to achieve more of their goals. To do this, KRWCDS consolidated the data on a higher level. The results of the women's association comparisons are illustrated in Figure 8.2. In this case, among the 521 women in 2006 who each answered the 5 economic goals in 2006 with 'yes' or 'no', 9.5 per cent of the goals were answered with 'yes'. This increased to 75.8 per cent (of 516 women) in 2009.[5] Goals on attitude, knowledge, and skills were achieved fastest, and the highest, political goals the least. The strongest increase, with 68 percentage points, was in the proportion of group members reaching economic goals.

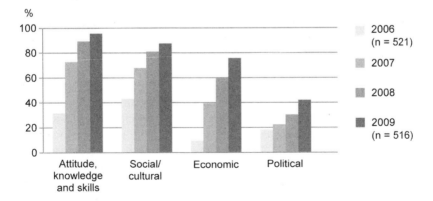

Figure 8.2 Women's Association goal achievement, 2006–09

Community-level reflection and action

Within communities, groups were able to aggregate data against their goal achievements, and then analyse the causes of change and the contribution of project activity to those changes. Taking the goal of safe drinking water, for instance, groups were able to list and analyse contributions to change (see Table 8.1) against the indicator 'I am working for safe drinking water'. Previously, they had a general perception that the development of the village was only possible through externally driven KRWCDS activities, but through the application of this tool, local people began to identify different contributions, including their own, and think more deeply about opportunities for, and obstacles to, further action.

Table 8.1 Cause–effect analysis on access to water, analysed by a women's self-help group

Group contribution	NGO contribution	Other influences
• Identified the problem of drinking water at family level • Identified different water distribution points • Approached Panchayat • Participated during the pipeline and tap fitting • Organizing water access • Utilization plan • People work for digging the well and pipeline as local contribution • Chapper Bothe villagers collected the water maintenance fund • From the tank, villagers have laid a pipeline connection to their house veranda on their own initiative	• Organized women's association in planning and accompanied the group to Panchayat for application and negotiations • At Chapper Bothe village, KRWCDS made the community well of 20ft depth – connected with 500m pipeline to the Panchayat-constructed water tank	• One of the woman members became the Panchayat member • Government mini water scheme • Farmers' associations support

The application of these tools also helped groups work collectively with a focus on the poorest members. Nirmala Belingatti, a group member in Devalwada Chilume village, reported:

> Akkamma Chikmat was the poorest in our group, as she is a widow and she has to feed three family members. It was very difficult with no income at all. She was not articulate. Before [the participatory impact monitoring], we did not give much thought for her, but when we saw that she is the poorest after doing the wealth ranking with no income at all, we as a group thought she has to be uplifted to a better position. We encouraged her to take up an Income Generation Project and she took bangle selling. Also when there was a scheme from the government for a post of the Govt. Kannada Higher Primary School cook, we did not compete

with each other but asked her to apply and she is now working as a cook. We are now happy that from poorest category she has moved to poor category.

Participatory statistics integrated into an NGO management tool

Outside communities, from an external planning perspective, KRWCDS was able to combine its own management tool – the logical framework plan – with the participatory impact monitoring data to measure the following indicator milestones: (a) increase of family income on an average of 35 per cent and (b) decrease of dependency from financial structures with high interests from present level. Table 8.2 illustrates the women's association's results that were utilized as evidence for KRWCDS' logframe. In this case, the proportion of households not in serious debt increased from 11 per cent to 88 per cent. Similarly, the proportion of households not taking loans from money lenders (with high interest) increased from 10 per cent to 88 per cent. That means that about 400 households became independent of loan sharks in a period of 3 years. This was a strong indicator for reduction of vulnerability and confirmed that the logframe impact indicator milestone (b) had been achieved. Meanwhile, the increase in savings, income, and involvement in income-generating projects substantiated that families had moved towards impact indicator (a).

Table 8.2 Impact indicator achievement 2006–09

Participatory impact indicator	Women Members Association			
	2006 (n = 521)	%	2009 (n = 516)	%
I am doing regular savings	120	23	513	99
I am involved in income-generating projects	13	2	389	75
My income has increased since I joined the group	5	1	354	68
I am not taking a loan from money lenders	51	10	455	88
I am not in debt	59	11	455	88
I have created assets in my name or jointly with my husband	8	2	221	42
I am repaying regularly a loan with interest	92	17	354	68

Participatory statistics in impact monitoring: a win–win for communities and NGOs

The experience in India is illustrative of the win–win benefits of this methodology implemented through the NGO collective experience. At the community level, participatory statistics helped group members to identify inbuilt weaknesses and strengths, and possibilities for improvement within the individual, families, groups, organizations, and the broader community. It helped group members prioritize tasks collectively and motivated group leadership to be more responsible for their own group members. It instilled confidence in the poorest group members, who were better able to articulate their own situation and reflections. As a result, the poorest were more accepted and respected by other group members.

Outside communities, through participatory statistics and the toolbox, NGOs increased their understanding of local conceptualizations of poverty and better target the poorest and most vulnerable. It also changed relationships with community groups, and was able to promote collaboration and joint ownership of initiatives. This collaboration was more timely and efficient through the rapid feedback and analysis of monitoring data. In the case of the experience of KRWCDS with local communities in India, it enabled the NGO:

- to identify the policy corrections and strategic review
- to build more linkages with local governments
- to initiate a rights-based approach
- to work on repayment based on short-, medium- and long-term bases
- to initiate community-based marketing mechanisms to save tribes from exploitation.

More broadly, KRWCDS staff reflect that the participatory monitoring of outcomes and impacts shifted their organization to a 'people-centred' system.

Conclusion: trade-offs in quantitative participatory outcome and impact assessment

The experience of the NGO-IDEAs collective with participatory outcome and impact assessment has prompted reflections on the trade-offs involved with this type of methodology. The first is one that is raised widely in this book, and is the trade-off between extractive data collection and empowering data collection and analysis. Frequently in the context of M&E we talk about 'data collection' or 'information systems'. The NGO collective's approach is to promote methods and tools that do not only serve for collecting data, but, already in the moment of asking questions and of documenting graphs, serve to empower, as results are shared and analysed, prompting debates about what has contributed to change and what could contribute in the future.

The second trade-off is between standardized measurement for aggregation vs measurement in context. The NGO-IDEAs methodology and toolbox certainly emphasizes the importance of learning about the context. In the context of self-help groups, it is often more important that the poor and marginalized people understand and act on contextualized meaning. If this is assured, the NGO-IDEAs tools contribute to considerably more accurate measurement of change by providing differentiated data on who benefited most from it: women and men, households below and above the poverty line. This data is group validated and documents a process over time. The toolbox was also designed deliberately to allow for standardization for aggregate poverty analysis and outcome/impact monitoring. Related to this is the question of 'whose perspective counts?'. With the methodology and toolbox approach of this NGO-IDEAs collective, the clear priority was given to the poor people's perspective. But with the practice of triangulation, it becomes obvious that this perspective has to be complemented by other perspectives of all those with agency and influence in the process, including the NGO staff and other involved external actors.

There is a further trade-off related to 'what is this data collection process for?'. Is it more about accountability to an external constituency or about internalized and protected learning? In order to promote empowerment, the NGOs and their target groups need a protected space where they can analyse the outcomes and impacts of their action without justifying themselves for not being perfect or for committing mistakes (if any). Accountability and reporting are always part of cooperation, but in self-help promotion this is subordinated to internal learning. Not all information has to be disclosed and certainly some information needs to remain confidential.

Another tension in monitoring and evaluation is between the short-term achievements (outputs) and longer-term changes in behaviour and well-being (outcomes and impacts). If monitoring is done during project implementation, it tends to focus on these shorter-term outputs closely tied to project inputs and activities. The NGO collective challenge was to monitor outcome and impact, aspects that frequently emerge after some time only. Furthermore, by looking at longer-term changes and loosening the chain of attribution to a project intervention, the initiative is designed to empower local communities to analyse and act on their own understanding of cause and effect, which goes well beyond the confines of the logical framework planning tool.

Additionally, empowerment and awareness creation mean more than democratic participation. Although democratic participation is required in the context of self-help promotion, there can be more. All project activities can contribute to the empowerment of the poor and marginalized people; and specifically the outcome and impact monitoring can serve as an eye-opener and create awareness about the results of their own actions, i.e. their self-effectiveness, and help to improve it. At the same time, visibility of changes at community and NGO level is continually improved, from the start of the project.

Two kinds of synergies emerge with the NGO-IDEAs approach and bridge these trade-offs. First, when focusing on the participatory, more unconventional option of the above-mentioned polarities, NGO-IDEAs often improved data collection for conventional ends: in other words, participatory data collection produced higher-quality data in some fields. Understanding of the context led to a higher accuracy of data. Learning processes increased the level of accountability. Second, the continuous sharing of the two autonomous monitoring systems (the grass-roots organizations' and the NGOs') does not simply reflect different perspectives, but contributes to mutual learning and bridge building.

Notes

1 Information on the utilization of the tools by the partnering organizations is provided in Rithaa, 2011.
2 The indigenous population is called 'adivasi' or 'tribals' in India.
3 SAGE (situational analysis and goal establishment) is used to identify the individuals' goals and to appraise changes at the individual and household levels. This tool works with the concept that people create their own vision of their future living conditions. The purpose is to make individuals aware of their own goals or objectives. This will then guide their actions and help them in monitoring to what extent each group member or each household has developed towards these objectives. Initially, SAGE was used with a yes/no rating. Over the years, many NGOs introduced scales between three and five points in the groups with good success.
4 PAG (performance assessment by groups) is used to identify goals to be reached by the group and to assess its performance with regard to these goals. PAG establishes changes in the performance of groups.
5 There was very little fluctuation in the group membership. Only five women had left the community during this period.

References

Causemann, B., Gohl, E., Cottina, G., Limotlimot, G., and Rajathi, C. (2011) *How do they do it? Civil Society Monitoring Self-Effectiveness*, An NGO-IDEAs Documentation of Field Experience, Association of German Development NGOs (VENRO) / NGO-IDEAs, Bonn. Available from: www.ngo-ideas.net/publications

Gohl, E., Causemann, B., Rithaa, M., Rajathi, C., Cottina, G., and Limotlimot, G. (2011) *NGO-IDEAs Impact Toolbox: Participatory Monitoring of Outcome and Impact*, VENRO / NGO-IDEAs, Bonn. Available from: www.ngo-ideas.net/publications

Rithaa, M. (2011) 'Review of NGO-IDEAs: survey of partners from the global south', NGO-IDEAS, Bensheim. Available from: www.ngo-ideas.net/publications

Susairaj, A. and Tantry, G. (2011) 'KRWCDS: 6 Years of Experience with the NGO-IDEAs Toolbox', in B. Causemann et al., *How do they do it? Civil Society Monitoring Self-Effectiveness*, pp. 11–26.

About the authors

Bernward Causemann is a sociologist and works as a development consultant and coach. He has 15 years' experience in evaluation, monitoring, and impact assessment for government and non-government agencies and international networks. As a project leader of NGO-IDEAs, he has cooperated with a North–South NGO collective to adapt participatory impact assessment tools for East Africa and the Philippines, and for sectors such as conflict resolution, street children, cooperatives, and persons with disabilities. He has developed strategies with NGOs for using such methods to quantify social, attitudinal, and behavioural change. He is an administrator of the [ngo-ideas] yahoogroup.

Eberhard Gohl is a sociologist and economist specialized in outcome/impact monitoring and evaluation. He has extensive experience in using qualitative research methods such as surveys with participatory approaches and the set-up of grassroots-based systems for monitoring self-effectiveness. As a project leader of NGO-IDEAs, he has developed participatory methods for quantifying social change together with a North–South NGO collective and practitioners.

Chinnapillai Rajathi has worked for 18 years in different capacities, as Danida Indian Adviser, Programme Director, Impact Adviser, and South Asia Regional Coordinator in International Rural Development projects with donor agencies and the Government of Tamil Nadu. In addition, she has worked for 10 years in research and development projects in rural areas. She has introduced and piloted new concepts and contributed to policy development for the Government of India and donor development projects.

Abraham Susairaj is the founder and Director of Karwar Rural Women and Children Development Society (KRWCDS) at Karwar, Karnataka, India. He has more than 30 years of experience in the rural development field. He is actively involved in socio-economic development, with a focus on women and children in Karwar and Joida in Karnataka State. He was one of the resource persons and trainer for the first phase of NGO-IDEAs tools development. Under his guidance, KRWCDS is implementing the NGO-IDEAs tools in its projects.

Ganesh Tantry has a background in agriculture sciences. He has been actively involved for 22 years as a Coordinator in the projects of KRWCDS for food security, watershed development, and income generation activities through organizing women and men farmers' self-help groups. He is actively involved in designing NGO-IDEAs tools application in the field of KRWCDS project areas.

Srividhya Tantry is a Documentation Officer in KRWCDS. She has more than 12 years of experience in KRWCDS in communication and data analysis of project achievement by using conventional methods and NGO-IDEAs tools, and gives qualitative and quantitative feedback to the core team members in the project as well as to the local stakeholders.

Chapter 9

Scoring perceptions of services in the Maldives: instant feedback and the power of increased local engagement

Nils Riemenschneider, Valentina Barca and Jeremy Holland

A longitudinal survey in the Maldives, collecting data at three points between 2006 and 2011, monitored and evaluated the contribution of a human development project to health and education outcomes on different islands. The research methodology included a perception scorecard, implemented as part of a survey module and also in a group-based setting. The group-based scorecard activity generated perception data that could be triangulated with the survey module, while prompting a deeper evaluative discussion to justify and explain the satisfaction scores that the group had given. During later rounds of the survey, the research team were able to increase the interactive nature of the scorecard method and the participatory elements in the survey grew stronger during its five-year lifetime. The effects of this methodological evolution were seen in substantially stronger local engagement, greater usefulness, and deeper insights. This chapter describes this evolution and serves as a case study to support the two central claims of this book, namely that participatory research can generate accurate and generalizable statistics in a timely, efficient, and effective way; and that participatory statistics empower local people in a sphere of research that has traditionally been highly extractive and externally controlled.

The Maldives Integrated Human Development Project

The Maldives consist of 2,000 islands, of which 200 are inhabited. They have a population of 300,000, of which two-thirds live outside the capital Malé. The average size of an island is 1,000 people, making it impossible to provide schools and health services to each island at a decent standard. As a consequence, the government decided to strengthen public services on four islands that serve as regional hubs. It secured a loan of about $12m from the World Bank to do so and set up a multi-year 'Integrated Human Development Project' from 2005 to 2011. The purpose of the project was to improve education, health, employment, and community services on these 'focus' islands. This was to be achieved through a mixture of construction work and improvement in the quality of services. The construction work consisted of building

http://dx.doi.org/10.3362/9781780447711/009

new classrooms, school halls, teacher resource centres, boarding facilities, and multi-purpose buildings. The quality of education services was to be improved through teacher training programmes and the provision of educational facilities. Health and other public services were to be improved through, for example, the introduction of standard operating procedures, telemedicine, nutrition programmes, job centre programmes, and community grants.

In addition, the project had a monitoring and evaluation (M&E) component which was carried out by Oxford Policy Management (OPM), a UK-based consultancy with a locally contracted research team. The authors of this paper were members of the OPM team. Three rounds of research were conducted: a baseline in 2006, a mid-term round in 2008, and an end-of-project round in 2011.

The scorecard method

The main instrument for the longitudinal M&E of the Integrated Human Development Project was a set of social surveys conducted with three social groups – parents, schoolchildren, and hospital users – on each island. With about 100 questionnaires per island per group, this generated a statistically representative sample of about 1,200 respondents in total.

As part of the monitoring and evaluation component, the government of the Maldives had requested that the M&E team carry out beneficiary assessments using a scorecard method.

The citizen report card tool was developed by the Public Affairs Centre, based in Bangalore, India, in the mid-1990s, by transplanting the market research techniques that are widely prevalent in the private sector into the public arena (Gopakumar, 2005; Gopakumar and Balakrishnan, n.d.). Citizen report cards are used with the following objectives (World Bank, 2004; Asian Development Bank, 2007):

- to generate citizen feedback on the degree of satisfaction with the quantity and quality of services provided by various public service agencies;
- to evolve an effective and easily accessible instrument to assess and highlight qualitative and quantitative dimensions of public service delivery in a community;
- to catalyse citizens to adopt proactive stances by demanding more accountability, accessibility, and responsiveness from public service providers;
- to serve as a diagnostic tool for service providers, external consultants, and analysts/researchers to facilitate effective prognosis and therapy; and
- to encourage public agencies to adopt and promote client-friendly practices and policies, design performance standards, and facilitate increased transparency in operations.

The efficacy of citizen report cards at achieving these results has been shown, for example, in a randomized study in Uganda. There, citizen report cards improved both the quality and quantity of local health service provision by increasing the efforts of health units to serve their users (Björkman et al., 2006).

In essence, citizen report cards consist of perception questions (such as 'how satisfactory is the education that your child is receiving at school?' on an ordinal scale from 1 to 4) that are asked to a random sample of service users and consequently aggregated to measure overall levels of satisfaction (see Figure 9.1).

1 = Fully satisfactory	‏= 1 ‏ ‏	‏(‏ ‏ ‏ ‏ ‏ ‏) ‏ ‏ Q10
2 = Mostly satisfactory	‏= 2 ‏ ‏	‏ ‏ ‏ ‏ ‏ ‏ ‏
3 = Not fully satisfactory	‏= 3 ‏ ‏	‏ ‏
4 = Not at all satisfactory	‏= 4 ‏ ‏	In summary, how satisfactory is the
8 = Don't know	‏= 8 ‏	education that (name) is receiving?

Figure 9.1 Example of a scorecard question

The research methodology: group-based and survey-based scorecards

Interactive vs extractive methods

As with many of the research instruments described in this book, the score-card can be used in an extractive research mode or in a more interactive mode. Extractive research removes the influence of the investigator, whereas interactive research promotes the agency of the investigator. Quantitative surveys are examples of extractive methods, and standard focus groups may also be considered as such. Scorecards, on the other hand, are designed primarily as interactive instruments.

The M&E methodology for the IHDP evaluation consisted of a quantitative survey, as well as focus groups, both asking a set of perception questions (scorecards) on satisfaction with public services. While the survey-based scorecards had the advantage of providing aggregate estimates of user satisfaction with the project outcomes, results from the quantitative data gave little scope to explore the reasons for those satisfaction scores and the processes triggered (or not) by project activities. For this reason, the same set of perception questions were also addressed in a group setting, promoting the agency of the investigator and the interactive nature of the research process.

To conduct the group-based scorecards, the team assembled random-stratified focus groups of 6–12 individuals, where possible representing a sub-sample from the social survey samples on each island. At the beginning of the focus group discussion, each participant was asked to complete a scorecard identical to those in the quantitative survey by filling in their satisfaction scores against each question. In the case of education, for example, the scorecard contained 15 questions that included satisfaction with the school buildings, teaching, confidence to ask questions in class, homework setting, and relevance of education for finding a job. These were completed individually and secretly by the participants and handed in. The group then came together for an hour or so and discussed each question on the scorecard, with the task of arriving at a collectively agreed satisfaction score for each question. The lively group discussion around each question, combined with the need for the group to justify the scores they gave, elicited rich evaluative insights underlying and explaining these scores.

The same sets of questions around satisfaction with health and education were also included as modules in the social surveys. The difference between group-based and survey-based scorecards in the context of this study is illustrated in Figure 9.2. The purpose behind repeating these satisfaction questions in a survey was to increase the sample size and the reliability of the results. We saw this as creating 'the best of both worlds': representative, externally credible, statistically significant findings, as well as an evaluative understanding of why parents, schoolchildren, and health users had scored the way they had.

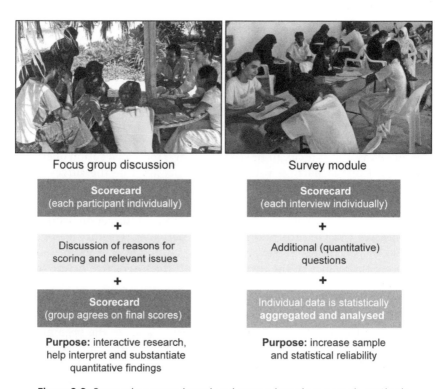

Focus group discussion

Scorecard
(each participant individually)

+

Discussion of reasons for
scoring and relevant issues

+

Scorecard
(group agrees on final scores)

Purpose: interactive research,
help interpret and substantiate
quantitative findings

Survey module

Scorecard
(each interview individually)

+

Additional (quantitative)
questions

+

Individual data is statistically
aggregated and analysed

Purpose: increase sample
and statistical reliability

Figure 9.2 Comparing group-based and survey-based scorecards methods

Qualitative and quantitative integration

One of the key advantages of using the same set of perception questions within a quantitative survey and focus group discussions was therefore the potential for integrating the two sources of information. It was also a way to generate 'participatory numbers' while not facing some of their underlying constraints: these constraints often are excessive standardization, issues of scale and resources needed versus quality of outputs, and problems of representativeness (Chambers, 2007; Garbarino and Holland, 2009), all of which were avoided in this study. Depth and quality could be achieved through the group-based discussions, while the standard survey helped to validate those perception scores in a representative fashion and at a relatively low cost.

In the first round of fieldwork in 2006, integration of qualitative and quantitative findings was done at a later analysis stage and presented at a national workshop with key stakeholders. As the literature on scorecards highlights, the quantitative aggregation of perception scores allowed for benchmarking of results across islands, with powerful consequences in terms of individual service providers' accountability. On the other hand, findings from the focus groups helped to contextualize those numbers, providing diagnostic solutions and highlighting which of the 'areas of dissatisfaction' were most pressing and important to users.

In the second and third rounds of research (2008 and 2011), the research team used mini-laptops (ultra-mobile PCs and netbooks) to collect quantitative data. This allowed us to do the qualitative and quantitative integration of results directly in the field. After three days of key informant interviews and focus group discussions, we sat down and reflected on the key emerging insights while these were still 'fresh'. We compared these to the results from the quantitative survey which happened in parallel, which we could relatively easily extract from the mini-laptops. We then prepared feedback presentations combining the two, as will be outlined further in this chapter. Other than the advantages which had already been witnessed in the national workshop, these 'interface' meetings with the community allowed for local stakeholders to challenge our conclusions and improve on our understanding of the results. In this sense, the instruments that we used proved to be efficient, i.e. results were generated quickly with greater value for money.

Comparing group-based and survey-based scores

In this context it was interesting to compare the results that we obtained from the individual scores at the beginning of the group discussions to the scores elicited from the household survey modules, even if the results simply confirm sample size theory. The quantitative results obtained by using individual scores as part of the group-based scorecard were similar to those elicited from the scorecard module of the household survey.

Figure 9.3 illustrates this comparison. The survey module showed a slight decline in satisfaction in 2008. The individual scores from the focus groups were elicited from a much smaller sample size, but nonetheless tell a similar story with a more pronounced dissatisfaction in 2008.

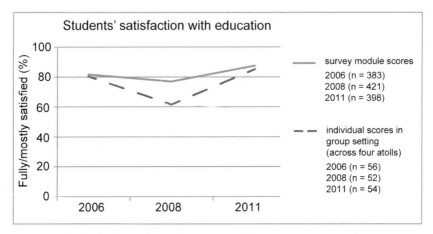

Students' satisfaction with education by island

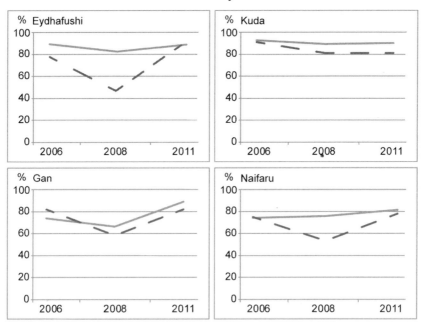

Base: 85–108 survey respondents per island per year; 9–22 group participants across several groups per island per year

Figure 9.3 Comparing group-based scores and survey-based scores

These results confirm the obvious point that a small sample will lead to slightly different results than a larger sample. However, the point of interest here is that while the household survey included a scorecard module in order to increase the sample size and reliability, there is no methodological reason why individual scoring could not have been conducted with a larger sample of students, parents, and hospital users in a group setting, as long as the selection of participants is done randomly using standard sampling procedures.

Emerging process

In sum, the combination of group-based and survey-based scorecards was useful in order to strengthen the insights and credibility of qualitative and quantitative results. It also generated accurate and generalizable statistics in a timely, efficient, and effective way. However, it was also the case that much of the research was initially largely 'extractive', partially due to the fact that M&E had been largely designed as an independent evaluative process rather than an integral part of the project implementation effort, as is all too often the case (see Figure 9.4). That said, even the baseline study already included a more participatory element in the form of a workshop held in the capital Malé, which brought local and central stakeholders together.

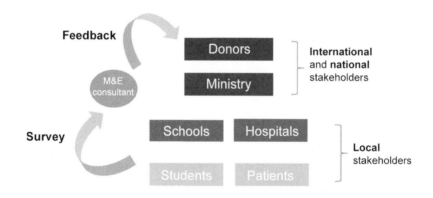

Figure 9.4 Scorecards used in extractive mode

Feedback and benchmarking at a national workshop involving all stakeholders

In the presence of central ministry and local stakeholders, including community representatives (such as delegations from the schools), we presented the research results at a national workshop and mixed the various stakeholders in working groups to discuss the findings. This led to revealing and unusual discussions between local and central stakeholders. One ministry person later told us that he was stunned by the stories he heard from the representatives of rural communities, including the constraints they faced. In other words, the presentation of results had facilitated a discussion between central and local stakeholders in a way that was unusual, and possibly more effective than the formal communication channels.

The importance of benchmarking service providers also emerged in the course of the workshop and the following research rounds. One anecdote illustrates this. A school deputy principal realized his school was rated the 'worst' of the schools on the four study islands on a whole range of perception indicators. He felt 'sad' about this, he told us, and went back to improve things. He introduced several inspired measures to improve the behavioural problems at his school. The school management started popular scout camps that only could be visited by students who did not disrupt lessons, and weekly meetings between parents, teachers, and students were introduced. The effect of these measures was a dramatic reduction of behavioural problems, which we could prove during the subsequent rounds of fieldwork. This was done through a further expansion of the participatory element of the research process: in-the-field feedback.

In-the-field feedback

As previously mentioned, during the mid-term assessment in 2008 we replaced the paper questionnaires with ultra-mobile personal computers, allowing the provision of instant feedback. Since we could obtain the data on the spot, we reported the results back to one school principal during fieldwork. At this session we also discovered the opportunity for impromptu qualitative–quantitative integration and for obtaining immediate feedback. Both helped us to further improve our analysis. However, the tight timeframe of the fieldwork did not allow for further feedback sessions in 2008.

This experience prompted us to extend the fieldwork in the final round of research in 2011. We scheduled an additional day in each community to provide feedback to the school management, the hospital management, and to 'the community'. We spent about five days in each community, carried out interviews, focus groups, and key informant interviews on days 1–4 and extracted the quantitative data, did the qualitative–quantitative integration and prepared the presentations on day 4. On day 5 we presented the findings in three separate presentations (always leading to insightful discussions and useful feedback): to the school management, hospital management, and finally, an assembly of students and parents (up to 300). Whenever we announced this process on day 1 to community representativeness we got the impression that it was exactly what they had expected all along, i.e. to be informed about the results of the survey straight away. For us, it felt that we were suddenly in a dialogue with the community, rather than just extracting information. Hence, we had moved substantially from an extractive to a participatory process (see Figure 9.5). While we did not give up control of the data and analysis, the rapid feedback allowed local stakeholders to interpret the results and use them for their own purposes. We did not share control of the data, but the results.

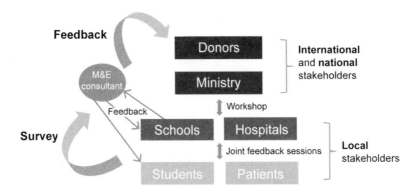

Figure 9.5 Scorecards in participatory mode

Once again, the example of the deputy school principal who had worked to change his school's 'scoring' after having participated in the 2007 national workshop is emblematic. Thanks to the immediate integration of qualitative and quantitative data, we could prove that the measures he had introduced had been effective in increasing student and parent satisfaction levels. This was done in the course of presentations to the school management, as well as to 200 students and parents. We felt that the rapid feedback of results further encouraged the school management to continue on this path, testifying to the utility of integrating the scorecard method into a participatory process that empowers and engages local people.

Process tracing and power mapping

During the third and final round of research in 2011 the team extended the participatory element of the research process still further, beyond the original scope of the study. Most project components were supposed to have been completed by 2008 and in full operation by 2010. However, many of these were only just about to be finished shortly before or after the final survey in 2011. Hence, many components could not have had an impact, and an end-of-project impact assessment became redundant to some extent. Instead, other questions gained importance: 'why has it taken so long?' and 'what can be learned for another project?'

In order to answer these crucial questions, the team introduced participatory visual tools such as process tracing and power mapping into diagnostic workshops with project stakeholders within central government. These included the sector ministries responsible for delivering various components of this 'integrated' project. We were taken aback by how much the participants welcomed them. They served as eye-openers not only to us, but also to them. On one side, comparing the different power-maps from different stakeholders clearly highlighted where the main blockages in project implementation

Feedback session with parents, students, and teachers

had occurred. It also simultaneously highlighted institutional arrangements that could have helped to circumvent this. Rather than 'shifting the blame', stakeholders were encouraged to view the project in its integrity, highlighting opportunities on how they could take things forward. On the other side, the process tracing exercise illustrated just how many steps needed to be taken for a successful project implementation. It helped to explain the many delays experienced. They partly resulted from the pioneering character of several project modules and the resulting unfamiliarity with implementing them. At the same time, it helped to anticipate future hurdles and encouraged improved forward planning.

The overall implication of these exercises was that the discussions with us suddenly became useful to the stakeholders as well. As a result, the engagement of stakeholders increased substantially. We also received critical feedback pointing out flaws in our conclusions and reasoning. As a consequence, we adapted the research design even further. Whenever one research question was settled, it brought up new questions which we followed up on. In the end, the high iteration of feedback loops and interactive research led to an overall conclusion that had been challenged and refined by so many parties, that it eventually represented the consensus among all levels of stakeholders (local, national, donors). This was in spite of the fact that there had been much finger-pointing between stakeholders during earlier interviews. Hence, we felt that the adaptiveness of the research agenda, coupled with insightful tools that key informants experienced to be useful for themselves, led to a substantially better overall research output.

Conclusions

The monitoring and evaluation methodology for the Maldives Integrated Human Development Project embraced a quantitative tool that could be used as part of a participatory process of reflection and learning. During the course of the five-year longitudinal study, this methodology evolved to include additional participatory elements at community and national levels. These included rapid feedback and discussion, aided by mini-laptops, at community level and institutional analysis, aided by process tracing and power mapping, with stakeholders at national level. The research team could have continued on the pre-defined methodological path, but felt that local feedback processes and dialogue would strengthen local ownership and change while increasing the robustness of the research.

In this study such methodological changes were possible and accepted, but this is not always the case. There often seems to be a tension between an externally driven monitoring and evaluation agenda with extractive data gathering that informs national stakeholders and donors on the one side and feedback of results to local stakeholders on the other side (let alone ceding even greater control of the research process to local stakeholders).

This is worth reflecting on, as there are several reasons that easily prevent rapid feedback to, and interaction with 'beneficiaries', and the chance to improve a project locally. The most powerful are budget constraints. There is also a widely perceived need to be seen as an external evaluator who does not influence the project. Indeed, as a result, if feedback loops are considered, they are often carried out by someone else entirely.

In our case we also had the opportunity to adapt the research agenda on the basis of the answers that we found to the initial research questions. This is often difficult in M&E and impact assessment studies that are pre-designed, and rely on a baseline and endline study done in exactly the same way (to obtain a difference-in-difference measure of the impact of a programme). In the case of the Maldives Integrated Human Development Project, we feel that changing the study design (completely within the budget) led to a substantial improvement in the usefulness and quality of results. The study thereby supports the two claims of the book, namely that participatory statistics can be accurate and help empower local stakeholders.

References

Asian Development Bank (2007) 'Improving Local Governance and Service Delivery: Citizen Report Card Learning Tool Kit', ADB, Manila.

Björkman, M., Reinikka, R. and Svensson, J. (2006) 'Local accountability', Seminar Papers, Institute for International Economic Studies, Stockholm University.

Chambers, R. (2007) 'Who counts? The quiet revolution of participation and numbers', Working Paper 296, Institute of Development Studies, Brighton.

Garbarino, S. and Holland, J. (2009) 'Quantitative and qualitative methods in impact evaluation and measuring results', GSDRC Issues Paper, Department for International Development, London.

Gopakumar, K.T. (2005) 'Can public feedback enhance public accountability? Experiences with citizen report cards', paper presented at the First International Forum on Citizen-Driven Evaluation of Public Services, Beijing, 29 September.

Gopakumar, K. and Balakrishnan, S. (no date) 'Citizens' feedback and state accountability: report cards as an aid to improve local governance', Public Affairs Centre, Bangalore.

Riemenschneider, N. (2010) 'Comparing quantitative results from three different stories: do they tell the same story?' *OPM Briefing Notes* 2010 (01), Oxford Policy Management, Oxford.

World Bank (2004) 'Citizen report card surveys, a note on the concept and methodology', *Social Development Notes*, No. 91, February.

About the authors

Nils Riemenschneider is a Senior Consultant at Oxford Policy Management, a UK-based consultancy. He has worked on surveys and M&E for 15 years, and pioneered the introduction of mini-laptops for data collection and the rapid feedback of integrated qualitative–quantitative results to local stakeholders. He has worked with scorecards both as part of social development studies and during his prior career as a market researcher, and has a keen interest in adapting successful business tools to development work.

Valentina Barca is a consultant at Oxford Policy Management working within the Social Development portfolio. Her expertise lies in combining quantitative and qualitative methods for research design, implementation, and analysis, as well as for innovative M&E approaches. Her recent work includes participatory research on cash transfer programmes in Africa and South East Asia, analysing issues of voice and accountability, and empowerment.

Jeremy Holland is a social development consultant and a Visiting Fellow with the Participation, Power, and Social Change team at the Institute of Development Studies, University of Sussex. He has 20 years' research and advisory experience in developing and transitional countries, working on poverty and policy analysis, gender equality, rights, participatory governance, and political economy. Jeremy has a particular interest in participatory and combined methods for measuring and analysing non-material dimensions of poverty.

Chapter 10

Are we targeting the poor? Lessons with participatory statistics in Malawi

Carlos Barahona

In Malawi in 1999–2002 a research team from the Statistical Services Centre at the University of Reading, with colleagues from the University of Malawi, conducted studies using participatory methods to generate population estimates, specifically estimates of the proportion of people in a population with certain characteristics (e.g. the very food insecure) and estimates of the proportion of people in a population that should be targeted by an intervention. A key requirement was to produce results from a representative sample from which conclusions for the population of interest could be inferred. This meant working in a larger number of sites than was common for most participatory studies. Other key requirements were for the study design to incorporate statistical principles and for participatory tools to be adapted to meet the demands of standardization and comparability of data produced across sites. The research team argued that this could be done without undermining participatory approaches, behaviours, and methods, concluding that if research studies using participatory methods followed this approach, the data generated would be suitable for standard statistical analysis. The statistics produced by such studies should be capable of informing policy at national level. This chapter reproduces an earlier paper written by one of the authors, and reflects on what has changed in the 10 years since this research was conducted and on what challenges need to be tackled in the push to mainstream participatory statistics within development decision making.

In this chapter I revisit a significant participatory poverty targeting study, nearly 10 years after its original publication (see Levy, 2003), to consider how we have moved on in the generation of participatory statistics and what are the new challenges and opportunities. At the suggestion of colleagues, the original paper is lightly edited and included here as an innovative example of the use of participatory methods for generating statistics. It is still relevant in many ways, particularly from a methodological point of view, insofar as highlighting some of the challenges faced by professionals considering the production of participatory statistics. Our impression from talking to younger professionals working in national and international agencies, however, is that experiences like the one described below are not filtering down effectively to many individuals and organizations working in development and interested in the generation of statistics that can be considered to have reliable quality.

http://dx.doi.org/10.3362/9781780447711/010

Levy makes some points that were important in 2003, but that remain as relevant today: the lack of information from official sources at the level of the aggregation that is required to inform decisions at local level and higher; the difficult issue of relative measurements against absolute measurements when working with communities; the imaginative way in which she and her Malawian colleagues designed a tool to record information at household level during the focus group discussions through the use of cards, which allowed them to construct databases that had complete information on the issues of interest for all the households in each of the communities; and in particular, the ethical issues that they were grappling with at the time when they were conducting field studies in Malawi. Remarkably these issues continue to be at the centre of generation of statistics through participatory approaches. The paper is a good example of how statistical principles can be used in the design of studies that use participatory approaches. Some of the principles highlighted in Barahona and Levy (2002) get direct application in a context of measuring poverty, and although her paper doesn't mention in detail many of the design innovations that evolved through the Malawi experiences, the papers in the references are a good source for this information.

Measuring poverty in Malawi with participatory statistics

Programme and project managers engaged in the day-to-day work of implementing poverty-reduction initiatives need to know whether or not their intervention is working. If it is, then they may decide to continue implementing it. If it is not, they may consider shifting resources to another, more successful initiative. Frequent small-scale evaluations are needed, in which a key question is: 'Did the intervention succeed in targeting the poor?'. Questions about the impact of specific interventions cannot be answered by the type of household surveys usually carried out by national statistical offices – even if appropriate questions were to be included in the questionnaire – because the population surveyed is unlikely to coincide with the population targeted by the intervention. Most studies based on participatory methods do not answer these questions either, because the measurements of human poverty elicited during participation tend to be relative (see discussion below), so it is difficult to compare findings between sites and over a period of time.

Between 1999 and 2002, ongoing evaluation research assessed the impact of the DFID-funded Targeted Inputs Programme (TIP) in Malawi. The 2000–01 and 2001–02 Targeted Inputs Programmes (TIPs) provided rural smallholder households with one Starter Pack containing 0.1ha-worth of fertilizer, maize seed, and legume seed. The TIPs followed on from the Starter Pack campaigns in 1998–99 and 1999–2000 (the subject of Elizabeth Cromwell's chapter in this volume). A key objective of these campaigns was to increase household food security amongst rural smallholders in Malawi. The 1998–99 and 1999–2000 Starter Pack campaigns were designed to cover all rural smallholder households, providing 2.86 million packs each year. The 2000–01 TIP (TIP1) was enough for roughly half this number of beneficiaries, while the 2001–02 TIP (TIP2) was further scaled down to 1 million beneficiaries.

The TIP evaluation examined a range of impact questions using a modular approach in which different types of research complemented each other. Within this modular approach, the evaluation team developed two ways of measuring poverty to assess the poverty-targeting effectiveness of the TIP interventions. The first used tailor-made surveys incorporating a rough-and-ready poverty index, the second, adapted participatory approaches. Both methods proved effective, but the first is only possible with a relatively large budget and the technical capacity for carrying out a survey. This chapter presents what was done with the participatory approach and discusses the challenges for similar participatory research in the future. The following are slightly edited extracts from Levy (2003).

Survey vs participatory statistics

Survey-based research can generate statistics that are 'representative' of a population, and, as such, tends to be seen by policymakers as more useful than research using participatory methods, which generates results that are valid at the local level but usually cannot be generalized in order to reach conclusions for a population of interest.

The experience with participatory research in the TIP evaluation in Malawi suggests that the dichotomy is a false one. It is possible to apply statistical principles to research using participatory methods and to generate both text- and numbers-based analysis that is 'representative' of a population. There are major differences between survey-based research and research using participatory methods, but these should not be because one approach is representative while the other is a collection of 'case studies'. By adopting certain statistical principles and making some adaptations to the PRA tools, this difference disappears in most cases. The key difference that remains is the type of information that can be collected.

Surveys collect simple pieces of data using questionnaires with closed-ended questions. Research using participatory methods studies uses discussions to explore deeper matters, often with tailor-made 'tools' or 'techniques'. Even if they generate numbers, these are the result of discussion and exchange of views rather than an on-the-spot reaction to a question. It is important to recognize that different types of data, fulfilling different objectives, require different approaches to information collection. It is not our intention here to argue that the type of research using participatory methods developed in Malawi could replace survey work. Rather, we believe that research using participatory methods complements survey work by collecting types of 'public' information that surveys cannot collect efficiently. The reverse is also true. It would be inefficient and impossible to attempt to collect some sorts of 'private' data that questionnaires capture using participatory methods. In many research exercises, both types of information have a role to play. The challenge is to ensure that policymakers give equal weight to the findings of research using participatory methods by making it representative of the populations of interest.

The participatory methodology to measuring poverty-targeting interventions was developed by a partnership between researchers based at the University of Reading and the University of Malawi. Development of the concepts has also benefited from discussions with members of the 'Parti Numbers' group (an informal group looking at the whole subject of deriving numbers from participatory approaches and methods). The methodology built on the publicly known and mutually understood nature of household poverty in many rural contexts and involved:

- absolute as well as relative measurements of poverty; and
- a technique called community mapping with cards.

Relative and absolute poverty

The first of the studies in Malawi, entitled *Consultations with the Poor on Safety Nets*, began by asking a group of five to ten participants in each community to define categories of wealth/poverty and vulnerability. It found that, 'Communities often distinguished many categories, with characteristics being a mixture of poverty and vulnerability' (Chinsinga et al., 2001). For instance, in Chikadza village in Chikwawa (Southern region), they classified households into three categories: poor; medium; and rich. In Chakuwereka village in Karonga (Northern region), they identified four categories: the relatively well-to-do; the 'struggling'; the very poor; and the vulnerable. And in Kasalika village in Lilongwe (Central region), they distinguished six categories of household: the 'struggling'; the very, very poor; the poor; the elderly; households with orphans; and 'average' households.

A major problem with this sort of approach, in which communities are asked to define the categories, is that they vary from place to place. How can we compare the outcomes in Chikadza and Kasalika? Even if we have asked the participants to divide the community so that we have an idea of the proportion of households belonging to different categories, we find ourselves on difficult ground. In Chikadza the participants identified 139 'poor' households out of a total of 181, representing 77 per cent of the village. In Kasalika only five households were described as 'poor' – 10 per cent of the village. Of course, other categories might also be regarded as poor in Kasalika. The problem is, which ones to include? And how poor are the ones we might decide to include in Kasalika, compared with the poor identified in Chikadza?

Perhaps we are more interested (from a policy perspective) in the 'very, very poor', as identified in Kasalika. But how can we compare the situation in Kasalika with that in Chikadza, where no such category was defined, or in Chakuwereka, where we cannot be sure if the equivalent is the 'very poor', or the 'vulnerable', or some households in both categories. This problem is one which many practitioners will recognize, because most participatory studies of poverty adopt a similar approach, using some form of wealth ranking based on local definitions. From the point of view of policymakers who need an answer to the question, 'Did the intervention succeed in targeting the poor?', these **relative** measurements of poverty within each community are not enough. They need a more **absolute** yardstick: something that will be able to distinguish consistently the 'poor' and the 'very, very poor' in all communities where the intervention has occurred.

The second of our series of Malawi studies, entitled *TIP Messages* (Chinsinga et al., 2002) worked with a more absolute definition of poverty. In our view, such definitions are quite specific to each developing country (or part of it), and should be developed through discussions with communities about how they see poverty, and by consulting previous research. We had the benefit of the *Consultations with the Poor on Safety Nets* study, as well as research by Van Donge et al. (2001), which assessed how the poor perceive poverty. Both of these studies found that food security is perceived as a key indicator of poverty in rural Malawi. Indeed, this is true for rural areas in many developing countries. Brock (1999), reviewing participatory work on poverty and illbeing worldwide for the World Bank's Consultations with the Poor workshop, observed that, 'Respondents in rural areas placed a strong emphasis on food security in their definitions of poverty, ill-being and vulnerability, as well as lack of work, money and assets'. We therefore decided to use food security as a proxy for poverty. We agreed to use the following definitions in all study sites:

> **Food secure (FS):** households that have enough to eat throughout the year from harvest to harvest
> **Food insecure (FI):** households that have enough food to last from harvest up to Christmas but not between Christmas and the next harvest. (The harvest in Malawi is in April/May)
> **Extremely food insecure (EFI):** households that have a longer period of not having enough to eat. These households start facing severe food shortages before Christmas.

Food security is by no means a perfect indicator of poverty, and it might be argued that others are better, but the principle is to find something that is:

- meaningful to participants (and means the same in every place);
- simple, so that it is clear which category each household fits into; and
- capable of differentiating between the groups of interest to the study, such as the well-off, the poor, and the extremely poor.

Unlike when asking communities to define poverty/vulnerability in their own terms, or when looking at the various aspects of 'human poverty', it should be stressed that the aim here is to **avoid complexity**. We only need to divide the village into different groups so that we can assess the impact of an intervention. Of course the two approaches are not mutually exclusive – it would be possible to have a broad discussion of poverty/vulnerability and then use a simple, absolute poverty indicator to divide the village into groups.

Community mapping with cards

The method used for dividing the village into food security/poverty groups and assessing whether or not the intervention (the TIP in this case) succeeded in targeting the poor was simple. We asked five to ten community members to draw a social map. The participants were asked to mark every household in the village on the map and to give it a number. Then they prepared a card for each household, with the name of the household head and the household number as shown on the map. It was vital that every household in the village appeared on the map and had a card with the same number as on the map.

The facilitator then introduced the discussion of food insecurity, explaining our definitions, and asking participants what were the characteristics of households in each category. After some discussion, participants were asked to put each household card into the appropriate food security category, and its food security status (FSS) was marked on the card by the facilitator. Finally, participants were asked to say which households received a TIP pack, and the facilitator marked the TIP status (TS) of the household on the card.

What have we achieved by using this method? We know for each village, and for all villages together, what proportion of households are extremely food insecure (very poor) and the degree of success achieved in efforts to target these households. Table 10.1 shows that 32 per cent of households in the villages visited were extremely food insecure in the 2001–02 season and that TIP was not very successful in targeting these households. The report concluded that, 'There should have been no food secure TIP recipients, and no extremely food insecure non-recipients. There were considerable "inclusion" and "exclusion" errors in the poverty targeting process' (Chinsinga et al., 2002).

Table 10.1 Correlation between receipt of TIP and food security status

Food security status	TIP recipients (%)	Non-recipients (%)	Total
Food secure	21.2	33.5	28.9
Food insecure	38.5	39.7	39.3
Extremely food insecure	40.3	26.8	31.8
Totals	100.0	100.0	100.0

Source: Chinsinga et al., 2002

What are the advantages of using this approach? Firstly, it is simple to do and can be understood by most participants. This means that it has a good chance of producing reliable results. Secondly, we have information for **all** households in the villages visited, which means that we do not run the risk of having a biased sample. In the case of the Chinsinga et al. (2002) study, information was collected on 1,343 households in 21 villages. Thirdly, it ensures that we have information at household level, but this has been produced quite quickly by asking participants to act as key informants.

The main disadvantages of the approach that we have identified so far are:

- it can be argued that using a proxy for poverty is too simplistic – even for measuring the impact of an intervention – as poverty is a complex issue;
- large villages present problems for mapping and producing cards;
- if you want reliable information at district or national level, you need to do the study in a relatively large number of sites – in Malawi we worked with a minimum of 20 sites for national-level studies – and these need to be selected at random (see Barahona and Levy, 2002).

Ethical considerations and future challenges

There are a number of ethical considerations associated with participatory learning that involves generating numerical data, such as community mapping with cards. They include issues of transparency, consent, and confidentiality. In particular, there is a responsibility amongst those commissioning and implementing participatory research studies to ensure that ethical issues are fully taken into account as community mapping with cards evolves and is adopted by more practitioners. There is an attendant obligation to develop ways of involving participants in the analysis of the numerical data generated in their villages and in feedback into actions that benefit the community. From an 'extractive data' perspective, there is an ongoing challenge to persuade policymakers of the usefulness of this approach, which can play a key role in the process of evaluating poverty-targeted interventions, so that developing countries can make the most of the resources for reducing poverty.

Conclusions: what now?

Ten years after this experience was written up we must ask what has changed, and what new opportunities have appeared after this time and the accumulation of experience. We would argue that the need for and power of statistics generated through participation have not changed and that the principles guiding the design of this type of study remain valid (something that is comforting, since otherwise they would not be useful principles!). However, there are some things that have changed, among them the fact that Levy's data was stored by her team in their own computers and today, potential users do not have access to the original information, and neither do the communities with whom they worked. I am sure that this was never the intention of the team, but at that time, the technology to store and make available information over the long term did not exist. In 2012 we have better developed Internet facilities, international public domain data archives, and much more awareness about the need to build accessible reservoirs of data that can be used in the future. This opens up a fantastic opportunity to communities, community organizations, and others interested in the development of statistics at local level through participation. We no longer are constrained by technology for access to easily maintained sources of data that can be used by the people and organizations connected to the Internet (even through a mobile phone). Of course, this is an opportunity that by no means has become an asset in the hands of those interested in locally developed statistics. Enabling communities to produce and store data about themselves and the issues they are concerned about remains a challenge for those who work in development as decision makers. It is now even more important to tackle this challenge when we can so much more easily access information about ourselves and relate it to other available information.

Interesting opportunities are now opening up to combine statistics produced by participatory processes, information from participatory mapping, and the satellite images. The issues highlighted by Levy about ethical considerations, and about the trade-offs between relative and absolute measurements, are crucial if these powerful tools are to be brought together. In particular, the ethical aspects become more important when it is possible to link information to geographical position and therefore to specific individuals/communities. This is a debate that is urgent among those who are working in this area, and that requires a balancing act between the interests of the wider population and external stakeholders, and the rights of the individuals or communities involved.

Finally, we need to consider the tendency amongst development agencies to push back against what might be perceived as localized research methods. Ten years ago we were seeing increased acceptance and even promotion of participatory approaches in mainstream development work. Now there is a push from many funding agencies away from the generation of information in close partnership with communities and more towards investing in the evaluation of interventions by external agencies, using methodologies that have gained momentum on the claim of being rigorous. This will probably mean that the big players in the world of development, at least in terms of capacity for investment, will divert resources away from participatory generation of statistics. However, the spread of participatory approaches among organizations that work close to the ground is unlikely to change in the near future. The extent to which good principles of design for the generation of statistics are known and understood by this large number of individuals and organizations is still unknown. This makes it all the more important to continue the discussion and sharing of experiences about how to produce good numerical information that applies to communities or populations and that can be used by decision makers to inform decision making at all levels.

Acknowledgements

I am grateful to *PLA Notes* for granting permission to reproduce sections of the original paper.

References

Barahona, C. and Levy, S. (2002) 'How to generate statistics and influence policy using participatory methods in research', Statistical Services Centre, University of Reading Working Paper. Available at: www.reading. ac.uk/~snsbarah/sscwp

Brock, K. (1999) '"It's not only wealth that matters – it's peace of mind too": a review of participatory work on poverty and illbeing', paper for the Global Synthesis Workshop, Consultations with the Poor, World Bank, 1999. Available at: www.worldbank.org/poverty/voices/reports.htm

Chinsinga, B., Dzimadzi, C., Chaweza, R., Kambewa, P., Kapondamgaga, P., and Mgemezulu, O. (2001) *Consultations with the Poor on Safety Nets*, Module 4 of the 2000–1 TIP Evaluation, Statistical Services Centre, University of Reading. Available at: www.reading.ac.uk/~snsbarah/TIP1

Chinsinga, B., Dzimadzi, C., Magalasi, M., and Mpekansambo, L. (2002) *TIP Messages: Beneficiary Selection and Community Targeting, Agricultural Extension and Health (TB and HIV/AIDS)*, Module 2 of the 2001–2 TIP Evaluation, Statistical Services Centre, University of Reading. Available at: www.reading.ac.uk/~snsbarah/TIP2

Levy, S. (2003) 'Are we targeting the poor? Lessons from Malawi', *PLA Notes* 47: 19–24.

Van Donge, J., Chivwaile, M., Kasapila, W., Kapondamgaga, P., Mgemezulu, O., Sangore, N., and Thawani, E. (2001) *A Qualitative Study of Markets and Livelihood Security in Rural Malawi*, Module 2, Part 2 of the 2000–1 TIP Evaluation, Statistical Services Centre, University of Reading. Available at: www.reading.ac.uk/~snsbarah/TIP1

About the author

Carlos Barahona has worked for nearly 20 years in the design, analysis, and communication of research. Over the years, his role has included providing technical inputs into planning, team coordination, resource management, and ensuring delivery of project outputs. As a consultant statistician he has developed skills in dealing with a wide range of clients in the UK and overseas, advising on survey design, survey management, experimental design, and analysis of statistical data. Over the last 10 years he has also worked on the design of training programmes. From a research point of view his interest is in how to integrate quantitative and qualitative methodologies to ensure robust and reliable research results.

PART III

Statistics for
participatory impact assessment

Chapter 11

Participatory impact assessment in drought policy contexts: lessons from southern Ethiopia

Dawit Abebe and Andy Catley

This research used standardized participatory impact assessment (PIA) methods to look at the impact of a 'commercial destocking strategy' on pastoralists in drought-affected southern Ethiopia in 2006. This destocking strategy involved encouraging private traders to purchase (often emaciated) stock from local pastoralists under drought conditions as an alternative to dependency-based food aid. PIA was conducted with a random sample of 'destocking' pastoralist households in Moyale woreda in the far south of Ethiopia. The PIA used proportional piling to determine the relative proportions of 7 sources of income and 11 sources of expenditure. Participants calculated the proportion of household income (54 per cent) sourced from destocking during the drought period and the proportion of destocking income (38 per cent) subsequently used to invest in the (remaining) livestock. The proportional piling findings led to the conclusion that livelihoods-based interventions, such as destocking, are partly justified on the basis of supporting local markets and economies. The PIA also used matrix scoring (with 30 stones allocated across 8 sources of support) to compare different food and non-food relief interventions using locally defined impact indicators. Destocking was considered to be the most useful intervention to help pastoralists cope with the effect of the drought, and to help fast recovery and herd rebuilding. Follow-up interviews confirmed the value of destocking over food aid. The PIA elicited robust, insightful, and timely data on the impact of the commercial destocking strategy that fed into key policy discussions, contributing to the development of national guidelines on destocking in pastoral areas of Ethiopia, as well as informing the development of global Livestock Emergency Guidelines and Standards.

It is widely recognized that recurrent drought has a major impact on the vulnerability of pastoralists in Ethiopia, and leads to repeated bouts of humanitarian assistance. Although food aid accounts for most of this assistance, experiences in Africa since the mid-1980s indicated how livestock-based support could help to protect the main assets of pastoralists, their livestock (de Waal, 1989; Oxby, 1989). Over the past 15 years, the concept of destocking has often been presented as an appropriate drought response in

http://dx.doi.org/10.3362/9781780447711/011

pastoral areas (see, for instance, Toulmin, 1995). When viewed from a livelihoods perspective, commercial destocking is a way to exchange some animals for money, thereby giving pastoralists the financial resources they need to buy food, maintain a core herd, and access the services that they want to (rather than those that aid agencies provide). This herd maintenance might involve the purchase of fodder or veterinary care, extending support to local markets and service providers.

More recently in Ethiopia, the Pastoralist Livelihoods Initiative, a USAID-funded programme, supported a commercial destocking intervention as an alternative to food aid. The programme was implemented by four consortia of non-governmental organizations (NGOs) working with regional governments and federal government departments – Save the Children US (SC US) headed one of the consortia. Almost as soon as the Pastoralist Livelihoods Initiative programme started in October 2005, it was evident that a major drought was evolving in parts of southern Ethiopia. The price of cattle in October 2005 was around Ethiopian birr (EB) 1,200 (USD 138) per head, but over the following months it started to fall, and by March–April 2006 stood at only EB 438 (USD 50) per head.

In response to the drought, a commercial destocking strategy was developed by the Pastoralist Livelihoods Initiative in Moyale district in the far south of the country, working closely with the Government of Ethiopia. Drawing heavily on experience gained in northern Kenya during its drought of 1999–2001, good-practice guidelines were prepared to assist agencies in designing livelihoods-based livestock interventions (Aklilu et al., 2006). It was also recognized that contrary to the Kenya experience, it might be possible to test alternative interventions such as commercial destocking, based on linking private livestock traders and drought-affected pastoral communities.

In early 2006, an Ethiopian Government working group encouraged private livestock traders to travel to the drought-affected areas to purchase livestock. Groups of pastoralists nominated a person to represent them in the destocking markets, and cattle prices were determined in negotiations between traders and pastoralists. Traders then purchased 20,000 cattle (many of them in very poor body condition), which were either transported directly to holding grounds or held in the Moyale area, where they were provided with fodder until they were healthy enough to travel. With an average purchase price of USD 50 per head of cattle, the total value of cattle destocked was approximately EB 8.76 million (USD 1.01 million), with some 5,400 households benefiting from the intervention.

Participatory impact assessment methods

As argued in the general introduction to this book, participatory approaches and methods are often viewed as purely qualitative, but some standardization and repetition of participatory approaches and methods allows numerical data to be collected and analysed using conventional statistical tests.

This adaptation of participatory approaches and methods has been widely applied by veterinary epidemiologists in marginalized areas (Catley, 2005; Thrusfield, 2005) and was used in Ethiopia prior to October 2005 to assess the impact of community-based animal health programmes (Abebe, 2005; Admassu et al., 2005). The PIA also fitted well with the development activities of many of the NGOs engaged in the Pastoralist Livelihoods Initiative, which were using community-based and participatory approaches that involved communities in project design and implementation. A final consideration when using PIA in this context was the need to utilize methodologies that NGOs could employ in the long term without too much specialized technical support.

The impact assessment of the destocking initiative combined participatory approaches and methods with conventional sampling methods and statistical analysis. The assessment was carried out in seven kebeles (a cluster of villages representing the smallest administrative unit in Ethiopia) where commercial destocking had been conducted. A list of 570 households that had destocked cattle during the drought was obtained from the Moyale District Pastoral Development Office. From each kebele, 20 per cent of destocked households were randomly selected, giving a total sample size of 114 households. Table 11.1 summarizes the participatory approaches and methods used in the assessment. The proportional piling and matrix scoring methods were standardized and repeated with all 114 participants. Semi-structured interviews formed part of each of these methods, providing a flexible opportunity to verify and probe responses, and to clarify information as necessary.

Table 11.1 Participatory methods used in the assessment of commercial destocking in Moyale woreda

Method	Use	Sample size
Timeline	To determine the times when the intervention started and ceased	Seven groups of informants (one group per kebele; 10–15 people per group)
Proportional piling	To determine relative proportions of different sources of income and expenditure	114 households
Matrix scoring	To compare different food and non-food relief interventions using community-defined impact indicators	114 households
Semi-structured interviews	Used with all other methods to cross-check information and clarify responses	114 households

Source: Abebe et al., 2008

The impact of commercial destocking on livelihoods

The PIA elicited robust, insightful, and timely data on the impact of the commercial destocking strategy in Moyale district. Figure 11.1 shows the relative proportions of seven different sources of income for destocked households, derived from proportional piling. On average, 54 per cent of household income was derived from the sale of animals during the drought, significantly higher than any other source (at the 95 per cent confidence level). In absolute terms, this amounted to approximately EB 1,618 (USD 184) per household, and therefore represented a substantial injection of cash. The second most important source of income during the drought was labour (safety net), which, on average, comprised around 21 per cent of total household income, significantly higher than all other sources apart from destocking (at the 95 per cent confidence level).

Figure 11.2 summarizes use by households of income derived from destocking; 11 main types of expenditure were identified. Although the purchase of food for people was the highest single item of expenditure (28 per cent), pastoralists also invested heavily in safeguarding their remaining livestock. Expenditure on livestock accounted for 37 per cent of the money

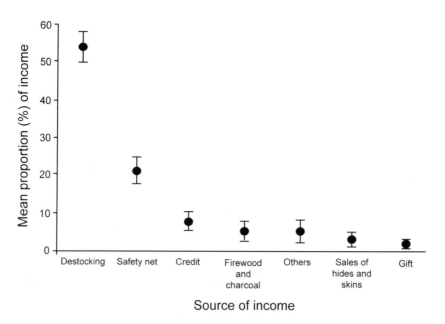

Figure 11.1 Mean proportion of income by income source for destocked households during the drought

Note: 95% confidence interval; n=114 households

Source: Abebe et al., 2008

obtained from destocking, comprising feed for animals (19 per cent), transporting animals to other grazing areas (12 per cent), and veterinary care (6 per cent). Livelihoods-based interventions, such as commercial destocking, are partly justified on the basis of supporting local markets and economies. With this in mind, 79 per cent of the money acquired through destocking was used to purchase local goods or services: food for people (28 per cent), feed for animals (19 per cent), trucking fees (12 per cent), human medicines (9 per cent), veterinary care (6 per cent), and clothes (5 per cent). In addition, people were able to use some of the money from destocking to pay school fees, repay debts, offer support to relatives, and augment savings.

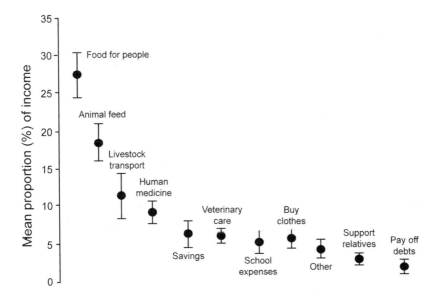

Figure 11.2 Proportional use of income derived from commercial destocking

Note: 95% confidence interval; n=114 households

Source: Abebe et al., 2008

Matrix scoring (with 30 stones allocated across 8 sources of support) compared different food and non-food relief interventions using locally defined impact indicators. Table 11.2 shows the results of the comparison of these relief interventions. The indicators reflect both short-term and longer-term needs, such as 'Saves human lives' and 'Helps fast recovery and rebuilding herd', respectively. Looking at each in turn, the indicator 'Helps us to cope with the effect of the drought' reflects the value of an intervention to buttress a household's capacity to cope with the shocks and stresses caused by the drought. Destocking was considered to be the most useful intervention (mean score 9.1), with a significantly higher score (95 per cent confidence limit) than any other intervention. In follow-up interviews after scoring this indicator, all participants confirmed that they were able to buy their own food with the money obtained from destocking, instead of having to wait for food aid as they did during droughts of previous years. They also described the advantage of destocking over food aid, explaining that money from destocking could be used to buy other things, such as medicines and clothes (as confirmed in Figure 11.2). Food aid was perceived as the second most important intervention to help people cope with the effects of drought (mean score 6.9).

The indicator 'Helps fast recovery and herd rebuilding' reflects the value of an intervention in terms of its ability to assist with post-drought recovery, particularly the rebuilding of herds. Again, destocking was scored significantly higher than any other intervention (mean score 11.1); participants explained this score by describing the applications of money derived from destocking. Almost all participants said that they were able to use some of the money from destocking to buy animal feed and veterinary medicines, thereby protecting their remaining livestock. Some also said that they saved some money from destocking and used it to restock after the drought (often purchasing goats). Feed supplementation (mean score 5.7) and veterinary support (mean score 4.4) were also important. Some food aid was fed to livestock, a practice that explains the scores allocated to food aid for this indicator (mean score 4.9).

The indicator 'Helps the livestock to survive' reflects the value of an intervention vis-à-vis saving livestock, and therefore, partly overlaps with the previous indicator. Destocking (mean score 10.3) and feed supplements (mean score 8.9) were considered to be the most useful interventions and again, income from destocking was mentioned as a means to buy veterinary care (mean score 4.9). Participants noted that unlike the past drought, it was possible to save most animals that otherwise would have died through destocking and feed supplement interventions.

The overall preference indicator was used to measure participants' overall preference in relation to the different relief interventions during the drought. The four most preferred interventions were destocking (mean score 10.6), feed supplementation (mean score 6.2), food aid (mean score 4.7), and veterinary care (mean score 4.2).

From participatory impact assessment to policy analysis

Another component of the Pastoralist Livelihoods Initiative focused on learning and policy development. In part, this component was a response to the limited information available on the impact of emergency interventions in pastoral areas of the Horn of Africa, particularly the consequences for livelihoods. Many agencies monitored and reported on the implementation of project activities, but their effect on people's lives was rarely assessed. Given the operational constraints in pastoral areas and the difficulties of using conventional research approaches, the Pastoralist Livelihoods Initiative aimed to build the capacity of partner NGOs in PIA and to use the results of the PIA to inform policy dialogue. More specifically, the programme worked with the

Ministry of Agriculture in Ethiopia to develop a national guideline for livelihoods-based drought response, and PIA was seen as an important approach for understanding the impact of past interventions.

Despite the involvement of only two traders in the destocking initiative, and the rapid design and implementation of the work, dramatic results ensued. Not only did destocking provide more than 50 per cent of household income during the drought (Figure 11.1), but also this income was used in very rational ways, to meet immediate household needs and to protect assets (Figure 11.2) – expenditure on livestock accounted for 37 per cent of income derived from destocking. The transportation of some remaining cattle to grazing areas is a novel approach to protecting assets and was organized in the absence of advice or support from government or aid agencies. This is a good illustration of people using their resources wisely, when resources are available. Up to 79 per cent of the money procured through destocking was used to buy local goods or services, highlighting livelihoods benefits in terms of supporting local markets and services required for post-drought recovery.

A comparison of livestock-based inputs, food aid, and safety nets (Table 11.2) reveals that food aid was the third most preferred option and was a particularly important type of support for poorer households. The safety net was not perceived as a useful approach during the drought, but it did account for 21 per cent of household income (Figure 11.1). These findings indicate a need for better integration of non-food and food-based responses, and suggest a need for analysis of the right balance of non-food and food inputs by wealth group.

Timing of the intervention

The commercial destocking intervention was rapidly designed and with limited prior experience of supporting this kind of initiative in Ethiopia. Although the results of the assessment show the advantages of destocking, the intervention occurred late in the drought – drought was declared in November 2005, whereas destocking took place in March 2006. As noted above, the price of cattle in October 2005 was around EB 1,200 (US$138) per head, but by March–April 2006 it had fallen to EB 438 (US$50) per head. If destocking had happened in January 2006, it is likely that pastoralists would have received twice the amount for their cattle, indicating that better contingency planning and preparation of traders are needed for future droughts.

Involvement of traders

Twenty-one livestock traders visited drought-affected areas and up to US$2 million was made available in the Pastoral Livelihoods Initiative budget, yet only two traders intervened during the drought. As noted above, the formal livestock export traders tended to be based outside pastoralist areas and many

Table 11.2 Community perceptions of interventions before and after the drought

Indicators	Mean scores for interventions							
	Destocking	Veterinary support	Livestock feed supplementation	Food aid	Water supply	Labour (safety net)	Credit	Others
Helps us to cope with the effect of the drought	9.1 (8.5, 9.7)	3.5 (3.2, 3.9)	5.7 (5.1, 6.2)	6.9 (6.5, 7.4)	3.0 (2.4, 3.6)	0.8 (0.5, 1.1)	0.5 (0.2, 0.8)	0.4 (0.2, 0.7)
Helps fast recovery and herd rebuilding	11.1 (10.5, 11.7)	4.4 (3.9, 4.9)	5.7 (5.0, 6.3)	4.9 (4.4, 5.6)	1.9 (1.5, 2.4)	0.9 (0.5, 1.4)	0.6 (0.1, 1.1)	0.4 (0.1, 0.7)
Helps the livestock to survive	10.3 (9.5, 11.2)	4.9 (4.4, 5.4)	8.9 (8.1, 9.7)	2.3 (1.8, 2.8)	2.8 (2.2, 3.5)	0.2 (0.1, 0.4)	0.3 (0.1, 0.6)	0.2 (0.0, 0.4)
Saves human life better	9.8 (8.9, 10.6)	2.4 (1.9, 2.8)	3.7 (3.1, 4.3)	8.8 (8.1, 9.6)	3.6 (2.9, 4.3)	0.9 (0.5, 1.3)	0.5 (0.2, 0.9)	0.3 (0.1, 0.5)
Benefits the poor most	7.6 (6.7, 8.6)	1.9 (1.6, 2.3)	3.2 (2.5, 3.8)	11.0 (10.1, 11.9)	3.7 (2.8, 4.3)	1.6 (0.9, 2.2)	0.7 (0.3, 1.1)	0.5 (0.1, 0.8)

Mean scores for interventions

Indicators	Destocking	Veterinary support	Livestock feed supplementation	Food aid	Water supply	Labour (safety net)	Credit	Others
Socially and culturally accepted	11.5 (10.6, 12.4)	5.1 (4.7, 5.6)	5.8 (5.1, 6.4)	3.4 (2.8, 3.9)	2.6 (2.1, 3.2)	0.9 (0.5, 1.4)	0.3 (0.1, 0.5)	0.3 (0.1, 0.5)
Timely and available	8.4 (7.8, 9.0)	3.3 (2.9, 3.7)	4.3 (3.0, 4.6)	8.5 (7.9, 9.1)	3.5 (2.8, 4.1)	1.2 (0.7, 1.7)	0.5 (0.2, 0.8)	0.3 (0.1, 0.5)
Overall preference	10.6 (9.9, 11.2)	4.2 (3.8, 4.7)	6.2 (5.5, 6.9)	4.7 (4.1, 5.2)	2.6 (2.1, 3.2)	1.0 (0.5, 1.5)	0.4 (0.1, 0.6)	0.3 (0.1, 0.6)

Note: 95% confidence interval

Source: Abebe et al., 2008

were unfamiliar with these areas. To a large degree, the commercial destocking intervention was an exercise in communication between traders previously unfamiliar with drought off-take opportunities in Moyale district, and pastoralists. However, there were still major communication gaps between traders and pastoralists, and hence there was a need for ongoing awareness-raising involving individual traders and the various livestock marketing associations in Ethiopia. The Marketing Department had an important role to play in convening events in which representatives from pastoralist communities and traders could discuss marketing opportunities.

Requirements for scaling up commercial destocking

This experience of commercial destocking provides useful indicators for the wider application and institutionalization of the approach in Ethiopia. Perhaps the first point to note is that although we sought initially to cover five districts, and traders were exposed to these districts, traders opted to focus on only two districts. The main reason for this restricted coverage was the appalling condition of the roads in the area, and therefore there was a desire to limit activities to the vicinity of the main asphalt road to reduce transaction costs. This shows how poor roads and infrastructure in pastoralist areas hinder opportunity and, in the case of commercial destocking, most likely limit the approach to relatively accessible communities. If stronger livestock marketing systems are to evolve in these areas, the need for better roads is self-evident.

The provision of loans to traders during the intervention was in response to requests from traders, and probably bridged a short-term gap in capital flow during the drought. Clearly, the purchase of animals by traders to the value of around US$1 million vastly exceeded the US$50,000 provided in loans. Given the current loan arrangements offered by the government and private banks in Ethiopia, particularly for livestock activities, there is a need to design and institutionalize 'fast-track' loan schemes to support large-scale destocking during the early stages of a drought. A central contingency fund option, for instance, could provide quick but carefully screened loans to traders, and could also finance other forms of livelihoods-based support, such as feed supplementation and veterinary care.

During a drought, livestock in pastoralist areas become thin and, in some cases, unfit for transport. Traders require holding facilities for these animals, either in pastoralist areas (for animals too weak to travel) or in or around abattoirs. At present, limited holding grounds are a constraint, and both traders and government need to allocate holding zones prior to the onset of drought and agree modalities for utilizing and maintaining these facilities. Moreover, frequent customs and taxation points along the route hindered the transport of purchased livestock away from drought-affected areas to holding grounds. Temporary suspension of these payments should be considered during drought periods.

Integrating PIA into policy processes

One component of the Pastoralist Livelihoods Initiative programme was the establishment of a National Livestock Policy Forum in Ethiopia, convened by the Ministry of Agriculture and Rural Development. Its initial task was to develop national good-practice guidelines for emergency livestock interventions in pastoral areas. Five working groups were set up to examine specific interventions, namely destocking, veterinary care, livestock feed and water, natural resource management, and restocking. By early 2007, the five groups comprised more than 65 participants drawn from government, NGOs, research centres and universities, international agencies, and the private sector. The process for developing the guidelines recognized the importance of government leading and convening the work, while also recognizing the considerable field experience outside of government.

This process took about two years, and participatory impact assessment was probably the most important approach for filling information gaps. The benefits of the approach relate to the information that is generated through participatory methods, but also the field exposure for government and academic stakeholders who might previously have had limited experience of pastoralist areas or emergency programmes. The assessment described in this chapter contributed to the development of national guidelines on destocking in pastoral areas of Ethiopia (Ministry of Agriculture and Rural Development, 2008), as well as informing the development of global Livestock Emergency Guidelines and Standards (LEGS, 2009).

An important principle applied in emerging Ethiopian guidelines was the notion of drought as 'normal' and therefore an event that ultimately should be predicted and planned for in long-term development processes rather than being treated as a recurrent emergency. This concept is not new, having featured in discussions on drought response in Ethiopia for at least 10 years (Hogg, 1997) and in the wider literature on drought management in pastoral areas (Barton et al., 2001). While livelihoods-based approaches to relief programming in pastoral areas can provide more appropriate assistance than typical emergency relief, to some extent livelihoods-based programmes necessitate the pre-existence of livestock services and markets. A strong, pre-existing livestock export trade will drive commercial destocking, and a strong, pre-existing network of primary veterinary service delivery will provide a system through which emergency veterinary care can be delivered.

There are considerable opportunities to improve linkages between pastoralists and livestock traders during normal periods and during drought. Based on the PIA research presented here, policymakers need to question the myth that pastoralists refuse to sell their animals during drought. Not only will pastoralists sell animals, but also they use the income in entirely logical ways to satisfy their immediate food needs and to protect their remaining livestock assets.

Box 11.1 Key steps in a successful policy process in Ethiopia

- A commitment by government to lead the process and convene the necessary meetings, workshops, and technical consultations.
- Commitment to a multi-stakeholder review process, involving government technical experts working together with communities, local research institutes, NGO staff, private sector, and other actors.
- A structured and systematic review of evidence of good practice, based on the following stages:

  1. Creation of technical working groups teams to review and compare specific technical options; each group has terms of reference, and a set of deliverables and milestones.
  2. Literature review and expert consultations – this is the first step in collating available evidence and identifying key information gaps.
  3. Fill agreed critical information gaps using methods such as:

     * Applied participatory research and **participatory impact assessments** with communities;
     * Benefit–cost analysis;
     * Field visits and local consultation;
     * Wider literature review;
     * Focused additional studies as needed, e.g. around very specific outstanding technical, economic, or other aspects;
     * Further expert consultations.

- Each team drafts a report on their findings, with a series of specific good-practice recommendations. The reports are presented to the wider stakeholder group, with feedback for additions, corrections, changes, and so on.
- Revised reports are collated into a single government good-practice guideline/strategy, with final review by stakeholders before finalizing.
- Final document is edited, formatted and printed, and translated.
- Document is promoted and distributed, and relevant awareness-raising and training events are organized.

Conclusions

This chapter illustrates how participatory methods, carefully designed and applied, can elicit robust, insightful, and timely statistical data for policy analysis. The PIA of the commercial destocking strategy showed it to be a viable and useful drought intervention. Through the Pastoralist Livelihood Initiative, this PIA analysis was effectively incorporated into national policy processes in Ethiopia. A strong message was that drought management requires government, relief agencies, and donors to assume that drought is inevitable in pastoralist areas and therefore to develop harmonized development and relief strategies. In the case of destocking, long-term investments in domestic and export livestock marketing could support better risk assessment of drought, contingency planning, clear triggers for intervention, and mechanisms for the rapid release of funds. In the event that strong livestock marketing systems are in place, the facilitating role of government and NGOs can be very cost-effective and might involve loans to traders. The potential for commercial destocking to reach the most vulnerable pastoralist households requires further research, as does the most appropriate combinations of livelihoods-based interventions such as destocking and food aid.

Acknowledgements

This chapter is a modified version of a paper originally published by Abebe et al. (2008). We are grateful to Wiley Publishers for granting permission for us to reproduce sections of the original paper here.

References

Abebe, D. (2005) *Participatory Review and Impact Assessment of the Community-based Animal Health Workers System in Pastoral and Agro-Pastoral Areas of Somali and Oromia Regions*, Save the Children US, Addis Ababa.

Abebe, D., Cullis, A., Catley, A., Aklilu, Y., Mekonnen, G., and Ghebrechirstos, Y. (2008) 'Livelihoods impact and benefit-cost estimation of a commercial de-stocking relief intervention in Moyale district, southern Ethiopia', *Disasters* 32(2), 167–89.

Admassu, B., Nega, S., Haile, T., Abera, B., Hussein, A. and Catley, A. (2005) 'Impact assessment of a community-based animal health project in Dollo Ado and Dollo Bay districts, southern Ethiopia', *Tropical Animal Health and Production* 37(1), 33–48.

Aklilu, Y., Admassu, B., Abebe, D., and Catley, A. (2006) *Guidelines for Livelihoods-based Livestock Relief Interventions in Pastoralist Areas*, USAID Ethiopia and Feinstein International Center, Addis Ababa.

Barton, D., Morton, J., and Hendy, C. (2001) 'Drought Contingency Planning for Pastoral Livelihoods', *Policy Series* 15, Natural Resources Institute, Chatham.

Catley, A. (2005) *Participatory Epidemiology: A Guide for Trainers*, African Union and Interafrican Bureau for Animal Resources, Nairobi. Available at: www.participatoryepidemiology.info/PE%20Guide%20electronic%20copy.pdf [accessed March 2006].

de Waal, A. (1989) *Famine that Kills: Darfur, Sudan, 1984–1985*, Clarendon Press, Oxford.

Hogg, R. (1997) *Drought Contingency Planning to Support Pastoralist Livelihoods in Ethiopia*, United Nations Development Programme Emergencies Unit for Ethiopia, Addis Ababa. Available at: www.africa.upenn.edu/eue_web/pastoral.htm%20 [accessed July 2007].

LEGS (2009) *Livestock Emergency Guidelines and Standards*, Practical Action Publishing, Rugby. Available at: www.livestock-emergency.net

Ministry of Agriculture and Rural Development (2008) *National Guidelines for Livestock Relief Interventions in Pastoralist Areas of Ethiopia*, Ministry of Agriculture and Rural Development, Addis Ababa.

Oxby, C. (1989) *African Livestock Keepers in Recurrent Crisis: Policy Issues Arising from the NGO Response*, International Institute for Environment and Development, London.

Thrusfield, M. (2005) *Veterinary Epidemiology*, 3rd edn, Blackwell Science, Oxford.

Toulmin, C. (1995) 'Tracking through drought: options for destocking and restocking', in I. Scoones (ed.), *Living with Uncertainty: New Directions in Pastoral Development in Africa*, Practical Action Publishing, Rugby.

About the authors

Dawit Abebe is a veterinarian with experience in community-based delivery systems, impact assessment and regional and national food security, livestock, and pastoralism policy in the Horn of Africa. He joined the Feinstein International Center in early 2006 as a Research and Policy Specialist on the Pastoralist Livelihoods Initiative programme in Ethiopia, where he used impact assessments with government and NGO partners to influence policy reform. From 2006 to 2009 Dawit was seconded to the Secretariat of the Common Market for Eastern and Southern Africa (COMESA), where he provided policy support to the COMESA Regional Policy Framework for Food Security in Pastoralist Areas, under the Comprehensive Africa Agriculture Development Programme (CAADP). He is currently working on a PhD on vulnerability and climate change in pastoralist areas of Ethiopia.

Andy Catley is a Research Director at the Feinstein International Center, Tufts University. He joined the Center in 2000, and during the past decade has worked on regional- and international-level policy and legislative reform to support community-based delivery systems in Africa. This included work on participatory epidemiology and the use of participatory impact assessment to influence policy. From 2005 to 2011 he directed the Center's Africa Regional Office in Addis Ababa, Ethiopia, and supported the use of participatory impact assessment in the Pastoralist Livelihoods Initiative and other programmes. He currently chairs the Steering Group of the Livestock Emergency Guidelines and Standards, published in early 2009. Andy's professional background is in veterinary medicine and epidemiology.

Chapter 12

Participatory impact assessment: the 'Starter Pack Scheme' and sustainable agriculture in Malawi

Elizabeth Cromwell, Patrick Kambewa, Richard Mwanza and Rowland Chirwa with KWERA Development Centre

This chapter reflects on early innovation in the development of rigorous methodology for participatory statistics in impact assessment. It reviews a participatory study undertaken as part of the Malawi Starter Pack Evaluation Programme (1999–2000). Focusing on the concept of 'sustainable agriculture', it describes how a participatory impact assessment was designed and implemented, and illustrates the kind of information that emerges from such an approach. The study explored how farmers themselves perceived the concept of sustainable agriculture and how this related to their livelihoods. Detailed information was collected from 30 villages and was used to determine variations in sustainability across regions, between different households, and trends over the previous 30 years. The types of inputs required for increased agricultural sustainability were also ascertained. The use of participatory approaches revealed that farmers' perceptions of sustainable agriculture were closely related to their concerns for immediate family food security. Crop diversity and the availability of seed to support this were regarded by farmers as the most important indicators of sustainable agriculture. Lessons learned from this early innovation with participatory impact assessment included the importance of upfront time and resources to identify standard indicators and evolve a robust methodology.

Malawi agricultural sector reform and sustainability

From the late 1980s, Malawi went through a period of substantial economic and political reform. At the time, fertilizer subsidies were dramatically reduced; the government agricultural credit system ended; ADMARC, the agricultural marketing parastatal, underwent substantial downsizing and retrenchment; and consumer maize prices were liberalized. Successive devaluations as part of the wider macro-economic reform programme caused a dramatic increase in fertilizer prices. All this served to increase the pressures on smallholder agricultural land, at the same time as reducing the economic rationale for farm

http://dx.doi.org/10.3362/9781780447711/012

families to use the hybrid maize/chemical fertilizer technology package that had been the lynchpin of Malawi's agricultural development strategy for the last 20 or more years.

Accordingly, a structural food deficit of several hundred thousand tonnes per year emerged. By the mid-1990s, the environmental and economic sustainability of Malawi smallholder agriculture was seriously in doubt in the immediate short term. The national agricultural research system responded to concerns about the environmental and economic sustainability of smallholder agriculture by identifying a 'best-bet technology' package as a short-term solution to ameliorating soil fertility in the smallholder sector (Rockefeller Foundation, 1998). This had two components: 1) increasing access to improved maize seed and chemical fertilizer inputs and the extension advice to go with it; and 2) diversifying the cropping system using grain legume rotations.

It was to supply this package that the 'Starter Pack Scheme' was implemented in 1998–9 and 1999–2000. The Scheme aimed to supply improved maize seed to cover 0.1 hectare (20kg), together with grain legume seed and chemical fertilizer to all rural households with land in Malawi. The objectives of the Scheme were to increase household food security; act as a forerunner to a wider social safety net programme; examine 'best-bet' agricultural technologies for smallholder farmers in Malawi; and introduce more sustainable agricultural practices. In both years, some 2.86 million packs containing seed and fertilizer were distributed by the government with NGO assistance. A reduced scheme – the Targeted Inputs Programme – was planned to supply similar inputs to 1.5 million farm families in 2000–1.

Evaluations of both phases of the Starter Pack Scheme were conducted (Longley et al., 1999; SPEP, 2000). This chapter reports on a module of the second-phase evaluation that focused on the Scheme's impact on sustainable agriculture. This was designed and implemented as a participatory impact assessment (PIA). As an early and innovative study it provided useful lessons on how participatory approaches could be used more widely and systematically for impact assessment, and what kinds of information could be collected compared to formal questionnaires and other conventional impact assessment methods.

Appropriately for a participatory study, the context for the PIA was to address long-term sustainability issues for agriculture in Malawi. This went beyond technical questions about inputs and management to look at underlying *institutional structures and processes*: 'Sustainable agriculture ... must become a process for learning' (Pretty, 1995). The PIA focused on one group of stakeholders in this institutional landscape – smallholder farmers – and used participatory approaches to develop an understanding of their own particular perspectives and definitions of sustainability.

Participatory impact assessment of agricultural sustainability: the methodology

At this time, amongst development practitioners worldwide there was a growing realization that an understanding of local needs and capabilities was central to any assessment of the options and potential for longer-term sustainability (see Box 12.1). There was also a well-established literature on how participatory approaches could be used for impact assessment (see, for example, Guijt, 1998; Abbot and Guijt, 1998; Guijt and Gaventa, 1998; Harnmeijer, 1999). Therefore, impact assessments based on participatory approaches were recognized as useful contributions to the ongoing debate. In particular, they could help to reveal the *diversity* of local needs and capabilities among different socio-economic categories of families and also within families according to gender, age, and so on.

Box 12.1   Key features of participatory approaches for impact assessment

- identifying which stakeholders want to be involved;
- establishing their expectations of the study;
- identifying their priority evaluation criteria;
- identifying indicators to provide the information needed for the evaluation;
- agreeing amongst stakeholders on the methods to be used;
- collecting and analysing information collaboratively with stakeholders.

Some of the lessons emerging about the practicalities of this approach were that decisions have to be made in advance about the range of stakeholders to be involved and the extent of their participation. The extent of stakeholders' participation ranges from their control over identification of evaluation criteria and data analysis, to a less extensive involvement focusing on participatory indicator identification and participation in information gathering. It is also important to note that participatory approaches do not necessarily generate *all* the information needed to identify options and potentials; rather, they focus on eliciting the views and understanding of selected stakeholders. This study focused on smallholder farmers, as their views on sustainable agriculture had not been sought systematically in Malawi before, and it involved them primarily in indicator identification and data gathering.

The basic framework of analysis chosen for this study was to adapt the approach and techniques of participatory well-being ranking to measure farm families' sense of agricultural sustainability instead of well-being. At that time, participatory well-being ranking had been used successfully by, for example, CARE in Zambia (Drinkwater and Rusinow, 1999) and by the HIMA-Njombe project in Tanzania (see Temu and Due, 2000). In adapting this method to the PIA in Malawi, the research team aimed in collaboration with farm families to develop sustainability categories, which we called 'Farming Practice Groups', which could be used to map actual short-term changes and potential long-term changes in sustainability. In each case study village, key informants ascribed farm families to a particular Farming Practice Group and this formed the basis for focus group discussion about movement between sustainability categories over time and reasons for this movement.

Because participatory approaches had not been used to explore sustainable agriculture issues in Malawi before, and yet time for fieldwork was relatively short, it was realized that preliminary participatory fieldwork would be needed to:

- identify which variables farmers themselves use to assess agricultural sustainability, i.e. to generate a set of sustainability indicators which could be used as a starting point for village-level discussions;
- assess which particular participatory tools and techniques would be most appropriate for facilitating discussions at community level.

Accordingly, an in-depth preliminary field study was carried out at three sites. The sites were chosen to represent the variability in one of the main factors that determines farming practices in Malawi, namely altitude. Within each site, the individual village was chosen to be of medium wealth and accessibility, to avoid extremes in these two variables unduly influencing results. The study team spent six or seven days in each village, starting with an open meeting to discuss farming activities (problem-objective tree), and moving on to identifying different farming practices within the village with key informants (transect walk) and discussing their sustainability (phrased as *ulimi okhazikika* – literally 'stable agriculture').

From the transect walk and discussion, the team was able to generate for each village a list of farming practices considered to be indicators of sustainable agriculture, with descriptions of how to distinguish 'high', 'medium', and 'low' sustainability for each practice (which we called Farming Practice Groups 3, 2, and 1, respectively). The team then spent time experimenting with different participatory tools – including institutional mapping, history timelines, pair-wise rankings, trend analyses, and dream/nightmare visions – in different formats (open meetings, key informants, focus group discussions, and so on), to assess approaches which would be most appropriate for the main study for generating the information needed within the limited time available. The preliminary fieldwork in each village concluded with a feedback meeting for the whole village, at which the team presented the results and incorporated comments from village members.

Using the results of the preliminary field study, the team got a clear vision of how the information needed for the study could best be obtained in the main study using participatory approaches. This was written up as a field facilitators' manual, which guided the main study fieldwork. The team was able to identify 15 sustainability indicators which were mentioned consistently across villages (Table 12.1). These were used as a set of standard indicators for which information was sought in each village during the main study.

The main study was carried out in 30 villages, with teams of 4 field facilitators spending 3 days in each village. Study sites were selected by proportional representation, based on a vulnerability assessment mapping exercise conducted in 1996 by the Famine Early Warning Unit (Moriniere et al., 1996). Within each study site, specific villages were randomly selected from the Starter Pack Logistical Unit national database of villages, excluding those villages with less than 30 or more than 300 households registered to receive a Starter Pack.

The fieldwork within each study village consisted of:

- introductions;
- background information: resource, social, and institutional mapping, transect walk;
- pair-wise ranking of relative importance of sustainability indicators;
- categorization of households into 'high', 'medium', and 'low' sustainability Farming Practice Groups, using the list of sustainability indicators;
- focus group discussions with each Farming Practice Group about the relative importance of different sustainability indicators;
- trend analysis of factors influencing the sustainability of their farming over time;
- impact (positive, negative, zero) of Starter Pack on their farming; and
- ideal contents of a 'Dream Pack' of inputs and extension advice for the future.

For the household categorization, two groups of key informants (one male, one female) took the household cards generated during the earlier social mapping exercise and placed each in turn in the box that best described that household's farming practices (high, medium, or low sustainability) for each sustainability indicator. Throughout these exercises, symbols selected by the community were used to represent the sustainability indicators.

The mixed-gender focus groups from each Farming Practice Group were composed of those households consistently placed within the same Group by both male and female key informants *and* who had received Starter Packs.

Each focus group in turn pair-wise ranked the 15 sustainability indicators according to their relative importance to the particular focus group (not the village as a whole). Each focus group then made line drawings of trends in the sustainability of their farming over the last 30 years, and highlighted the key influential factors in each decade. When proposing the 'Dream Pack', focus groups could introduce new items or varieties (as long as this did not increase the weight of the Pack beyond the 20kg of the Starter Pack) and could also suggest changes in distribution logistics and extension methods. They ranked the proposed changes through pair-wise rankings.

Table 12.1 Sustainability indicators of Farming Practice Groups

		Farming Practice Group 1 (high sustainability)	Farming Practice Group 2 (medium sustainability)	Farming Practice Group 3 (low sustainability)
1	Tilling or weeding by retaining weeds and crop residues in soil	Farmers retain maize leaves and stalks, and bury weeds while weeding (vundira or kugaula, kuojeka). Residues are buried immediately after piling maize for harvesting. If done by hand ridging is carried out at this time; if using cattle tilling is undertaken during this time, usually between June and July	Farmers in this group mostly do the same as FPG1 but the tasks are performed a bit later, usually in August or September. This, it was said, does not give enough time for the residues to decompose. In other areas late retention means trouble with termites and poor germination rate	Farmers usually gather stalks and weeds in piles and burn them (kusosa), or set the garden on fire to clear it before ridging. Others in this category wait until the first rains when the soils are wet and then ridge immediately. Though residues are retained in soil there is no time for decomposition
2	Application of organic manure (animal and compost)	Able to apply manure to whole fields and usually have means of transporting manure to their farmlands (ngolo). Most farmers also apply fertilizer because it is less laborious. This is done in good time, just before the rains in November	Put manure on each plant station to economize. May not have enough to apply to all farm plots. Usually just apply to farm plots near homesteads for lack of transport to carry manure to distant farm plots and for limited access to animal manure	Do not apply any manure because they usually do not own any animals and may not be able to purchase manure. FPG1 farmers rely on Starter Pack as only source of improving on soil fertility
3	Livestock farming	Keep a diverse type of livestock e.g. chickens, goats, pigs, and cattle. These help in production of animal manure; and animal power in terms of transport and farming; and as a source of income to buy fertilizer	Keep some livestock, but only chickens, goats and pigs	Keep only a few chickens
4	Agroforestry trees	Plant agroforestry trees such as rantana, pigeon peas (nandolo), with systematic spacing. Other trees mentioned include msangu and tifonia	Scattered agroforestry trees in garden / farm plots	No agroforestry trees planted in farmland. Trees such as gmelina and eucalyptus occur in farmland, which disturb crop growth

	Farming Practice Group 1 (high sustainability)	Farming Practice Group 2 (medium sustainability)	Farming Practice Group 3 (low sustainability)
5	Land husbandry practices	Use SWC measures including contour bunds, storm drains, and contour ridges where their gardens are sloping. Make ridges across slope following contours and also make box ridges. Ridges are well spaced, 90 cm apart	Have contour bunds where their gardens are sloping. Have ridges across some slopes but may not necessarily follow contours. No box ridges. Ridges may be too close or far apart	No contour bunds even where garden is on slope. Ridging along slope. Improper spacing of ridges, too close together or too far apart
6	Farm implements and tools	Have tools and implements such as ploughs, ridgers, oxcarts, plus hoes, sickles, axes	Own a few suitable farm tools such as axes, hoes, sickle, and panga knives	Own just some basic tools e.g. a few hoes and an axe. Farmers borrow most of the other tools from other people
7	Access to seed	Save enough seed for all crops and can also buy seed. Able to follow recommended planting methods per plant station and spacing	Save enough seed for 1 or 2 crops only. Plant following recommended methods per plant station and spacing	Rarely save any seed and rely on ganyu labour or Starter Pack to access seed. Characterized by late planting because time is wasted in searching for seed. May not always follow recommended planting methods
8	Farmland size	Enough land to plant all crops needed to feed family. Farmers able to lend some land to others	Own land may be inadequate, but some farmers can afford to rent to expand their farm area	Small land size, limiting cultivation area
9	Application of fertilizer	Farmers are able to buy fertilizer to apply on all farmland, thus ensuring production and allowing them to buy more fertilizer in subsequent years. Do not have much trouble to repay fertilizer loans	Only manage to buy some bags of fertilizer and may have some trouble repaying loans.	Cannot afford to buy any fertilizer, rely on Starter Pack as a source of fertilizer
10	Crop diversification	Grow a number of staple crops	Grow only 1–2 staple crops	Grow only one staple crop

continued overleaf

		Farming Practice Group 1 (high sustainability)	Farming Practice Group 2 (medium sustainability)	Farming Practice Group 3 (low sustainability)
11	Mixed cropping (intercropping, relay cropping)	Intercropping usually involves maize and beans mixed with tree legume crops grown just around the edges of the field. Farmers tend not to mix more than two different crops but may divide plots within the garden for different mixtures	Make sure the crops grown in same garden relate well by mixing nitrogen fixing [crops], such as beans, pigeon peas and maize. You will also find some complementary crops in the garden such as pumpkins, and different types of the beans mixed in the garden	Improper mixing of crops, such as mixing cassava, pigeon peas, maize and beans in the same garden. Overloading the garden with many crops beyond capacity. Just grow crops that they access at the planting time
12	Fallowing	Farmers leave land fallow for three or more years with total control of animal grazing in the field. This ensures that the purpose of leaving land fallow is not defeated by overgrazing or hardening of the soil by hoof stamping of animals	Farmers leave land fallow for a period of only 1–2 growing seasons, with some controlled grazing in the fallow fields	Cannot willingly leave any land fallow. Fallowing only occurs when farmers cannot farm the land for some reason such as illness during farming season
13	Application of chemicals	Apply recommended measures and types of chemicals to their fields, e.g. SMITHION mixed with SEVEN for termites, caterpillars and borers. Practise integrated pest management	Apply recommended measures and types of chemical to their fields, as with FPG3 farmers	Apply detrimental chemicals to fields such as DUAL for weed control instead of keeping weeds as green manure. Farmers also use sulphate of ammonia fertilizers on their fields
14	Crop rotation	Practise proper rotation: maize followed by groundnuts or tobacco. In another year tobacco follows maize or groundnuts, while groundnuts may follow where millet was previously planted	There is much change: rotation between two crops such as maize and tobacco, with millet planted on fallow land	Plant same types of crops on same pieces of land every year. If there are changes then the crops that follow each other are not appropriate, for example a maize plot followed by cassava or vice versa
15	Institutions[1]	Farmers are members of farmers' clubs for both cash and food crops and the family has access to a range of credit sources for the purchase of inputs. Farmers have access to and are able to act on good extension advice	Farmers receive some credit, often from within the village, not outside institutions. They are members of some farmers' clubs and receive some extension advice	Farmers do not have access to extension services and advice. Farmers do not have access to any credit schemes for inputs, either for cash or food crops

1 Institutions is used here to refer to extension, credit and community organizations, NGO projects, seed supply, marketing, and agricultural

The types of households within the 30 villages selected for the main study fieldwork are given in Table 12.2. There was a high incidence of female-headed households in the Northern Region because husbands had migrated from the villages for work, leaving their wives behind. Because only 4 of the 30 randomly selected villages were in the Northern Region, results from the Northern Region are possibly less reliable than those from the Central and Southern Regions.

Table 12.2 Total households in study villages, by region

Region	Male-headed household	Female-headed household	Total
Northern (4 villages)	257 (70.4%)	108 (29.6%)	365
Central (14 villages)	998 (78.6%)	271 (21.4%)	1,269
Southern (12 villages)	985 (76.4%)	305 (23.6%)	1,290
All regions (30 villages)	2240 (76.6%)	684 (23.4%)	2,924

Throughout the main study, the emphasis was on collecting information that could be used to make comparisons between sites as well as generalizations across sites. Thus, for example, scores were used in preference to relative rankings wherever feasible (e.g. see Table 12.3). Where ranks were used, the ranking was always done considering the same set of ranked items.

For each village, results were recorded in a debriefing document. One copy of the debriefing document was left in the village and the study team kept one copy. The information in the debriefing documents was then summarized in various simple Excel tables and charts. These were used for analysis, with the emphasis being on exploring regional variations (experience in North, Centre, and South) and differences in the experience of Farming Practice Groups (high, medium, low sustainability), as well as national trends and patterns.

Farmers' perceptions of sustainable agriculture

Sustainability indicators

Out of 15 possible choices, farmers in the study villages across Farming Practice Groups (FPGs) and regions picked out the following (in descending order of importance) as the five most important indicators of sustainable agriculture in Malawi:

1   Crop diversification – growing a range of staple crops
2   Access to seed – enough seed for timely planting at recommended spacing for all crops
3   Farmland size – enough land to feed family

4   Tools and implements – owning all the necessary farm tools and implements
5   Mixed cropping – optimal mix of crops for in-field soil fertility management through inter-cropping and relay planting.

Tables 12.4a and 12.4b show that, overall, the sustainability indicators chosen were fairly consistent across Farming Practice Groups and between male- and female-headed households.[1] The two significant differences between male- and female-headed households were that the cropping patterns of male-headed households are seen as more diversified than those of female-headed households; and, while all households relied on seed from off-farm sources, a greater proportion of female-headed households did so.

Table 12.3 Importance of sustainability indicators ranked by study villages

| Sustainability indicator | Means of pair-wise ranking across villages | | | |
	North	Centre	South	Total
Crop diversification	5.5	3.6^h	3.6^h	4.2^h
Access to seed	5.5	4.2^h	4.5^h	4.7^h
Farmland size	7.9	4.1^h	4.1^h	5.4^h
Tools and implements	5.1^h	5.5	5.8	5.5^h
Mixed cropping	7.1	7.9	3.1^h	6.0
Fertilizer application	9.0	5.8	6.3	7.0
Institutions	1.3^h	10.0	10.7	7.3
Crop rotation	8.8	3.2^h	12.2^l	8.1
Land husbandry	9.1	9.5	9.0	9.2
Livestock	10.1	8.8	9.6	9.5
Tilling or weeding	11.1	10.4	8.0	9.8
Manure application	10.6	10.0	13.1	11.2
Chemical application	9.6	12.1^l	12.2^l	11.3^l
Agroforestry	11.6^l	13.1^l	10.9	11.9^l
Fallow	8.9	14.3^l	13.5^l	12.2^l

Note: the sustainability indicators were weighted using pair-wise ranking. The top-ranking indicator was assigned one point and the lowest-ranking was given 15 points. An indicator was considered to be highly important if its rank was below the mean minus its standard deviation, and was considered of low importance if its ranking was above the mean plus its standard deviation.

Sustainability indicators were classified as: high (h = mean – standard deviation); medium (no superscript); and low (l = mean + standard deviation). Low figures imply that an indicator was highly ranked.

Table 12.4a Distribution of study households between Farming Practice Groups – perceptions of male key informants

Sustainability indicators	Male-headed households (%)			Female-headed households (%)		
	FPG1	FPG2	FPG3	FPG1	FPG2	FPG3
Crop diversification	40	24	36	30	24	46
Access to seed	23	31	47	13	27	61
Farmland size	34	32	34	26	32	42
Tools and implements	13	57	40	1	37	62
Mixed cropping	24	28	48	18	34	48
All 15 indicators[1]	17	34	46	8	36	56

FPG1 = highly sustainable, FPG2 = medium sustainable, FPG3 = lowly sustainable
Note: figures arrived at by dividing percentage of households in specified FPG in all villages by total (male and female) households in all villages.
1 Mode of all 15 indicators, as perceived by key informant group, not arithmetical mean

Table 12.4b Distribution of study households between Farming Practice Groups – perceptions of female key informants

Sustainability indicators	Male-headed households (%)			Female-headed households (%)		
	FPG1	FPG2	FPG3	FPG1	FPG2	FPG3
Crop diversification	45	33	22	33	35	32
Access to seed	31	26	44	19	28	52
Farmland size	40	37	24	46	31	23
Tools and implements	3	62	34	1	48	51
Mixed cropping	17	31	52	15	33	53
All 15 indicators[1]	20	42	38	14	34	52

The numbers produced allowed for statistical comparison of sustainability indicators across regions, with some minor differences emerging (Table 12.3). Respondents in the north ranked institutional contact highly. Those in the centre and the south ranked farmland size highly, while respondents in the north did not – presumably because the centre and the south are more densely populated than the north. Farmers in southern Malawi had adopted mixed cropping because of land scarcity; therefore, mixed cropping was ranked highly in this region. Groups in central Malawi ranked crop rotation highly – because the centre has relatively more land, which enabled farmers to practice crop rotation.

The statistics challenged preconceptions. Despite our initial assumptions that sustainable farming among smallholders might be indicated by the practice of agroforestry, the availability of fallow land, and low chemical application, these were ranked lowly across the country. Land shortage was one of the main reasons respondents gave for not maintaining fallow or practising agroforestry, and lack of knowledge or availability of inputs were also cited as reasons for the lack of use of crop chemicals and agroforestry. These findings suggested that experts' recommendations for sustainable agriculture that include these practices might not be feasible given farmers' natural and human capital base.

Trends over time

Table 12.5 shows that farmers in Farming Practice Group 3 perceived sustainability to have declined more markedly than those in Farming Practice Group 1. Farmland size was perceived to have decreased across nearly all Farming Practice Groups.

Seed availability was also considered to have declined by between one third and one half of farmers in all Farming Practice Groups. But over one half of farmers in all Farming Practice Groups indicated there had been an *increase* in crop diversification. This might have been due to the increasing impact of land pressure over time: many focus groups mentioned that growing a diverse range of crops was not necessary 30 years previously because there had been sufficient fertile land to support monoculture of maize at that time. Crop diversification had also been promoted over a number of years by various NGOs and the Ministry of Agriculture and Irrigation.

Baseline crop and variety diversity in the Malawi smallholder sector over the previous 30 years, as presented in the trend analyses, appeared to have been relatively low. Many farmers in the study villages mentioned that the Starter Pack was their first access to seed of some crops and varieties. Malawi's experience did not therefore appear to fall within the commonly assumed paradigm of highly biodiverse small farm agriculture at risk from the interventions of the formal seed sector. In fact, it appeared closer to the experience documented in, for example, Wood and Lenné (1993), of small farmers being *short* of crops and varieties, and keenly seeking new sources.

Dream Packs

A majority of the groups indicated that the Starter Pack had had a positive impact on some sustainability indicators: crop diversity, seed availability, mixed cropping, fertilizer application, and farm size. These were mentioned because of the seed and fertilizer that the Starter Pack provided (Figure 12.1). As regards farmland size, respondents said the availability of the seed enabled farmers to plant a relatively larger land area than normal. This suggested that the availability of seed remained a major constraint among smallholder farmers.

In some cases, some indicators that were not directly related to the Starter Pack Scheme were mentioned. For instance, while the Scheme did not provide any tools and implements, some groups indicated that it had a positive impact

Table 12.5 Trends in sustainability indicators in study villages, 1970–2000

| | FPG1 | | | FPG2 | | | FPG3 | | |
	Constant	Increase	Decrease	Constant	Increase	Decrease	Constant	Increase	Decrease
		%			%			%	
Northern region									
Farmland size	75	0	0	25	0	25	25	0	50
Access to seed	0	25	0	50	0	0	0	25	50
Mixed cropping	25	25	0	0	25	0	25	50	0
Crop rotation	0	50	0	0	75	0	0	50	0
Crop diversity	0	75	0	0	25	0	0	50	0
Central region									
Farmland size	0	7	57	0	79	0	0	0	100
Access to seed	7	14	36	0	14	50	14	7	50
Mixed cropping	7	29	21	0	21	7	14	36	7
Crop rotation	0	7	0	0	29	0	7	7	0
Crop diversity	7	64	36	14	43	14	14	57	21
Southern region									
Farmland size	17	67	0	0	0	67	0	92	8
Access to seed	0	17	33	0	17	67	8	8	50
Mixed cropping	17	75	0	0	58	8	8	83	0
Crop rotation	8	25	0	0	0	0	0	8	0
Crop diversity	0	17	8	8	17	8	8	25	0

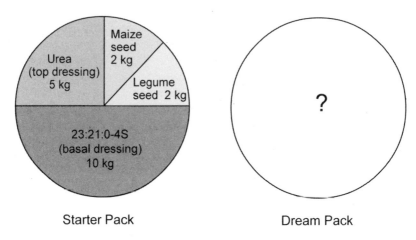

Starter Pack   Dream Pack

Figure 12.1 Pie chart of Starter Pack contents

on the availability of these to farmers. They argued that after harvest, they sold some produce whose proceeds were used to buy tools and implements. Some groups indicated that, through the provision of legume seed, the Scheme had a positive impact on crop rotation, mixed cropping, tilling, and crop diversification, and thus on soil fertility.

The process of registration and distribution of the Starter Pack enabled farmers to have access to various agricultural service institutions, sometimes for the first time, and that was why institutional contact was said to have been affected positively by the Scheme.

The focus groups also gave various reasons for Starter Pack having a negative or zero impact. For example, for indicators such as tools and implements and chemical application, while not directly being negatively affected by the Scheme, respondents said they were not provided and therefore the Scheme did not assist them. The other indicators were mentioned because the packs were distributed late, or the seed was rotten or broken. In such cases, the farmers never used the pack and therefore did not benefit through mixed cropping, crop rotation, or crop diversification.

Box 12.2 summarizes farmers' descriptions of their 'Dream Packs'. Responses were similar across regions. Overall, alternative seed types came out clearly as the top-most priority for farmers, with improved logistics in second place. Changes to extension were much less important, but focused on the desire for 'hands-on' demonstrations rather than written leaflets. (The main extension tool in the Starter Pack Scheme was leaflets detailing plant spacing, fertilizer application, etc. included in the Starter Packs. The many illiterate farmers could not read them and those who could, said they found them confusing.) Few farmers wanted any changes to fertilizer. The desired changes all indicate a desire to see the *quality* of the packs improved, both in terms of content and delivery systems.

Box 12.2   Dream Pack contents, ranked in order of importance to farmers in study villages

Maize: seed of flinty (hard) varieties rather than dent (soft) varieties, the former being more similar to local varieties in taste and poundability.
Legumes: groundnut and bean seed, not soyabean seed which is perceived as unsuitable to local agro-ecological conditions and without a local market.
Logistics: provide the Pack early, i.e. before the first rains.
Extension: introduce demonstration plots, and give face-to-face instructions, not just written leaflets.
Fertilizer: no change to basal fertilizer or top dressing for most Farming Practice Groups.

Farmers' perceptions of sustainable agriculture

Time and again in the problem-objective tree exercise in the preliminary field-work, farmers emphasized that their main concern was immediate family food security, and that they would use whatever farming practices were most likely to achieve this. If monocropping of modern varieties with chemical fertilizer was accessible and was likely to achieve this in the coming season, farmers would use this package, even though they were aware that this might not be sustainable economically or environmentally over the longer term.

From the ranking of sustainability indicators, it was clear that farmers' overriding concern was with cropping practices (diversification, rotation, etc.) and the availability of seed to support these. Frequently during the ranking exercises, farmers explained the low priority given to other farming practices, such as agroforestry or manuring, that were often promoted by extension, in terms of lack of physical resources (e.g. cattle for manure) or knowledge (e.g. advice about the planting and care of agroforestry species).

In farmer-led discussions, the longer-term economic and environmental impact of prevailing farming practices – for example, the impact of land clearance on local ecosystem functioning – never arose. The participating farmers might well have understood many of the relationships involved, but it is interesting to note that they did not include them in their framework of sustainable agriculture. Many farmers were aware of the influence of institutions on their own farming practices, and expressed the desire for more and more relevant institutional contact (extension advice, credit institutions, etc.), but they did not have a detailed understanding of the institutional structures and processes that influence agricultural sustainability. To fully understand the reasons for the institutional situation and the options for change would require the participation of other stakeholders. This was necessary given that the Starter Pack Scheme was originally conceived as a means of helping to transform Malawi's agricultural research and extension institutions into real participatory mode – an essential component of longer-term sustainability. These other stakeholders include the donor agencies involved in the design and implementation of schemes such as Starter Pack.

Conclusion: impact assessment using participatory approaches

The formative experience with innovating with participatory statistics in the Malawi Starter Pack Scheme impact assessment contributed to methodological lesson learning as PIA expanded during the past decade. Perhaps most important was that this type of participatory research is not undertaken lightly. Time and resources are needed to design and implement a rigorous PIA methodology properly. In this case, as discussed above, the research team engaged in 3 weeks of intense participatory fieldwork just to identify the 15 indicators (listed in Table 12.1) and evolve the methodology for the study proper.

Overall, the seven months of time available and the resource constraints limited the extent to which the study could embrace all the features of participatory approaches in a number of ways. This signals the trade-offs that need to be made, transparently, when conducting participatory research in general. In this case, the study managers had to decide on one group of stakeholders to involve, and identified smallholder farmers. Therefore, the study did not include the equally relevant and possibly different views of other stakeholders. Nonetheless, the focus on smallholder farmers was felt to be justified, as the views of this group on sustainable agriculture had not been sought systematically before and many new insights were obtained.

Underlying these trade-off decisions is the issue of 'who owns the research process?'. As in most research contexts, the institutions commissioning the impact assessment had specific questions they wished to see answered, so the criteria for the impact assessment were pre-set: farmers had no input in deciding these. However, it was farmers who identified appropriate sustainability indicators for assessing the pre-set impact assessment criteria. This was an extremely important aspect of the study, as many of the indicators selected – and the parameters dividing the three Farming Practice Groups – were not obvious to the study team. Thus, as we have seen earlier in this chapter, they gave the team, and ultimately the commissioners of the study, several new insights into farmers' perceptions of sustainable agriculture.

Farmers were also involved in the selection of fieldwork exercises during the preliminary field study, and in the collecting of information. In fact, most exercises were organized so that key informants or focus group members led the discussions and study team staff acted only as facilitators and note-takers – for this reason, the study team field staff were called field facilitators, rather than enumerators. In this way, a number of important issues were raised that may not have arisen if the field facilitators had been more actively involved in directing the discussion, e.g. by using checklist approaches.

As regards the nature of the information obtained by using participatory approaches, a number of points emerged from the study. First, there were the usual problems inherent in participatory work of needing a long time to explore issues adequately (and therefore some issues had to be missed out, for example differences *within* families). Also, of community leaders and dominant men leading discussions, although this was dealt with to some extent by organizing discussions in groups that were objectively selected (e.g. the focus groups were made up of members of each Farming Practice Group). Second, as mentioned earlier in this chapter, the sustainability indicators chosen by farmers related closely to farmers' goals of meeting immediate livelihood needs, with no reference being made to longer-term horizons or to wider ecosystem functions. A number (not all) were also closely related to prevailing notions of best farming practices. By definition, none related to the overall institutional sustainability of the Starter Pack Scheme, an unavoidable but important omission. Related to this, farmers had very little knowledge or understanding of *upstream* linkages and causal factors relating to the organization of research and extension and other institutions, so analysis of these was based instead on extrapolation by the study team.

In conclusion, by using participatory approaches to assess the impact of Starter Pack on sustainable agriculture in Malawi, the PIA reviewed here was able to collect detailed information relevant to both national and more local levels. By working in a relatively large number of sites, the study team could be confident of capturing the main trends and variations across the country. By using participatory approaches, we obtained a much clearer understanding of the underlying relationships involved in sustainable agriculture in the smallholder sector in Malawi than if we had relied solely on quantitative survey data. In sum, the participatory impact assessment approach used in this study was able to get the best of both worlds within the parameters set for the study.

Acknowledgements

This chapter is a modified version of a paper originally published as Cromwell et al. (2001). We are grateful to ODI for granting permission to reproduce sections of that paper here.

Note

1   Though data were collected for all 15 sustainability indicators, only the five most important are listed in Tables 12.4a and 12.4b. The complete tables can be found in the full report (Cromwell et al., 2000).

References

Abbot, J. and Guijt, I. (1998) 'Changing views on change: participatory approaches to monitoring the environment', *SARL Discussion Paper* No. 2, International Institute for Environment and Development, London.
Cromwell, E., Kambewa, P., Mwanza, R., and Chirwa, R. with Kwera Development Centre (2000) 'The impact of Starter Pack on sustainable agriculture in

Malawi', Report for Ministry of Agriculture and Irrigation, Government of Malawi and Department for International Development, UK.

Cromwell, E., Kambewa, P., Mwanza, R., and Chirwa, R. with KWERA Development Centre (2001) 'Impact assessment using participatory approaches: "Starter Pack" and sustainable agriculture in Malawi', *Network Paper* No. 112, Agricultural Research and Extension Network, Overseas Development Institute, London.

Drinkwater, M. and Rusinow, T. (1999) 'CARE's livelihoods approach', presented at DFID Natural Resources Advisers' Conference (NRAC '99), CARE International UK. Available at: www.eldis.org/go/topics/dossiers/livelihoods-connect&id=40253&type=Document [accessed October 2012].

Guijt, I. (1998) 'Participatory monitoring and impact assessment of sustainable agriculture initiatives', *SARL Discussion Paper* No. 1, International Institute for Environment and Development, London.

Guijt, I. and Gaventa, J. (1998) 'Participatory monitoring and evaluation: learning from change', *IDS Policy Briefing*, Issue 12, Institute of Development Studies, Brighton, UK.

Harnmeijer, J. (1999) 'From terms of reference to participatory learning: using an evaluation's creative space', *PLA Notes* No. 36, International Institute for Environment and Development, London.

Longley, C., Coulter, J., and Thompson, R. (1999) 'Malawi rural livelihoods Starter Pack scheme, 1998–9: evaluation report', Overseas Development Institute, London.

Moriniere, L., Chimwaza, S., and Weiss, E. (1996) *Malawi Vulnerability Assessment & Mapping (VAM) Baseline 1996: A Quest for Causality*, USAID/FEWS project, Lilongwe, and University of Arizona Office of Arid Land Studies, Arizona.

Pretty, J. (1995) 'Participatory learning for sustainable agriculture', *World Development* 23 (8): 1247–63.

Rockefeller Foundation (1998) 'Malawi: soil fertility issues and options', Discussion paper, Rockefeller Foundation, Lilongwe.

Starter Pack Evaluation Programme (SPEP) (2000) *Starter Pack Evaluation Archive*, CD-ROM, Statistical Services Centre, University of Reading, Reading, UK.

Temu, A. and Due, J. (2000) 'Participatory appraisal approaches versus sample survey data collection: a case of smallholder farmers' well-being ranking in Njombe District, Tanzania', *Journal of African Economies* 9 (1): 44–62.

Whiteside, M. (1998) *Living Farms: Encouraging Sustainable Smallholders in Southern Africa*, Earthscan Publications Ltd, London.

Wood, D. and Lenné, J. (1993) 'Dynamic management of domesticated biodiversity by farming communities', paper presented at Norway/UNEP Expert Conference on Biodiversity, Oslo.

About the authors

Elizabeth Cromwell is the Research Development Manager (Life Sciences and Medicine) at Warwick University. Her professional background is in agricultural economics, specializing in seed sector economics, especially the analysis of conservation and sustainable use of crop diversity at household level. Elizabeth was previously a Research Fellow at the Overseas Development Institute, an independent think-tank on development policy issues.

At the time this research was originally conducted, **Patrick Kambewa** was an agricultural economist specializing in farming systems research, resource management research, and institutional analysis of agricultural programmes. He was also an Associate Professor of Economics at the University of Malawi's Chancellor College.

During the original research period, **Richard Mwanza** was a social development scientist experienced in participatory development. He was also a Programme Manager for the Concern Universal Sustainable Livelihoods and Food Security Programme in Malawi.

At that time, **Rowland Chirwa** was Principal Agricultural Research Scientist at Chitedze Agricultural Research Station, with special interests in grain legumes, cereals and oilseed crops, and sustainable soil fertility amendment and conservation options.

Chapter 13

Participatory impact assessments of farmer productivity programmes in Africa

Susanne Neubert

The Competitive African Cotton Initiative (COMPACI) builds capacity and strengthens livelihoods amongst cotton farmers across Africa. An innovative and participatory approach – the Method for Impact Assessment of Programs and Projects (MAPP) – was used in COMPACI communities to analyse changing well-being categories and to give value scores to the contribution of COMPACI interventions to different aspects of economic and social well-being. The quantitative and qualitative data elicited was used for local reflection amongst farmers and by programme managers and implementing partners to reflect on programme design and prioritize future interventions. The standardization of aspects of the methodology partly allowed for aggregation of the data across COMPACI sites and even across countries. Future applications of MAPP can strengthen local participatory planning processes that emerge from local statistical analysis.

The Competitive African Cotton Initiative (COMPACI)

The Competitive African Cotton Initiative (COMPACI) operates in the cotton-growing African countries of Zambia, Mozambique, Malawi and Benin, Burkina Faso, and Ivory Coast. Since its inception in 2009, or in some countries in 2008, COMPACI has sought to increase cotton farmers' productivity and income, and improve their livelihoods overall. COMPACI is implemented and financed by a mix of stakeholders. While the largest financial share comes from Bill and Melinda Gates Foundation (BMGF), most technical support is given by German Development Cooperation Agencies, with DEG (Deutsche Entwicklungsgesellschaft/KfW group) in the lead. COMPACI delivers its support differently in each country, and where possible, the funds are channelled through private firms, such as cotton-ginning companies, in the cotton sector. These firms then implement COMPACI's programmes, which include training on cotton-growing methods as the most important activity, but also initiatives such as credit programmes, school construction, and the delivery of education materials. In Benin, for instance, where the government still plays a large role in the cotton sector, COMPACI runs as a programme in partnership

http://dx.doi.org/10.3362/9781780447711/013

with the German Development Cooperation (GIZ) and the national steering organization of the cotton sector.

In 2010 the National Opinion Research Centre at the University of Chicago (NORC) was commissioned to conduct an impact assessment to deepen understanding of the programme's contribution to changing incomes and livelihoods. Aside from a quantitative impact evaluation, which will be finalized only at the end of the programme, COMPACI proposed a participatory methodology which would enable farmers to generate data and analyse their own situation while uncovering strengths and weaknesses in order to fine-tune and improve the programme during its implementation phase. The methodology adopted – the Method for Impact Assessment of Programs and Projects (MAPP) – was tailored to the programme's needs and implemented across all COMPACI countries.

A participatory impact assessment methodology

MAPP is a group-based participatory impact assessment methodology. With this methodology, it is possible to evaluate the impact of a programme over a certain period of time and in the context of development trends affecting programme beneficiaries and their communities. In this case, since the research design used the same set of tools and a scoring system for measuring beneficiary responses, MAPP results could be partially aggregated, allowing the data and related impacts to be compared across different communities and even countries.

In this chapter we simplify the MAPP methodology and present it as a three-stage process. First, farmers influenced by COMPACI interventions analysed trends in cotton yield and cotton prices. They then broadened their trend analysis to consider four dimensions of change in well-being relating to living standards, resources, knowledge, and power. The third step was to analyse the contribution of COMPACI activities to those impacts. MAPP evaluated the programme in relation to other ongoing activities in the community to avoid the tunnel vision of other evaluation methods that focus only on the programme itself. At the end of the MAPP process, both farmers and outside programme managers could identify the overall impacts of the programme and in addition realize the challenges and shortcomings of the same programme from the perspective of farmers. This analysis could be used by farmers and programme managers alike to develop a vision and improve the programme.

The completed MAPP reporting forms (corresponding to the MAPP tools described below) are primary data, reflecting the farmers' views at the community level only. The evaluators (who facilitate and structure the discussions) take notes and summarize the results, transforming the primary data into narratives where aggregated tables of primary data cannot be formed.

In each country, the programme assembled its evaluation teams in a similar way: one supervisor from NORC was accompanied by the local cotton expert and three staff members from a local partner institution. All members of the team participated in short (one- to three-day) training in the MAPP methodology before starting the impact assessment in the field.

All in all, NORC and its local partners facilitated 25 MAPP focus group discussions, each lasting 2 days for a total of 50 days of discussion. The research teams kept detailed qualitative notes of each session, which could be used to explain and interpret the participatory quantitative data that was collected and aggregated.

The COMPACI communities participating in the impact assessment were sampled from the baseline survey communities in consultation with the COMPACI grantees, local cotton experts, and local partners. The communities were selected in order to represent the range of performance in the programme, including low, typical, and high-performing communities.

Within communities, the focus groups consisted of 15–60 male and female participants, giving a total of some 850 farmers of both sexes. Between 20 and 30 per cent of these farmers were female, who, when necessary, were encouraged to speak up on gender-related questions, but also when general questions were discussed. We didn't form separate women's groups in order to understand gender-related differences better and in order to discuss them with both male and female farmers at the same time. At the beginning of the session, the group was informed that men and women could always give different points to questions if they wanted to, and of course they could also give different explanations. In such cases, both views were noted. Women attributed less importance to the impact of radio announcements, for instance, than their male counterparts (see Table 13.3). Their reasoning was that they had less time to listen to these forecasts, lower access to radios, and no money for batteries. Of course, this approach of gender-mixed groups is only suitable when women are still able to express their views. The experience of the team was that, with careful facilitation, women in the COMPACI communities did speak up with careful facilitation.

The majority of farmers in the focus group discussions were so-called 'ordinary' or 'follower' farmers, who got training by so-called 'lead farmers'. Depending on the country, only lead farmers were trained directly by extension staff of the companies or by governmental extension services. These lead farmers were usually more experienced and achieved higher yields than the 'ordinary' ones. However, some 10 per cent of the focus group participants were 'lead' farmers and 5 per cent were service providers for land preparation or spraying, where these approaches existed.

After completing the MAPP FGDs, the research team presented the farmers' most significant concerns to the COMPACI grantees and then to the COMPACI programme management. The identified shortcomings were discussed in stakeholder meetings or during visits, and suitable improvements or resolutions for challenges were planned or implemented for the next season to come.

Generating participatory quantitative data on COMPACI impacts

Determinants of quality of life and overall development

A **quality of life curve** shows the overall development trends in the community along a timeframe that starts before COMPACI was implemented and ends at the present. We used a point system from 1 to 5, in which 1 means very low quality of life and 5 very high quality of life, in order to enable famers to value the different aspects of quality of life. In most countries, quality of life was clearly associated with the quantity of crop production, the quality and availability of inputs, and of course with the income from marketing these crops, for which the cotton prizes were the most important. In all communities, agriculture was the most important and mostly the only source of income, with the exception of one near-urban community in Malawi, where other economic activities such as trade also had significance.

In the typical Zambian COMPACI community (see Figure 13.1), for instance, farmers' quality of life had clearly improved over the last 10 years. The course of the curve closely followed the fluctuations in cotton prices as its most significant determinant. The Zambian farmers in all communities expressed that cotton prices were the decisive factors in their lives and that unpredictable price fluctuations were their biggest problem.

Until 2009, cotton prices fluctuated between the different seasons but never within one selling period. In 2009/10, however, a small crop came in when world market prices steadily increased. Being in hard competition for a small crop, ginneries had to raise prices as the season continued. Farmers who followed the cotton companies' advice and sold their cotton early

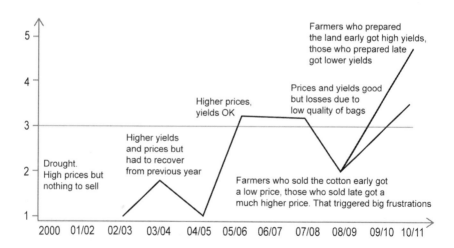

Figure 13.1 Quality of life trend curve produced by COMPACI farmers in Zambia

Note: 1 = very poor quality of life; 2 = poor; 3 = average; 4 = good; 5 = very good watched in frustration as the farmers who ignored this advice and sold later received higher prices for their crop. As a consequence of this experience, ginning companies in Zambia agreed to stick for the whole 2011 season to a unique cotton purchase price. This agreement was respected, and a large crop combined with good world market prices helped farmers to raise their income in this year.

As Figure 13.2 demonstrates, aside from climate variability and price shocks, the availability and quality of inputs, such as pesticides, sprayers, and high-quality seeds, determined the state of Malawian cotton farmers' livelihoods. In contrast to the other COMPACI countries, Malawian cotton farmers do not get inputs on credit from the cotton companies and instead have to purchase them on the open market. The government does not allow contract farming, with the exception of farmers organized in cooperatives. Hence, the key point raised in the focus groups with Malawian farmers was the threat to their quality of life posed by risky markets and the low quality, availability, and affordability of inputs (treated seed, pesticides, sprayers).

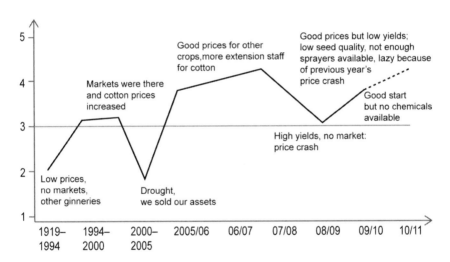

Figure 13.2 Quality of life trend curve produced by COMPACI farmers in Malawi

Note: 1 = very poor quality of life; 2 = poor; 3 = average; 4 = good; 5 = very good

Trend analysis

A **trend analysis matrix** identifies development trends and evaluates them in more detail with the same 1–5 point system, covering the same timeframe as the quality of life curve (or as here at least 4 years). The research design defined upfront the following four key standard indicators of quality of life: (a) improvement/degradation of living standards; (b) access to or exclusion from resources; (c) expansion or reduction of knowledge; and (d) participation in or exclusion from rights and power according to concepts in the literature and formulated common sub-indicators. This standardization involved negotiating a familiar trade-off in participatory research between accommodating the contextual priorities of the participants and, as decided here, maximizing the opportunity to standardize and compare indicators between populations and over time.

For aggregation purposes, the points of the trend analysis in the communities were turned into numbers, all matrices of each country were summarized, and the average was formed against each of the categories. Table 13.1 shows the overall trends cross country for all categories. Table 13.2 shows the aggregated cross-country trend analysis for three sub-categories: cotton yields, food security, and family income as an example.

Table 13.1 Overall trends in COMPACI communities in six countries

Overall change of life quality	Burkina Faso	Benin	Côte d'Ivoire	Mozambique	Zambia	Malawi	Overall
Living standard (health, yields, income)	–	+/–	++	+	++	+	+
Access to resources (credits/loans, infrastructure)	+/–	+/–	+/–	+/–	+/–	–	+/–
Knowledge and skills (school enrolment, agricultural skills)	+/–	+	+/–	+/–	+	+	+
Rights and power (fair arrangements and price negotiation power)	+/–	+	+/–	+/–	+/–	+/–	+/–
Overall	+/–	+	+	+/–	+	+	

Source: NORC Analysis

The statistics show positive development trends in the period from 2006 to 2010 in the COMPACI communities in Zambia, Côte d'Ivoire, Benin, and Malawi. In Mozambique the situation stayed more or less the same during the observed time period. One reason for this is that COMPACI started with delay in this country and only a few months before the focus groups discussions were conducted. In Burkina Faso results of focus groups discussions were influenced by the fact that the communities selected were extremely affected by heavy floods in 2010, which destroyed the yields and hence offset earlier positive developments.

Table 13.2 Trend analysis for three sub-categories conducted by farmers in COMPACI communities in six countries

	Western Africa						Southern Africa						All countries
	Burkina Faso		Benin		Côte d'Ivoire		Mozambique		Zambia		Malawi		
	Status quo	Trend	Status quo	Trend	Status quo	Trend	Status quo	Trend	Status quo	Trend	Status quo	Trend	Status quo in 2010 and trend

Cotton yields — Yields fluctuate according to the factors: 'timing of land preparation' (Zambia), 'availability/affordability of inputs' (Malawi) and 'climatic factors' (Burkina Faso). When farmers are frustrated because of low cotton prices they don't give so much attention to cotton in the following season and prepare the fields later (after having prepared the maize field). This again lowers the yields for the next season. In Burkina Faso adverse climatic conditions are regularly threatening the yields. Until now, no coping mechanism or adaptation strategies to buffer these climatic fluctuations are in place.

	Burkina Faso SQ	Burkina Faso Trend	Benin SQ	Benin Trend	C.d'Ivoire SQ	C.d'Ivoire Trend	Mozambique SQ	Mozambique Trend	Zambia SQ	Zambia Trend	Malawi SQ	Malawi Trend	All countries
2006/07	4.0		4.1		2.0		3.5		3.3 (3.7)		4.8		
2007/08	1.0	+/− until 2010, then − −	3.8		2.0		2.3		3.0 (3.7)		4.3		In 3 out of 6 countries positive and very positive trends
2008/09	3.0		4.4		2.8		3.5		4.0 (4.0)		5.0		
2009/10	4.0		3.5		4.8		4.3		3.7 (4.5)		2.7		
2010/11	1.0	+/−	n.a.	+/−	n.a.	++	3.5	+	n.a.	+	n.a.	+/−	

Access to food / food security — Farm households in all visited communities claimed to have sufficient access to food and during the analysed period food security appears to have slowly increased in all countries except Burkina Faso. In all countries and communities, coping mechanisms are weak. Communities with livestock can buffer one difficult year by selling some or all animals, whereas communities without livestock are more vulnerable since they have no compensation mechanism. But since communities without livestock are usually situated in more humid regions, complete crop failures appear less frequently there.

	Burkina Faso SQ	Burkina Faso Trend	Benin SQ	Benin Trend	C.d'Ivoire SQ	C.d'Ivoire Trend	Mozambique SQ	Mozambique Trend	Zambia SQ	Zambia Trend	Malawi SQ	Malawi Trend	All countries
2006/07	3.0		3.6		2.3		2.5		2.3 (4.5)		3.7		
2007/08	5.0		4.0		4.0		3.5		2.7 (4.3)		4.0		In 4 of 6 countries positive and very positive trends
2008/09	3.0		4.3		3.0		4.5		3.7 (4.7)		4.5		
2009/10	4.0		4.9		4.3		4.5		4.3 (5.0)		5.0		
2010/11	1.0	−	3.9	+	3.8	+/−	4.5	++	n.a.	++	n.a.	++	

Family income — Though incomes are still very low in all countries, on average they are on the increase mainly in Zambia, Mozambique and Côte d'Ivoire. In absolute terms incomes in Benin and Malawi are evaluated as much higher than in Mozambique. In Burkina Faso income is seen as a direct function of yields. However, income trends are mostly not consistent: they fluctuate greatly and vary between communities and households.

	Burkina Faso SQ	Burkina Faso Trend	Benin SQ	Benin Trend	C.d'Ivoire SQ	C.d'Ivoire Trend	Mozambique SQ	Mozambique Trend	Zambia SQ	Zambia Trend	Malawi SQ	Malawi Trend	All countries
2006/07	4.0		3.8		1.3		1.3		2.0 (5.0)		3.8		
2007/08	3.0		3.5		1.8		2.0		4.0 (4.3)		3.8		In 3 out of 6 countries (very) positive trends
2008/09	3.0		4.1		2.5		2.3		3.7 (4.3)		2.5		
2009/10	4.0		3.7		3.3		2.0		4.3 (4.5)		3.5		
2010/11	1.0		n.a.	+/−	3.8	++	2.5	+	n.a.	++	n.a.	+/−	

Note: 1.0 = very low, 2.0 = low, 3.0 = average, 4.0 = good, 5.0 = very good
Decimals are the result of forming the average

Influence matrix

The third tool in this sequence is the **influence matrix**, which allows farmers to score and evaluate the influence of individual programme interventions on each development indicator. This also allows the 'passive sum' to be calculated, which shows which development indicators did or did not perform well, and the 'active sum', which shows which interventions had impacts on the most development indicators. These calculations can be done together with the farmers at the end of the session and conclusions for action can be discussed on the basis of this. The point system for the influence matrix also includes negative numbers (from −4 to +4) in order to make negative ratings possible. The negative and positive ratings are analysed separately rather than merged, as they cannot compensate for each other. Usually, the aggregation of different influence matrices is not suitable, because in each community the set of activities mostly differs, which means that an influence matrix is contextual in principle and therefore mostly stands alone. However, when a standardized set of activities is used in all communities, the aggregation is possible. But also when standing alone, several influence matrices can be compared in a qualitative way, and region-specific impact patterns with similarities and deviations can be detected.

These scores are accompanied by a qualitative summary of the impacts from the farmers' perspective. In Zambia, for instance, the research team summarised the passive sum and active sum impacts as follows:

- Passive sum: access to capital, fair arrangements with cotton companies and price negotiation power are not developed and there is no activity addressing these issues yet. Condition of feeder roads does not develop quickly enough.
- Active sum: the clinic and school should have been completed since started long ago. This should be cross-checked by visiting them and asking the concerned organizations. Conservation farming and other training on agricultural skills (including Cargill trainings) have a high impact on many development indicators and are key measures. However, it is not clear how the training on IPM is designed. Farmers don't fully understand IPM as a concept. Cross-checking would be necessary. Radio programmes are appreciated but access to radio is a problem, especially for women (cost of batteries).

In Zambia, COMPACI had a measurable positive impact on livelihoods. From all measures, the trainings on early land preparation and the propagation of conservation farming, including minimum tillage, made the most decisive differences for yields in cotton and other crops, including vegetables. Contrary to this positive example, in which COMPACI had resounding positive impacts, this was not yet possible in Malawi, because several unsuitable framework conditions hampered progress and limited impacts. The most

Table 13.3 Influence matrix produced by farmers in Zambia

Question: How strong is the influence of activity 'a' on indicator 'b'?	Activities/trainings/projects/programmes										
Development indicators	School construction	Clinics	Vegetable growing	COMPACI: early land preparation	Boreholes	Orphan assistance	Conservation farming	COMPACI radio announcements	Feeder roads	COMPACI: (integrated) pest management	Σ passive sum
Living standard											
Community health	n.a.	n.a.	3	4	4	3	4	2 (women) / 3 (men)	2	3/–4	25–26 /–4
Cotton yields	n.a.	n.a.	0	4	2	0	4	2	3	3	18
Family incomes	n.a.	n.a.	4	4	1	0	4	2	3	4	22
Access to food	n.a.	n.a.	4	4	0	0	4	2	3	3	20
Access to resources											
Conditions of feeder roads	n.a.	n.a.	0	0	0	0	0	0	2	0	2
Access to capital	n.a.	n.a.	4	4	0	0	4	2	2	0	16
Knowledge and skills											
School enrolment	n.a.	n.a.	0	0	0	0	0	0	1	0	1
Agricultural management skills	n.a.	n.a.	4	4	2	2	4	4	1	4	25
Rights and power											
Fair arrangements with cotton company	n.a.	n.a.	0	0	0	0	0	0	0	0	0
Price negotiation power	n.a.	n.a.	0	0	0	0	0	0	0	0	0
Σ active sum	n.a.	n.a.	19	24	9	5	24	14/15	17	17 /–4	

important hampering factor was the low availability of good-quality chemicals, spraying equipment, and certified seeds. Another important factor was the price crash in 2009 which, together with the input scarcity, offset most COMPACI impacts until 2010.

In contrast to this, political improvements regarding the framework conditions contributed to essentially positive impacts of COMPACI in Benin. Here, positive impacts of the programme were boosted by a reform of the regulatory framework on cooperatives. Before, some farmers escaped from debt repayment by migrating from one cooperative to another. With the reforms, this collectivization of debts was no longer possible and therefore more farmers were motivated to grow cotton and to collaborate with COMPACI.

Beyond the larger picture assessment of impacts, the group analysis sessions allowed for more nuanced discussions of both negative and positive impacts (see Box 13.1). In Zambia, for instance, farmers complained about the lack of functional protective clothing against pesticides and some female farmers in Malawi complained about the mal-comprehension of the concept of gender equality of their husbands, who regarded women as 'nowadays more equal' because, for instance, in food-for-work programmes they could work as hard as men. Nonetheless, some men would try to hide the income from cotton from their spouses. All concerns which were raised during these discussions were listed by the evaluation team, then summarized and reported back to the cotton companies later.

Linking analysis to action

The decision of the programme managers to report back farmers' major concerns to the cotton companies was very important in order to enable the programme to progress in the right direction. This feedback loop of information allowed programme managers to understand farmers' views and positions better and in some cases resolve tensions. Sometimes, when obvious shortcomings of the firms or the programme were addressed by the farmers, the resolution was actually very straightforward and could be facilitated either by the firms or by COMPACI. For instance, in the case of lacking protective clothing, the firms corrected the shortcomings by including adequate equipment in the chemical packs for the next season.

In other cases, the addressed weaknesses had deeper or wider causes, which either lay beyond the influence sphere of a single or even all cotton companies or the COMPACI programme managers, or which took a longer time to change. In Zambia, for example, farmers complained about the fluctuating cotton prices, while in Mozambique they criticized the authoritarian style of the extension service by stressing that they felt forced to follow advice against their will. Finding solutions to these problems can be very complex and time-consuming. The complex change process includes, for instance, the formation of a regulatory cotton board in Zambia or converting the authoritarian extension approach into a participatory farmer-centred communication culture in

Box 13.1 Zambian farmers' comments on influence matrix

School construction
'Construction is ongoing and doesn't have any impact yet'
(Evaluation team: should be terminated since long [time] because started in
2000, please cross-check)

Clinics
'Construction is ongoing and doesn't have any impact yet'
(Evaluation team: should be terminated since long [time] because started in
1991, please cross-check)

Vegetable growing
'Has very high impacts on income (we make a lot of money with it) and health
as well as access to high value food (nutrition). Some of us can also build
capital with it (for buying fertilizer)'
(Evaluation team: is actually not capital but money for further production)

Pesticide spraying
'Spraying has high effects on yields, income and access to food. But sometimes chemicals are not effective. In addition to that, they have very negative
effects on our health. Cargill doesn't provide us protective clothes.'

Early land preparation
'Has a huge impact on our income and thus on many other indicators.'

Boreholes
'Fosters our health (no water-borne diseases) and is also needed for production
(watering) and spraying.'

Orphan assistance
'Is important but doesn't impact on many indicators.'

Conservation farming
'Impacts on yields, income and food and at the same time lowers work load.
It is very important.'

Radio programmes
'Are important but not so for women. Women have access to radios only sometimes and less time to listen than men.'

Road construction
'This activity would have a very high impact on many indicators, but in reality,
this is only moderate because progress is slow.'

Mozambique. But of course, it is still easier to manage these types of problems than to influence risks caused by completely external factors – such as external economic shocks or climate change – which are beyond the influence of the programme. In such cases, adaptation measures such as conservation agriculture, which buffers these fluctuations, are the only possible options.

All in all, focus group discussions empowered farmers in different ways. Firstly, they increased group understanding of context and the interconnectedness of problems, thus allowing farmers to make more informed decisions on what to grow and how to grow it. COMPACI programme managers could support the cotton companies to foster such discussions, for instance by founding 'cotton schools' in which farmers and other stakeholders as programme or extension staff regularly meet and solve problems collectively. The founding of more cotton schools for enhanced mutual learning has to be regarded as a key measure, which was promoted and implemented especially by one cotton company in Zambia.

In this way, participatory development planning enables farmers to use impact assessment results for further action. In the classical MAPP methodology, development indicators that did not perform well (i.e., those that showed minimum passive sums in the influence matrix) are isolated, and the MAPP participants develop a vision of how to change the situation. Several people from the community are assigned to start concrete actions towards achieving that vision. In the case of a multi-stakeholder programme like COMPACI, such a process should be fostered from outside or higher levels in order to bring stakeholders together and to accelerate the empowerment and cooperation process.

Conclusion

MAPP is a context-oriented participatory method, with which beneficiaries assess the value as well as the shortcomings of programme impacts in the light of their entire livelihoods. With MAPP, a fixed set of tools is used, which as a whole shows positive as well as negative development trends and impacts of activities on these trends. This approach can be incorporated into a more randomized and quasi-experimental impact assessment design, including the identification of 'control' communities where appropriate. Demands for fully random (probability-based) sampling of communities for PIA have to be offset against logistical and resource constraints that may mitigate widespread activities. In all cases there is a need for trade-offs in the sampling methodology to be made transparent and fully justified. Certainly, if the selection criteria during a more 'qualitative' (contextualized) sampling process are pursued carefully, 'small n' can still generate quantitative and qualitative data that strongly indicate positive impacts and important shortcomings of a programme. If this selection process is not pursued deliberatively, then of course there is a risk of bias. This was the case in Burkina Faso where – by accident – only flood-affected communities were chosen. Therefore, the risk of biased sampling should always be mitigated in 'small n' designs through well-reasoned stratification and selection criteria combined with data cross-checking.

MAPP includes a quantification step by using ordinal-scale scoring methods, and hence is a semi-quantitative method, as some of its core results can be aggregated. With these scoring methods, systems trends, impacts, and changes can be assessed and differences in the views of actors involved made transparent. The multi-country experience with the COMPACI programme shows that trend data can be aggregated over sites and even over countries, although with attendant trade-off in loss of local control over identifying indicators. On the other hand, some of the other tools – like the quality of life curve or, when the set of activities is not standardized, the influence matrix – are context specific and hence aggregation doesn't make sense. For these tools, typical matrices and curves can be drawn from several examples, summarized, and compared more qualitatively.

In addition to being an impact assessment method, MAPP can be also used as an instrument for participatory planning. For this purpose, the assessment results are fed back to programme managers, sub-grantees, or other stakeholders in order to discuss the most crucial points and to find ways for improvement. In the COMPACI experience, the members of the focus group discussions were all farmers. Cotton company representatives and programme managers were excluded from these discussions. On the one hand, this meant that feedback loops had to be organized by the evaluation team as extra steps, requiring more time and being not participatory regarding the inclusion of farmers. On the other hand, this 'closed setting' chosen for COMPACI empowered farmers to articulate their concerns more clearly and to overcome their fear to speak up, since they could discuss the issues firstly among themselves. This was particularly important given the long-standing tendency for cotton companies, especially in southern Africa, to treat farmers in a hierarchical and top-down fashion. However, in other programme contexts it can be more productive to bring a wider group of stakeholders together to analyse, reflect, and plan.

References

National Opinion Research Centre at the University of Chicago (NORC) (2010) 'COMPACI farmers voices 2010: cross-country results of the interim MAPP assessment of COMPACI', unpublished paper, Cologne.

Neubert, Susanne (2004) 'Impact analysis of development cooperation is feasible', DIE Briefing Paper, 4/2004, German Development Institute (DIE), Bonn.

Neubert, Susanne (2010) 'Description of the method MAPP (Method for Impact Assessment of Programmes and Projects)', German Development Institute, Bonn, and Centre for Rural Development, Lusaka/Berlin.

About the author

Susanne Neubert is the Director of the Centre for Rural Development (SLE), Humboldt University, Berlin. Before that she lived in Zambia for three years, where she coordinated parts of the evaluation of COMPACI (Competitive African Cotton Initiative) with participatory methods. From 1997, Susanne was a senior researcher at the German Development Institute (DIE), where she worked in the field of agriculture, water resource management, and empirical methods of social research with the regional focus on Africa. She has been on temporary leave from DIE since 2009.

Afterword

Robert Chambers

This book presents evidence of a methodological breakthrough. This has for too long been unrecognized. Since 1991, when ActionAid Nepal facilitated a mapping study in over 130 villages to find out how many people had received services, the evidence has been there, and has been diversifying and accumulating, that participatory methods can generate excellent statistics. There has been a quiet methodological revolution. Great opportunities and potentials have been revealed. But the mainstreams of research, monitoring, and evaluation have been almost totally untouched.

Far from adopting participatory statistics, the direction of funding and fashion has sponsored and favoured a wider application of conventional methods for statistics and evidence in development. This book challenges such methodological conservatism and the direction it is taking. It shows that for many contexts and purposes there are alternatives which are more pro-poor, more accurate, more insightful, and more cost-effective, and that these, as Jeremy Holland points out in the introduction, are 'win–win': they can generate better statistics closer to ground realities to inform, influence, and improve policy and practice; and they can empower local people through their own analysis, learning, and data for use in action and advocacy.

Much has been learnt. Statistics generated through participatory processes can be and have been subject to the same tests as any other statistics (Barahona and Levy, 2003, 2007; Catley et al., 2008). They can be presented in tables just like any other numbers. They can be used for new indices: in 1996, in Bangladesh, a composite Prioritized Problem Index of Poor Communities was constructed for rural women, rural men, urban women, and urban men from problem rankings in 159 focus groups (UNDP 1996); and more recently, also in Bangladesh, a Group Development Index has been based on indicators assessed by thousands of groups (Jupp with Ibn Ali).

Beyond such normal approaches and uses of statistics, there are important differences and new insights.

'They can do it'

With good facilitation, often light and almost hands-off, local people have been found to have a far greater ability to model, map, assess, and quantify than most professionals have supposed. There are many illustrations in this book, for instance the participatory 3-dimensional modelling done by close to 120 villagers in Oromiya, Ethiopia (Rambaldi), the morbidity and

http://dx.doi.org/10.3362/9781780447711/014

mortality maps made by health field workers in the Philippines (Nierras), participatory indicator identification with farmers in Malawi (Cromwell et al.), group self-assessments of performance against 132 indicators by members of a social movement in Bangladesh (Jupp with Ibn Ali), and participatory impact assessments by farmers (Neubert), groups (Causemann et al.), and pastoralists (Abebe and Catley).

Methodological diversity and versatility

It is striking how diverse and versatile the approaches and methods are. Statistics can be generated in many ways for many purposes. We have mapping and modelling (Rambaldi, Shah). In Malawi, through a process including community mapping with cards, a table could be compiled showing food security status against the receipt of a government programme (Barahona). Aggregation from focus groups is well represented (Jupp; Moser and Stein; Neubert; Causemann et al.; Shah). In a participatory mode, almost anything that is qualitative, valued, and open to comparisons can be quantified, such as changes in empowerment and capabilities (Jupp and Ibn Ali); attitude and knowledge skills (Causemann et al.: 116); the importance of institutions (Moser and Stein); 'quality of life' (Neubert); poverty and wealth (Causemann et al.); wealth ranking into six standard categories at scale in the whole of rural Rwanda (Shah); trends in sustainability indicators (Cromwell et al.); and scoring satisfaction with services (Riemenschneider et al.). Versatility extends beyond census and service counting to, for instance, estimating changes in gender relations over a decade (MYRADA in Chambers, 1997: 174), or through matrices attributing effects or impacts to causes (Neubert; Catley et al., 2008). Indicators are again and again identified in a participatory mode, as in Bangladesh through listening study techniques, PRA methods, and participatory drama (Jupp), and in Malawi through extended interactive processes (Cromwell et al.), in both cases leading to many more indicators, of greater relevance, than would otherwise have been thought of. Diversity and versatility are evolutionary and adaptive, as Riemenschneider shows, with how what started as a longitudinal impact assessment becoming interactive research. Participatory approaches and methods can also generate statistics on hidden and sensitive subjects: as Shah points out concerning wealth and poverty, the *Ubudehe* maps in Rwanda make the invisible poor visible; and as others have shown, sensitive realities can be represented as with violence (Moser and McIlwaine, 2004), volumes of shit produced by a community (Kar, 2005), and teenage sexual behaviour and partner characteristics and preferences (Shah et al., 1999).

Participatory statistics tend to be more accurate than those from conventional methods

Accuracy comes from triangulation, cross-checking and processes of successive approximation. When participating analysts have overlapping knowledge of all the people in a community, there is little reason why any error should creep into a census: all participants can see and correct what is being shown. One common form of triangulation with tangible visualizations such as social mapping, matrix scoring, and pile sorting, is group-visual synergy,[1] where the facilitator can observe members of a group acting and interacting to converge successively on an agreed estimate or representation. Coverage of all project beneficiaries makes the NGO-IDEAS toolbox more rigorous than many research methods (Causemann et al.). Generally, rigour comes from relevance to the group, their overlapping knowledge and values, and their energy and commitment to 'trying to get it right'. These can be observed by the facilitator and assessed critically. Triangulation can also be between different groups and methods.[2]

Win–Win

As Jeremy Holland points out in his introduction, participatory statistics are a 'win–win': they are credible, often illuminate aspects that would otherwise be missed, and at the same time empower and enlighten participants. All learn together in the processes. Surprise insights can be valuable to all concerned and have policy implications. When participants in the Philippines workshop compared the maps they had made, they saw that the transition from communicable to degenerative diseases was beginning to manifest and that road accidents were the third most frequent cause of death (Nierras). Farmers in Malawi showed that they did not value the agroforestry that professionals believed to be a priority for them (Cromwell et al.). In the Maldives, researchers were taken aback by how much the methods were welcomed by key informants and how all gained from the feedback of findings (Riemenschneider et al.). Participatory well-being ranking can also identify those who are vulnerable and involve the rural rich in taking responsibility for the rural poor (Causemann et al.). P3DM in Ethiopia created a learning environment, and the elders who took part came to see more clearly the ecological changes that had taken place; and mapping brings peer-to-peer interactions and diagnostic analysis (Rambaldi). Knowledge embodied in the maps in Rwanda was democratized and made visible (Shah). Local governments in the Philippines became more responsive (Nierras) and downward accountability resulted in Bangladesh (Jupp). People found it empowering to become more aware of the effects of their actions (Causemann et al.). Consistently through all these examples, good statistics informed outsiders and empowered local participants.

Participatory statistics can have applications at the national level. In Rwanda, social maps offer a real-time census of populations in villages that can be and often are updated regularly by the communities themselves; and the Ministry of Health has used the maps for targeting households for free services and identifying who should be contributing to health insurance, and has invested in a data processing centre to capture and aggregate data from the maps more systematically (Shah). National statistics can be calibrated and corrected: in Malawi, participatory mapping in 54 carefully selected communities, cross-checked with a one-page household question-naire, indicated a population 35 per cent higher than in the national census (Barahona and Levy, 2003, 2007). Discrepancies between national question-naire surveys and participatory methods can raise questions of validity and credibility, as with the Uganda National Household Survey (Kagugube et al., 2007). All census studies and all household surveys might gain from such triangulation. In the Philippines workshops of health staff, statistics aggre-gated from midwives' records were found to be more accurate than those reported in the official data-gathering system, which they then replaced (Nierras). When health workers' statistics identified road accidents as the third cause of death, immediate action brought the death rate down. The 'robust, insightful and timely' statistical data from the participatory impact assessment of destocking in Ethiopia fed into key policy discussions and guidelines (Abebe and Catley).

Potentials

Many potentials are evident from what we have learnt. Given local people's capabilities and the versatility, accuracy, win–win character, and other advantages of participatory statistics, future adaptation, innovations, and applications promise to be innumerable. The power and sophistication of visual and tactile analysis with group-visual synergies in a PRA mode is an abiding strength, and has many applications. In addition, we now have ICTs and digital technologies. These open up unbounded new fields. Geospatial information technologies can express and assert local knowledge and rights (Rambaldi). Ultra-mobile personal computers bring opportunities for rapid analysis, feedback, and triangulation of participatory data (Riemenschneider et al.). Mobile phones, SMS, and crowdsourcing add to the proliferation of participatory methods and methodologies, raising new questions of inclusion, exclusion, representativeness, and data quality.

National and local statistics are one frontier (Barahona and Levy, 2007). The use of cloth maps in each of the 14,837 villages in Rwanda as a source of national statistics for health (Shah) takes us far beyond anything that could have been conceived a few years ago, and points to opportunities with moni-toring other sectors, and social and economic change, in Rwanda and other countries. Sarah Levy (2007), reflecting on her experience with participatory research in Malawi, has outlined a vision of locally managed resource centres that would generate statistics as tools for local decision making and advocacy, while also producing timely and accessible data for national and decentralized evidence-based policymaking. In sum, in research, monitoring, and evalua-tion, and for local and national statistics, there seems to be almost no limit to the frontiers that participatory statistics have opened up and which are now waiting to be explored and exploited.

Practical and professional blocks

The evidence in this book and elsewhere in the literature indicates, again and again, that if participatory statistics were more the norm, there would then be substantial gains all round. But examples that have been written up are not a mainland, but an archipelago, small and scattered islands in a vast ocean of business-as-usual. Anyone reading the cases in this book will recognize their win–win potential. Though the power of participatory statistics has been known for over two decades, they have not taken off to become widespread practice in research, in social development, or in national statistics. We have to ask what is stopping them. Three practical and professional blocks stand out and each can be confronted.

The first is paradigmatic, to do with rigour. Rigour has come to be associated with the canons of some scientific and medical research, especially randomized control trials. These belong in a reductionist Cartesian–Newtonian paradigm and can make sense in some standardized, relatively controlled and uniform conditions. For conditions of complexity, diversity, emergence, and unpredictability they are a bad fit. For these conditions, more timely, relevant, and credible learning can be sought through the rigour of a paradigm of adaptive pluralism.[3] But 'rigour' and 'rigorous' are embedded in many professional mindsets as referring only to the reductionist paradigm; other approaches have tended to be dismissed as anecdotal, soft, and unrigorous. Paradigms, mindsets, vocabulary, and often the power of funding reinforce methodological conservatism. But now we see that participatory statistics can span and transcend the paradigms by combining the (Cartesian–Newtonian) rigour of statistical methods with the (adaptive, pluralist) rigour of a close fit, with complex and emergent local realities. Through the good practices of both paradigms, they can be doubly rigorous, and promise the best of both worlds.

The second explanation is risk-aversion, routinization, and inertia. Participatory statistics are generated through innovation, often creatively and interactively evolved for context and purpose. This takes time and money. It may also be felt to be risky. It is seen as easier and safer to follow approaches and methods that are routinized and embodied in manuals and which are taught in education and training institutions, and with which field workers are familiar. Professionals in aid organizations have expressed enthusiasm for piloting participatory statistics, but no action has followed. This does not necessarily mean that they have not tried: it may mean that they have met objections. Anyone promoting participatory statistics can expect professional and bureaucratic resistance. Inertia and the path of least resistance mean more of the same. Caution and convenience combine in a compelling case for questionnaires. Promotion of participatory statistics needs convinced and courageous champions. But on their own they may not be able to succeed. They need colleagues who do not oppose them, but who actively provide support.

The third explanation is the shortage of creative facilitators and lack of efforts to record and spread their innovations and skills. Not many researchers, whether academic or based in research institutes, have the orientation, experience, or competence to innovate and pilot participatory methodologies or to train others in them. Outstanding exceptions are to be found in this volume. Two trainer champions in the Rwandan Government have been key to the roll-out of *Ubudehe*. Those with competence are often freelance consultants, but they are in short supply. Moreover, when they have completed their contracts, neither they nor their sponsors have interest or resources for writing up, let alone training others and disseminating a new methodology they have developed. Their innovations are then not an enduring legacy, but one-off and transient.

Ethics

Ethical issues with participatory statistics were recognized and explored in detail by a network in the early 2000s.[4] No succinct summary can do justice to the principles and prescriptions of the *Guidelines and a Code of Conduct*[5] which the network collectively produced and which remains an important source. What follows should be read together with Barahona's chapter on ethical considerations in which they stress transparency, consent, and confidentiality.

The guidelines outline the principles of participatory research. They then describe ideals of good practice with participatory research designed to produce numbers. Many of these apply to most or all research, like not raising expectations, assuring consent, not assuming approval of personal exposure or willingness to share data, not exposing people to risks, respecting confidentiality, and being sensitive to power relations. Others are of particular relevance to good practice in the participatory numbers context:

- being transparent when introducing externally driven research questions and ensuring a locally approved research agenda;
- feeding back findings to communities and maximizing the impact of community-generated data on external audiences, and doing these especially when a study has an extractive element, eliciting information for use elsewhere;
- empowering participants through their own data generation, analysis, action, and ownership;
- optimizing trade-offs between representativeness and empowerment and standardization and empowerment, and when they occur between external pressures for results and ethical ideals.

Inevitable trade-offs demand that practitioners are continuously aware and reflective, struggle to optimize, and are transparent about the compromises and trade-offs they are making. Care is needed to avoid either of two extremes: one, being driven by contracts, deadlines, and external demands to cut corners and, under pressure, exploit and expose local people; and the other, striving towards ideals and seeking to follow principles to a point of paralysis. The first is the greater danger. To achieve a balance, managing the tensions and optimizing the trade-offs inherent in participatory statistics work, requires resolution and commitment on the part of facilitators and researchers to ethical principles, and awareness and understanding on the part of those responsible for commissioning and funding.

Ways forward

To realize the potentials of participatory statistics requires transformative revolutions which are at once professional, institutional, and personal.

First, professionally, evidence of the rigour, win-win, and strengths and weaknesses of participatory statistics needs repeated analysis, articulation, and dissemination. Jupp records how there was a breakthrough in acceptance of the participatory processes and statistics of the Bangladesh social movement. It was when an expensive external evaluation corroborated the movement's own data. It was then that other donors began to accept the data. More such studies are needed, including on cost-effectiveness and trade-offs. In paradigmatic and practical terms, it has to be recognized that time, commitment, and flair are needed to develop, adapt, pilot, and refine methods. To develop the methodology for the Malawi sustainability study took a team three weeks of intensive hands-on participatory trials and innovations in the in-depth preliminary field study, leading to the production of a field facilitators' manual with the 15 standard indicators (Cromwell and Fiona Chambers, pers. comm.). Good professional practice for participatory statistics has to include time and space for developing methodology in the early stages as a condition for quality and speed later, and overall cost-effectiveness.

Second, institutionally, teaching and training curricula need to incorporate participatory statistics, and participatory approaches and methods more generally. For this to be effective, faculty have themselves to gain field experience. Again and again, hands-on fieldwork has proved vital for conviction and confidence. Breakthroughs into the mainstream can take various forms: an example is when the well-known textbook *Veterinary Epidemiology* (Thrusfield, 2005, cited in Catley, 2009) included a section on 'participatory epidemiology', a field in which participatory statistics were prominent. Institutionally, the transformation needed requires the widespread incorporation of the principles, practices, and range of applications of participatory statistics in tertiary education, in training institutes, in textbooks, and in courses, and involving students in real-life practicals.

The third, personal, dimension is universal and fundamental. The way in is always through people and agency. Innovation needs champions. It is individuals who can change professional norms and methods, who can introduce participatory statistics into contracts and into courses, and who can foster and provoke institutional change. It is creative facilitators who can invent and pilot approaches and methods to fit purpose and contexts of local diversity and complexity. It is creative champions and those who support them who will be the transformers. And it is more than innovation that is needed. In Dee Jupp's words (2007: 122), 'It is not innovation but innovativeness ... that needs to be nurtured'.

Such innovative champions are among the authors in this book. Some work in NGOs. Freelance consultants are well represented. A common pattern is for a creative innovator to become frustrated with the constraints of her[6] organization, and to take the plunge of leaving and launching out as an independent. Unlike embedded academics or trainers, such freelancers have a degree of freedom, depending on their assignments, to innovate. What they need is time and tolerance on the part of their sponsors, often in governments or donor agencies, so that they can develop and test methodologies – a process which, if done well, will take a matter of weeks. And then when implementation is complete, they need support to write up the experience for a wider audience, and sometimes to train others. But these before and after blocks of time are rare in contracts, or severely squeezed. It would be a significant breakthrough, with high payoffs, if it became the norm for those who sponsor innovation with participatory statistics to set aside resources and time for these activities: through time and capacity before application, to enhance the quality and local fit of innovations; and through time and capacity after it, to disseminate generalizable learning, approaches, and methods.

If participatory statistics are to fulfil anything like their potential, they need resolute, imaginative, and sustained support. The establishment of participatory statistics in livestock epidemiology in East Africa was the result of sensitivity to professional concerns, a decade of methodological innovation, field exposure of university faculty and government officials, and a track record of high-quality data (Catley, 2009). This is inspiring, but may be difficult to replicate without sustained external support. Unfortunately, such support tends to be short term. There is no organization in our world dedicated to developing and disseminating participatory statistics. This is a glaring gap and omission, and a testimony to conservatism, ignorance, and lack of imagination. It also reflects a failure on the part of those of us who have long been aware of the potentials. I am angry with myself for not having done more. I am frustrated at the failure of any organization to see the need and seize the opportunity. For a few years over a decade ago, the Statistical Services Centre at the University of Reading conducted annual 10-day courses in participatory statistics, but lack of demand brought them to a close. I hope that after this book such a closure could never happen again. One of the most pro-poor and cost-effective investments a funding agency could make now would be to sponsor and support a global knowledge and innovation hub for participatory statistics. Its activities would include commissioning innovators to document and share their experiences, training and mentoring creative facilitators, and networking and nurturing a worldwide community of practice.

In conclusion

After this book, there can be no more excuses of ignorance. Those who do not explore participatory statistics can plead lack of time, lack of resources, lack of creative and innovative facilitators, the power and conservatism of others, their own or others' reluctance to take risks, or their own lack of confidence in making the case, but they cannot plead ignorance. Let me hope that the evidence presented here will inform and energize teachers, trainers, researchers, officials, funders, and other professionals; that it will give them confidence and ammunition to use in making the case for participatory statistics; and that in consequence, much professionalism, teaching, training, and commissioning of research will not just change, but be transformed.

The vision can then be of a future in which many millions of those who are poor, marginalized, and excluded are empowered through what they learn through their own analysis and the statistics and maps they generate, and those in power are better informed and driven to action as a result. It is a future in which modes of research, monitoring, and evaluation are determined not by conventional routines, but by creative innovation. It is a future in which core academic and official perceptions are more up to date and in touch with grass-roots realities. It is a future of win–win, empowering poor people, and giving those with power more timely, accurate, and credible information and insights into rapidly changing realities. Let me hope that this book and its contributors will inspire many, many others to join them in the vanguard of pioneers to bring that future about.

Robert Chambers, 23 June 2012

Notes

1   For a fuller discussion of the rigour of group-visual synergy and of participatory methods and approaches, see Chambers, 1997: 158–61.
2   For a helpful discussion and diagram, see Catley et al., 2009: 57–8.
3   I have tried to elaborate the contrasting paradigms in Chambers, 2010.
4   The Parti-Numbers Network of Southern and Northern practitioners and academics was established by members of the Institute of Development Studies (University of Sussex), the Centre for Development Studies (University of Wales, Swansea), the Statistical Services Centre and Integrated Rural Development Department (University of Reading), the Overseas Development Institute, and the International HIV/AIDS Alliance. It was much concerned with ethics. This led to *Guidelines and a Code of Conduct* on which this brief section is based.
5   Access at http://www.reading.ac.uk/ssc/n/publications/participation.htm
6   Empirically, most of them, at least those based in the UK, are women.

References

Barahona, C. and Levy, S. (2003) 'How to generate statistics and influence policy using participatory methods in research: reflections on work in Malawi 1999–2002', IDS Working Paper 212, Institute of Development Studies, Sussex, UK.

Barahona, C. and Levy, S. (2007) 'The best of both worlds: producing national statistics using participatory methods', *World Development* 35, 2: 326–41.

Catley, A., Burns, J., Abebe, D., and Suji, S. (2008) *Participatory Impact Assessment: A Guide for Practitioners*, Feinstein International Center, Tufts University, Medford, MA.

Chambers, R. (1997) *Whose Reality Counts? Putting the First Last*, Practical Action Publishing, Rugby, UK.

Chambers, R. (2010) 'Paradigms, poverty and adaptive pluralism', IDS Working Paper 344, IDS Brighton, UK.

Jupp, D. (2007) 'Keeping the art of participation bubbling: some reflections on what stimulates creativity in using participatory methods', in Pettit and Brock (eds), *Springs of Participation*, pp. 107–22.

Kagugube, J., Ssewakiryanga, R., Barahona, C., and Levy, S. (*c.*2008) 'Integrating qualitative dimensions of poverty into the Third Uganda National Household Survey' (UNHS III), *Journal of African Statistics* 8: 28–52.

Kar, K. (2005) *Practical Guide to Triggering Community-Led Total Sanitation*, IDS, Brighton.

Kar, K. with Robert Chambers, R. (2008) *Handbook on Community-Led Total Sanitation*, IDS Sussex and Plan International, UK. Available from: www.communityledtotalsanitation.org

Levy, S. (2007) 'Using numerical data from participatory research to support the Millennium Development Goals: the case for locally owned information systems', in Brock and Pettit (eds), *Springs of Participation*, pp. 137–49.

Moser, C. and Holland, H. (1997) *Urban Poverty and Violence in Jamaica*, World Bank, Washington, DC.

Moser, C. and McIlwaine, C. (2004) *Encounters with Violence in Latin America: Urban Poor Perceptions from Colombia and Guatemala*, Routledge, New York and London.

Pettit, J. and Brock, K. (eds) (2007) *Springs of Participation: Creating and Evolving Methods for Participatory Development*, Practical Action Publishing, Rugby, UK.

Shah, M.K., Degnan Kambou, S. and Monahan, B. (eds) (1999) *Embracing Participation in Development: Worldwide Experience from CARE's Reproductive Health Programs with a Step-by-step Field Guide to Participatory Tools and Techniques*, CARE, Atlanta, GA.

Thrusfield, M. (2005) *Veterinary Epidemiology*, 3rd edn, Blackwell Science, Oxford.

United Nations Development Programme (UNDP), Bangladesh (1996) *UNDP's 1996 Report on Human Development in Bangladesh, Vol. 3, Poor People's Perspectives*, UNDP, Dhaka.

About the author

Robert Chambers is a Research Associate at the Institute of Development Studies, University of Sussex. Robert has a background in biology, history, and public administration. His current concerns and interests include professionalism, power, the personal dimension in development, participatory methodologies, teaching and learning with large numbers, agriculture and science, seasonality, and community-led total sanitation.

Index

accuracy: GIS 10; and local knowledge 199, 200; NGO-IDEAs 120, 121; OSM 24; P3DM 28, 29, 31, 35; scorecards 131; social mapping 3, 9
Action Aid 5, 197
'active sum' 190
adaptation, phases of 39
Afghanistan 6
Afrobarometer indicators 7
agriculture, sustainable: farmers' perceptions 177, 178; indicators, Farming Practice Groups 168t–70t, 171–4; methodology 165–71; reform and 163–4
animal welfare 158

Bangladesh 97–110; and donor aid 98–100; GDI 197; land rights 13; self-evaluation of empowerment 100–1
benchmarking 7, 129, 131–3
Benin 183, 188
'best-bet technology' 164
bias, researcher 9
Bill and Melinda Gates Foundation (BMFG) 183
blocks 201–2
bribery 109

Burkina Faso 183, 188, 194
Burma 6

capacity, information management 92
CARE 165
CBOs (community-based organizations) 39
census mapping, participatory 9
Central American University 39
Citizen Report Cards 7, 126–7
citizen science 24

climate change and urban vulnerability 37–46; methodology 38–40; quantification 40–3; policy process 43–5
'cluster sampling' 5
collaboration 24, 28, 120
communication, visual 33
community-based organizations *see* CBOs
community census 3
'community facilitators' 52
community level action 118, 119
community mapping 90, 142–3
Community-Based Animal Health Workers 15
Community-Led Total Sanitation *see* CLTS
COMPACI (Competitive African Cotton Initiative) 183–95; influence matrix 190–2, 193box; MAPP 184–5; quality of life curves 186–7; standardization of methodology 16; trend analysis 187–9
comparing 5
confidentiality 143
conflict areas 9
conflict management 33
Conflict Reduction Programme *see* CRP
Consultations with the Poor on Safety Nets 6, 140, 141
cooperatives 192
corroboration, external 110
corruption 102, 103
Cotabato province 67–76; actions from workshop 72–4; issues 74–5; methodology 68–71
Côte d'Ivoire (Ivory Coast) 183, 188, 189t
cotton farming *see* COMPACI
counter mapping 26

CRM (Crisis and Recovery Mapping) 79, 82–7, 89
CRMA (Crisis and Recovery Mapping and Analysis) 12, 79, 82, 88, 89, 93
'crowdsourcing' 10
CRP (Conflict Reduction Programme) 89
CLTS (Community-Led Total Sanitation) 3

Darfur 93
data aggregation 68–70, 120, 129, 138, 188, 190, 195
decentralization, health sector 12, 65–76; actions from workshop 72–4; issues 74–5; methodology 68–71
Democratic Republic of Congo see DRC
destocking 149–61; impact on livelihoods 152–4; PIA 150–1; policy analysis 154–8; policy process 159–60
DFID (Department for International Development) 5, 6, 14, 138
Digital Atlas 82
discussion, diagnostic 11
diversification, crop 174
donor project funding 97
double-loop learning 13
DRC (Democratic Republic of Congo) 10
Dream Packs 174, 176, 177box
drought, adaptation to 39 see also destocking

East Sudan 91
Eco Build Africa Trust 39
education 102
e-government 92
elite control 53, 55
empowerment: control of economic resources 104, 105t; and engagement with local authorities 10; political 104–5; quantification of 97–8; self-empowerment 104; self-evaluation of 97; social 104, 105t; through PGIS 25
Estelí 38, 39, 40, 44, 45
ethics 143, 202, 203
Ethiopia 149–61; community environmental rehabilitation 29–30; drought 149, 150; food aid

154; PIA 150–1; policy process 160box
European Union 51, 52
'evaluative practice' 13

facilitation 9, 52
Famine Early Warning Unit 167
'Farming Practice Groups' 166, 167
feedback 132–3
Feinstein International Center 15
female-headed households 171, 172
food security, as indicator of poverty 141–3
Freedom Fighters 99box

Gaza 10
GDI (Group Development Index) 107, 108, 197
gender equality 192
geographic information systems see GIS
geospatial information technologies see GIT
German Development Cooperation (GIZ) 183
GIS (geographic information systems) 28, 82
GIT (geospatial information technologies) 24, 25
GIZ see German Development Cooperation
global positioning systems see GPS
goal setting 14
GOLD (Governance and Local Democracy) Project 67
Google Maps 24
governance, and state fragility 81
governance, local 67
Governance and Local Democracy) Project see GOLD
GPS (Global Positioning Systems) 28
Group Development Index see GDI
group-based analysis 5, 9
'group-visual synergy' 3
Guidelines and a Code of Conduct 202

Haiti 10
Health Insurance Scheme 49
'Health Sector Review Workshop' 68–74
hierarchical statistical sampling 9
HIMA-Njombe 165

Ibrahim Index of African
   Governance 7
ICTs (information and
   communication technologies)
   9–10, 129, 132, 144, 200
identity building 32
impact assessment 6, 14–16, 107,
   119–20, 151, 165
IMWG (Information Management
   Working Group) 82
India 113–22; community action
   118–19; election monitoring 10;
   goal setting 116–17; NGO-IDEAs
   114–15; poverty analysis 115,
   116fig
indigenous spatial knowledge see ISK
influence matrix 190, 191t, 193box
information and communication
   technologies see ICTs
Information Management Working
   Group see IMWG
infrastructure requirements 158
Institute for Applied Research
   and Local Development see
   NITLAPAN
Integrated Human Development
   Project 14
integrated pest management see IPM
integration, qualitative and
   quantitative 129, 133
International Centre of Insect
   Physiology and Ecology 15
interventions, drought 156–7t
IPM (integrated pest management)
   190
ISK (indigenous spatial knowledge)
   26, 27
'issue box' 84, 85
Ivory Coast see Côte d'Ivoire

Jamaica 6, 7
justice, local 102

Kagame, President Paul 52
Karwar Rural Women and Children
   Development Society see
   KRWCDS
Kenya 7, 10, 15, 37
khas land 98, 99
knowledge: community owned 3,
   53; intergenerational exchange
   33; local 26, 32; management
   91–2, 93; and mapping 28; tacit
   31; as valued 2

KRWCDS (Karwar Rural Women and
   Children Development Society)
   115, 117, 118, 119, 120

land policies, lack of 44
land rights 98, 99box
Latin America 6
'lead farmers' 185
'learning organisation' 13
'learning reversal' 8
legend making, participatory 32
Leprosy Control Program 67
'listening study' 100
literacy 108, 176
livestock 149–61; commercial
   destocking 152–4, 158; timing of
   intervention 155; and traders 155,
   158
Livestock Emergency Guidelines and
   Standards 15, 149
loans to traders 158
'Local Special Bodies' 66

M&E see monitoring and evaluation
Malawi 137–44, 163–79; agricultural
   sustainability 163–78; COMPACI
   183, 186–7, 188, 192; community
   mapping 142–3; food deficit 164;
   impact assessment 6; measuring
   poverty 138–9; population
   estimates 8; poverty measurement
   138–9, 140–2; reform 163–4;
   wealth ranking 6
Malawi, University of 137, 140
Malawi Targeted Inputs Programme
   see TIP
Maldives 125–35; education 126;
   health 126; 'Integrated Human
   Development Project' 125–6;
   scorecard use 14, 126–9
Map Kibera 10
MAPP (Method for Impact
   Assessment of Programs and
   Projects) 183, 184–5, 194
mapping: communication 25–6;
   technology 23–4
matrix scoring 5
measuring 5
MELCA-Ethiopia 29–30
'meta analysis' 10
Method for Impact Assessment of
   Programs and Projects see MAPP
methodology, and outcome 2fig
mind maps 84

Mombasa 38, 39, 40, 41, 42, 44, 45
monitoring and evaluation (M&E),
    participatory 12–14
'monitoring and learning' 13
morbidity analysis 69–70, 73, 74
mortality analysis 69–70, 71fig, 73
Mozambique 183, 192

Nairobi 10
National Institute of Statistics
    see NISR
National Opinion Research Centre,
    University of Chicago
    see NORC
natural resource management 5
Nepal 197
NGO-IDEAs (NGO Impact on
    Development, Empowerment and
    Actions) 114–17
NGOs (non-governmental
    organizations) 113–22; capacity
    building 154; IMWG 82; and
    monitoring 14; need for optimal
    use of funds 113; participatory
    'toolbox' 114–15; PIA 151; and
    ranking of wealth/well-being 5
Nicaragua 37
NISR (National Institute of Statistics)
    59
NITLAPAN (Institute for Applied
    Research and Local Development)
    39
non-governmental organizations see
    NGOs
NORC (National Opinion Research
    Centre, University of Chicago)
    184, 185

observable outcomes 6, 109
OpenStreetMap (OSM) 24
OPM (Oxford Policy Management)
    126

P3DM (Participatory 3-Dimensional
    Modelling) 11, 23, 28–33
PAG (Performance Assessment by
    Groups) 116
'Parti Numbers' group 140
Participatory 3-Dimensional
    Modelling see P3DM
participatory analysis 87–9
participatory climate change
    adaptation appraisal see PCCAA
participatory democracy 55–6

Participatory Geographical
    Information Systems see PGIS
participatory grass-roots review 100,
    104
Participatory Impact Assessment see
    PIA
Participatory Learning and Action
    see PLA
Participatory Rural Appraisal
    see PRA
participatory statistics: as stimulant
    to change 7
participatory statistics,
    standardization of 7–9
Participatory Wealth Ranking 115,
    116fig
'passive sum' 190
Pastoralist Livelihoods Initiative
    150, 151, 154, 155
pastoralists see destocking
PCCAA (participatory climate
    change adaptation appraisal) 39,
    44
Performance Assessment by Groups
    see PAG
PGIS (Participatory Geographical
    Information Systems) 23–33;
    contexts 26; and importance of
    participation 27; practice 25–8
Philippines 65–76; decentralization
    of health sector 12, 65–8; Health
    Sector Review Workshop 68–75;
    NGOs 14
PIA (Participatory Impact
    Assessment) 14–16, 149, 159–60
PLA (Participatory Learning and
    Action) 25
Plan International 5
population estimates 8, 9, 137
poverty: categorization of 120,
    140–2; and resilience building 44;
    urban 11, 37–8
Power Mapping 133–4
PRA (Participatory Rural Appraisal)
    8, 23, 51, 100
'precision of inference' 8
preference ranking 5
prioritization of intervention 87, 91
Prioritized Problem Index of Poor
    Communities 197
problem trees 84
Process Tracing 133–4
proportional piling 5
Provincial Traffic Code 12, 72

qualitative changes, measurement of 6–7
quality of life curves 186–7
quantification 103–9; asset adaptation 41; community-level assessments 104–6; data analysis 106–8, 109; effectiveness 6; institutional maps 42, 43t; listing and ranking of assets 41; reporting obligations 109; weather hazards 40, 41t

RCPM (Reconciliation and Peaceful Co-existence Mechanism) 89
Reading, University of 8, 137, 140, 204
research paradigm, participatory 2, 3box, 43–5
resilience 39, 93
Results-Based Management 103–4
Rwanda 49–62; census 56–7; centralization 50; district policy 57, 58; genocide 1994 50; national policy 59; policy making 57, 59–61; political system 50; poverty as locally defined 54t; *Ubehede* community mapping 11

SAGE (Situational Analysis and Goal Establishment) 116–17
Save the Children US (SC US) 150
Scorecards: community mapping 142–3; extractive 131; group-based scores 128fig, 129–31; methodology 126–31; participatory 133fig; survey-based scores 128fig, 129–31
seasonal food calendars 5
self-esteem 32, 120
self-facilitation 106
Sensemaker 10
sequencing 9
sexual harassment 102
Situational Analysis and Goal Establishment *see* SAGE
sketch mapping 29
smallholders, rural 138–9, 163, 164
social categorization 53
Social Dimensions of Climate Change (2008) 39
social mapping 3, 4fig, 14, 49, 53, 56–7
social protection 61
South Darfur 84box

South Sudan 79
spatial data, accessibility of 23–4, 25
'Starter Pack Scheme' 163–79; agricultural sustainability 163–4, 171–8; methodology 165–7
state fragility 80–2
State Situation Analysis 88, 89
statebuilding 81–2, 90–1
Sudan 79–94; community mapping 82–7; conflict prevention and peacebuilding 89, 90; information, role of 82; statebuilding 90–1
Sudan, Eastern 85, 86fig, 87
Sudan, Southern 12
survey-based research 139–40

Tanzania 165
Targeted Inputs Programme *see* TIP
Ten Seed Technique 5
TIP (Targeted Inputs Programme) 14, 138–9, 164
TIP Messages 141, 142
transparency 55, 143
triangulation 125
Trocaire 13
Tuft University 15

Ubehede: adoption as official policy 51; Community Development Fund 54; community mapping 11; community planning 49–62; evolution of 51, 52; and governance reform 50–1; influence on government policy 57; methodology 51, 52–6; role of 49–50; social mapping 56–7
Uganda 6, 126
Uganda National Household Survey 6, 200
UNDAF (UN Development Assistance Framework) 89
UNDP (United Nations Development Programme) 13–14, 79, 88, 89
United States Agency for International Development *see* USAID
UPPR (Urban Partnerships for Poverty Reduction Programme) 13
Urban Research Symposium on Cities and Climate Change (2009) 39
urban violence 6, 7

urbanization 38
USAID (United States Agency for International Development) 67, 150
Ushahidi 10, 24

Vision Umurenge Programme 49, 59–61
voluntarism 24, 52, 68, 152
vulnerability 39, 140

water: and climate change 38; Community Development Fund 55, 56; and disease 74, 191box; ISK 27; inadequate access to 37, 84, 118, 155t, 157t

wealth ranking 5, 6, 115, 116fig, 141
weighting 107
well-being ranking 5, 49, 115, 116fig, 165
West Darfur 85
Wikimapia 24
women 84, 101–3, 116–18, 171, 173, 185, 190, 192
Women's Association 117, 119t
World Bank 7, 13, 14, 39, 125, 141
Worldwide Governance Indicators (World Bank) 7

Zambia 165, 183, 186, 188, 190, 191t, 192, 194